Head Start on Holidays

Jewish Programs for Preschoolers and Parents

Roberta Louis Goodman
and
Andye Honigman Zell

A.R.E. Publishing
Denver, Colorado

Published by:
A.R.E. Publishing, Inc.
Denver, Colorado

Library of Congress Catalog card Number 91-070841
ISBN 0-86705-026-8

© A.R.E. Publishing, Inc. 1991

Printed in the United States of America
10   9   8   7   6   5   4   3   2   1

Dedication

To my mother, Wendy, who facilitated my
earliest and best holiday memories.

Andye Honigman Zell

To my parents, Maynard and Judy, from whom I
inherited *haimish* ways, and to my husband,
Bob, who saw me though every computer
crisis.

Roberta Louis Goodman

To all the parents and facilitators who will use
this book to make memories for generations
present and future.

Roberta and Andye

Acknowledgements

To our teachers and students, from whom we have gained wisdom: Joanne Barrington, who continued the tradition of the preschool parties at the Temple in Atlanta and who contributed to the revision of the programs. Dona Wise, whose music contributed to the success of these programs at the Temple in Atlanta. David Zell, whose computer talents assisted greatly in the presentation of the patterns. Mark Jacobson, who always thought of these preschool programs as one of the Temple's best kept secrets and as one of the Temple's best programs. The Temple in Atlanta and all of its leaders, who have supported the programs throughout the years. The Sisterhood of The Temple in Atlanta and all the Sisterhood members, who supported these programs in the beginning and continue to do so. The parents, some of whom have been coming for five years, and children of the Temple in Atlanta, who challenged us to fine tune the programs. Temple Adath Yeshurun, Syracuse, New York, and Holy Blossom Congregation in Toronto, Canada for hosting these programs and proving that they are successful in other settings. Sheila Taratoot for typing the original manuscript. Lonnie and Pete for taking good care of the programs. And, of course, a very special thank-you to our editors, Audrey Friedman Marcus and Raymond A. Zwerin, and to our typesetter, Steven Brightbill.

Contents

Introduction
A Guide for Implementing Holiday Programs

The preschool holiday programs outlined in this book are family education programs for children 2 to 4 years old and their parents. Each of these programs centers around a holiday. In each, holiday symbols, customs, terms, and concepts are introduced. Each holiday program features activities such as storytelling, making and enjoying Jewish foods, reciting blessings, singing and moving to holiday songs, and creating holiday objects to take home and use.

About This Book

In this book, a three year cycle of holiday programs for preschoolers and their parents is presented. Each program is carefully designed and, with a little advance preparation, ready to implement.

Included herein is an explanation of how to begin and carry out an ongoing series of pre-school programs and a rationale for doing so.

For each program there is a complete list of materials and supplies needed, suggestions for the physical set up, a schedule for and instruc-tions on how to accomplish each activity, pat-terns for all the art projects, and recommended songs to sing. Each program is described in detail so that anyone can run it, regardless of expertise, experience, or artistic ability.

A Unique Approach

This series of holiday programs represents a unique approach to family education for this target group. Characteristics that demonstrate this uniqueness are:

1. A triennial cycle – Three years of non-repetitive holiday programs are presented, enough to take a two-year-old and his/her parents through all the preschool years. Each holiday program is appropriate for ages two through four.

2. Interactive model – During each of the programs, family members interact with one another as they explore the Jewish holidays through a variety of activities. Most of these activities encourage and enable parents to assist their children. The group leader serves as a Facilitator who prepares and organizes materials and guides families through the activities.

3. Preparation for holiday observance – Each of the programs prepares families for observing and celebrating an upcoming Jewish holiday. Because these programs change from year to year, this allows families to explore a range of holiday symbols, rituals, and concepts. The take-home project families make may be used for their home holiday celebration. Thus, the holiday experience is translated from the program site into the home.

4. Projects and activities with a purpose – The holiday programs are content oriented in a creative, exciting, and substantive way; they are not just "sing a song, make a food, hear a story" programs. For each program, there are themes around which the story, music, activities, and take-home projects revolve.

5. A "win-win" situation for everyone – These holiday programs fulfill a variety of needs. For the child, the programs foster a sense of membership — a sense of belonging to an institution or group. The children who

participate feel welcome and comfortable in a Jewish setting.

For the sponsoring organization, programs provide a way to involve families and to make them feel comfortable and wanted. These programs also help to identify emerging young leadership and serve to recruit families as members for other activities.

For the parents, the programs integrate and empower, rather than differentiate and intimidate. Parents are given resources and opportunities to be transmitters of Judaism. Because of this, the programs are suitable for the single parent and the married couple, the born Jew, and the Jew by Choice, and are attractive to fathers as well as mothers, and to grandparents, too.

6. Tested and proven – This series of holiday programs has been instituted successfully in three congregations, led by three different individuals, in three different cities in North America.

Target Audience

Preschool holiday programs are appropriate for a particular group, such as a *Havurah*, or for a broader constituency, such as all congregational families with children of preschool age. The programs may be limited to group or institution members, or may include non-members. Additionally, the programs are useful for recruiting members, to showcase the advantages of belonging to the sponsoring group or institution. These holiday programs are successful with a minimum of four families present at a session to a maximum of forty families. (For more than forty families, it becomes necessary to form a second group.)

What will happen when these programs are implemented? First of all, a core of faithful attendees will emerge. Secondly, certain holidays, such as Chanukah, Passover, and Purim, will draw more participants. And finally, the families who attend will most likely represent a wide range of home and synagogue holiday observance. You will find these programs attract those who are already observing the holidays, as well as those who would like to do more in the way of holiday observance.

Possible Settings and Schedules

Holiday programs are adaptable to a variety of settings. The programs can be used by: synagogues, Jewish preschools, Jewish Community Centers, day-care centers, camps, Jewish Teacher Centers, parenting centers, central agencies for Jewish education, day schools, and *Havurot*.

Any single holiday program can be used for: a parent-child open house, an alternative festival service/program for families with preschoolers, a Jewish library (or school library) holiday program, Brownies or Cub Scouts, home holiday parties, retreat for families, a *Havurah* get-together.

It is possible to utilize all of the programs included in this book as a three-year cycle of programs, to utilize just one year's worth of programs, or to offer just a few programs. Families may attend one session or all the sessions. A family need not attend consecutive sessions nor begin attending at the start of the year. Families may join the group for any one program at anytime during the year. The more sessions they attend, of course, the more beneficial the program. As programs for the same holiday vary in theme and activity, families may participate for three years with the same preschooler without repeating activities.

Goals of the Programs

Each year of holiday programs is designed to fulfill the following goals:

1. To augment interaction between parent and child around a Jewish subject.

2. To increase participation in holiday celebrations at home and at synagogue.

3. To foster a commitment to Jewish life and living.

4. To connect participants to the Jewish community.

5. To enable the sponsoring Jewish institution or group to provide a setting that is warm, comfortable, and nurturing.

6. To create community by providing a network for families to meet and interact with one another.

7. To help families live Jewishly year round.

ORGANIZING PRESCHOOL HOLIDAY PROGRAMS

To guarantee the success of a holiday program series, it is essential to select a target audience based on the needs of families and the needs of the sponsoring organization. Once this has been done, the next task is organizing the program(s). The following personnel and aspects of the program must be arranged first:

1. An Administrative Caretaker

2. A Facilitator for the holiday programs

3. A music specialist (optional, but very desirable)

4. A space where programs will be held

5. A calendar of the programs for the year

6. A budget

7. Publicity for recruitment and ongoing participation

Descriptions of and recommendations for each of these elements follow.

The Administrative Caretaker

The sponsoring institution or group must designate an Administrative Caretaker who will be responsible for handling all the administrative concerns. This person oversees the making of the calendar for the year, prepares and oversees the budget, sends out publicity to recruit families and makes reminders for programs, supervises the Facilitator of the program and the music specialist, and coordinates the room set-up. Many of these tasks can be shared with committees of parents as a way of involving families in the actual preparation of the programs.

The Administrative Caretaker should be an individual who is well organized, knows how to publicize programs, and can handle the logistical arrangements, especially room set-ups.

The Administrative Caretaker and the Facilitator work together, coordinating their responsibilities. If desired, the tasks of the Administrative Caretaker and the Facilitator may be combined into one job.

The Facilitator

The responsibilities of the Facilitator include: purchasing and gathering all the supplies and snack; preparing the project materials, including duplicating, cutting out patterns, and assembling sample projects; setting out the materials the day of the session; conducting the session; organizing the clean-up of the materials; and evaluating each program.

Estimated preparation time for each holiday program is from four to ten hours, depending on the size of the group. The larger the group, the more time it will take to prepare many of the projects.

A good Facilitator may be a lay leader, a special education teacher, a nurse, a social worker, a person involved in communal service, a teacher, a storyteller, an artist, a day care worker, a grandparent, a parent, etc. Using this book as a guide, just about anyone, regardless of experience or training, can be the Facilitator for these holiday programs.

In deciding upon a Facilitator, look for these characteristics. The person must be flexible, but organized. He/she needs to interact well with adults as well as children, needs to feel comfortable telling a story and assembling an art project, and must be aware of the fact that people work at their own pace.

Remember that the Facilitator facilitates. The Facilitator gives simple instructions. The Facilitator floats from table to table, from family to family, encouraging, clarifying, and assisting only as needed. This position is not for a person who demands quiet, or the total attention of all, or the same response from everyone. Most of the Facilitator's work is done before a program begins. The key to the success of these programs is advance preparation.

A Music Specialist

Music and movement augment these holiday preschool programs. There are wonderful and appropriate holiday songs and new and old tunes to blessings. Young children enjoy doing body motions, marching, clapping, swaying, and even dancing to the music. After a program, families can share the music at home.

The ideal situation is to have a music specialist at each of the programs. If it is not possible to do so, here are some other ways to approach the inclusion of music in the holiday programs:

1. Entice a music lover and instrumentalist to learn a few tunes on the piano, accordion, or guitar.
2. Invite an individual with decent pitch and a middle range voice to learn a few tunes.
3. Sing along with a cassette tape or videotape of holiday tunes.
4. Dance, sway, and do movement exercises to the accompaniment of a tape.

A Space for the Program

Programs may be held in a standard preschool classroom, a lunchroom, a social hall, a multi-purpose room, a gymnasium, or in someone's home. A large, roomy space is preferable to a crowded one. Close access to a sink is desirable.

For items needed for the physical set-up of the space, see page xiii.

A Calendar of the Sessions

The calendar for the year is best made before the start of the first session. Each holiday program is designed to last an hour and a half. The Administrative Caretaker and the Facilitator, in consultation with the principal or director of the sponsoring agency or group, decide how many of the programs to do. They choose a weekday or weekend, a Sunday, or a Shabbat. (If the latter, some groups will need to make appropriate adaptations to accommodate Shabbat observance.) They decide upon a time of day for the programs. It is highly recommended that all of the programs be scheduled at the same time of the day.

When scheduling the sessions, planners should keep in mind the actual day of the holiday; school vacations; conflicting events that involve the Jewish community, such as an Israel anniversary celebration; and secular events, such as local football games and Super Sunday. Distribute copies of the annual calendar of holiday programs to participating families.

Budget

The actual cash outlay for the holiday program will vary from place to place based on resources and resourcefulness. Here are the necessary budgetary items:

- Use of a room
- Custodial help for room set-up and take down
- Salary for the Administrative Caretaker

- Salary for the Facilitator
- Salary for the music specialist
- The duplication of the announcements of programs
- Postage for mailings
- The purchase of non-consumable items (e.g., scissors, hole punches, etc.) and consummable items (e.g., glue, paper cups, construction paper, etc.)
- The purchase of special materials for each session
- The snack

The budget can be kept lower by using volunteers, obtaining donations, and borrowing staff from other institutional/agency programs.

It is recommended that the Facilitator have available a supply of scissors, single hole punches, staplers, gluesticks, markers, crayons, masking tape, transparent tape, paper cups, napkins, and pencils. These items should be exclusively for the use of the holiday programs.

The cost of the special materials and snack for any single holiday program generally runs between a dollar per family to a few dollars. Most often, the price per family averages in the middle of these figures.

The goals of the overall series should influence budgetary decisions, such as whether or not to charge a fee to each family. Consider finding a sponsor to underwrite the activity and the snack. To keep down costs, ask families to bring a novelty item, such as the fly swatter for Passover, Year 1.

Publicity

Publicity is vital for the success of the holiday programs. There are two constant publicity needs. The first involves recruiting families for the program. Since children grow up and move on to kindergarten, the need to recruit is present each year. The second is keeping families informed of each forthcoming program throughout the year.

Here are some ways to identify and recruit potential participants:

- Identify a few parents with preschool aged children. Ask them for names, addresses, and phone numbers of other families with preschoolers.
- Send a letter to a list of families with preschoolers asking for more names of families with children in that age range.
- Ask a few interested parents to allow the use of their names on publicity.
- Make phone calls explaining the holiday program.
- Advertise and place articles in the bulletin/ newsletter of the sponsoring organization.
- Publicize the holiday programs in the local Jewish newspaper(s) and in secular papers.
- Put up fliers in Jewish gift shops, delis, grocery stores, bagel stores, kosher butchers, etc.
- Advertise through networks: Sisterhood or Women's League, preschools, day-care centers, Jewish childbirth classes, classes for Jews by Choice, family worship services, etc.
- Using the membership list of the sponsoring organization, find a co-sponsor or two for the holiday programs. People in the co-sponsoring group come because they are members of that group and stay because they like the program. Co-sponsorship promotes the formation of networks.
- Get names from membership forms filled in by new members.
- On all school registrations and program applications, ask for the names and birthdates of other siblings.

- Send children a birthday card on their second birthday along with an invitation to their first holiday program.

- Have enthusiasts bring a family they know as guests to a holiday program.

- At the end of the first year of the holiday programs, ask families to indicate if they will be continuing in the following year. Ask them for the names of other families they know who might be interested in participating.

Here are some recommendations for publicity that promote ongoing participation:

- Print and give to all participating families a one page calendar of all the holiday programs for the year. Suggest that parents place this on the refrigerator door.

- Create a mailing list for the year. Send this group a postcard or flier reminding them of a program.

- On all publicity, include the dates of all upcoming holiday programs and the name and phone number of a contact person.

- Make phone calls to potential participant families.

- Have a volunteer greeter at each holiday program. This makes people feel welcome and part of the group.

- At each program, have people sign in so that any new people may be placed on the mailing list.

A few other tips for publicity round out this area:

- At each holiday program, promote other programs of the sponsoring group or institution that are approriate for the families.

- Invite board members and other leaders of the sponsoring organization to see a holiday program in operation and to welcome the attendees.

- Write up the holiday programs as an article for bulletins and/or Jewish newspapers.

Visibility is vital for the continued success of these preschool holiday programs.

A TOUR THROUGH A HOLIDAY PROGRAM

Following is a step-by-step guide through a typical holiday program. This section contains an explanation of the rationale for each segment of the program, as well as suggestions for successful implementation.

Each program contains the following elements:

Pre-Program Information
    Title
    Announcement of Program
    Physical Set Up
    Holiday Symbols, Customs, Terms
      and Concepts
    The Schedule and Timing
    Supplies and Materials

The Program Itself
    Preparation
    Procedure
    Mind Warmer
    Introductions and Announcements
    Story
    Snack
    Activity
    Closure: Music and Movement

Each of these elements is described in detail below.

Pre-Program Information

Title

Every session needs a title. The title includes the holiday presented and the year in the triennial cycle.

Announcement of Program

For every session, a flier or postcard should be sent to all prospective participants. This notice should contain the following information:

Program Title

Name of sponsoring organization or group

Audience (age group, members only or general public, etc.)

Date

Time

Location

Cost (if applicable)

RSVP or For Further Information
(Always include the name and phone number of a contact person.)

Special Requests for the Day
(Requests for specific supplies to bring, such as a paper towel roll, family picture, or type of clothing to wear.)

Ongoing and attractive communications with families are essential. Enliven all announcements with graphics adapted from the patterns provided in this book or use Jewish clip art obtained from A.R.E. Publishing.

Physical Set Up

The standard items needed for the physical set-up of each program are: 1) a work area for families consisting of tables and chairs; 2) supply table(s) or surfaces on which to lay out all the materials and supplies; 3) a table at which participants check in and receive name tags and on which fliers or publicity about other programs can be placed; 4) large trash cans and trash bags.

Furniture size – Use either preschool-size tables and chairs or adult-size tables and chairs. (Parents, even grandparents, can sit in preschool chairs for a short time. Preschoolers are used to sitting and eating at an adult-size dinner table.)

Putting furniture in place – In every program a story is told and at least one project is under-taken. For the work area, set up tables and chairs for easy movement for both the participants and the Facilitator. Put the tables in a horseshoe or in rows. For announcements and story time, it is preferable to have children and parents sitting together in a circle or semi-circle on the floor.

Special Set up needs – From time to time, additional items will be needed. These will be indicated under "Physical Set-up" in the outline for that session.

A Diagram of the Set-up – Diagram the set-up for each program. This makes it possible to visualize the traffic flow and movement from one activity to another. The diagram should be shared with maintenance people.

Holiday Symbols, Customs, Terms, and Concepts

For each holiday program, the activities revolve around the symbols, customs, terms, and concepts for that holiday. The particular symbols, customs, terms, and concepts emphasized in a program vary from year to year, allowing families to experience and explore many different ideas in depth. Aside from making each year's program novel, this expands the families' vision of what the holidays are about and what the holidays can mean to them.

Schedule and Timing

Just about every holiday program includes the following segments. (In a few of the programs the format is slightly different.)

Mind Warmer

Introductions and Announcements

Setting the Stage

Story

Snack

Activity

Closure: Music and Movement

Each program is designed to flow and build from one segment to another. The Mind

Warmer, Introductions and Announcements, and Setting the Stage are necessary introductory elements of the programs. The other segments may be sequenced differently if desired.

The program is designed for an hour and a half time period. Without music, an hour and fifteen minutes is sufficient.

Each program included in this book is broken down into time periods. As an example, here is an actual schedule for the Chanukah Program, Year 3:

00:00 – 00:15 – Mind Warmer: A Lights Museum

00:15 – 00:25 – Introductions and Announcements

00:25 – 00:45 – Story: Rekindling the Light

00:45 – 00:55 – Snack: Chanukah Delights

00:55 – 1:10 – Activity: Catching the Light — A Chanukah Sun Catcher

01:10 – 01:30 – Music and Movement: A Little Light Music

The amount of time allocated for each segment of a program varies from session to session. Read the schedule closely.

Accurate pacing of the program is essential. The time allotments are reasonable and achievable, and are adequate for every project, provided all the materials are prepared in advance as indicated and all the supplies are ready for quick distribution.

Helpful Hints on Schedule and Timing
- Stay on schedule. If an aspect of the session tends to take much longer than scheduled, shorten other aspects of the program.
- Advance preparation is one key to staying on time. Materials for projects must be readied as instructed.

- On the day of the program, plan on one hour for set up. Lay out materials and supplies for easy distribution on the supply tables.
- Write out the real times for each segment of the program (e.g., 2:00 P.M., 2:15 P.M., etc.).

Supplies and Materials
Keep a supply of the following items solely for the use of the holiday programs.

name tags
markers
gluesticks
scissors (have a few left-handed scissors)
staplers
staples
crayons
single hole punches
pencils

Consider purchasing specialty scissors for two-year-olds, the kind that have additional holes for an adult's fingers.

Margarine tubs or paper cups are handy for use as containers for small items such as cloves or glitter.

Individualized supply container of reusable items – For each of the projects that families do at tables, they will need specific supplies. Place standard supplies, those that are frequently used and that can be used again, each in its own container. For example, the scissors are stored in the scissors container, markers in the marker container, etc. This arrangement makes set up and clean up easier. The containers can be shoe boxes, baskets, margarine tubs, etc. Containers with tops stack more easily when storing. All of these containers are placed on the supply table during the program for easy access for all families.

The materials necessary for each project or activity are listed in the description of that activity. Some of the materials are standard supplies used in most programs. Other materials are special to a specific program. Some materials may be purchased, others collected, others copied from the Directions and Patterns section at the end of each chapter.

All pages in the book are perforated so that they can be removed and copied easily. When making copies of these pages, you may want to white out or tape over the information at the bottom of the page that pertains to this book (e.g., the name of the holiday, the suggested year of the program, the color and size of the paper, the page number). Those pages that are to be copied back-to-back are back-to-back in this book.

Here is an example of a list of materials for the Mind Warmer of the Simchat Torah program, Year 2:

> name tags
> markers
> sign-in sheet
> 1 Simchat Torah Letter Flag Pattern I per two
>   children copied on white paper (see
>   Directions and Patterns)
> 1 Simchat Torah Letter Flag Pattern II per two
>   children copied on white paper (see
>   Directions and Patterns)
> 1 6" x 11" piece of poster board per child
> 1 paint stick per child
> wiggle eyes
> feathers
> ribbon
> sequins
> gluesticks
> staplers
> staples
> scissors

Each list of materials includes the following information:

1. The quantity and size of each item needed per family is indicated. (When quantity is not indicated, the amount depends on the size of the group. Use your own calculations for these items.)

2. The standard supplies needed for each activity.

3. "See Patterns and Directions" indicates that a ready-made, easy to copy pattern is included in this book. When no pattern is included, e.g., for a sign or the like, make your own.

4. The form that materials should be in when presented to families (e.g., the Hebrew letters need to be copied on card stock or poster board using the patterns provided in this book).

Helpful Hints on Materials

- Secure the storybook for the day well in advance. If you rely on a library, make arrangements for the book early. If you need to order the book, allow several weeks.

- Be resourceful when gathering supplies. Put out lists of what is needed.

- Save leftover scraps and the like. These often come in handy for other programs.

- Keep everything bright and colorful.

- Many specialty items, such as wiggly eyes, stickers, glitter, and feathers, make projects look special and are often worth the extra expense.

- Substitute readily available items when appropriate. Always make a sample to check on whether your substitution works.

- Bulk purchasing is less expensive. If there is an art room or supply room, try to share resources and purchasing costs.

- Places to search for items include: grocery stories, art stores, bakeries, paint stores, art supply shops, school supply stores, novelty shops, fabric stores, and costume stores.

- Have a recycling bin for recyclable goods like plastic cups, paper, etc., to help the environment.

The Program Itself

In this section, the various segments of a holiday program are described.

Preparation

The sections called "Preparation" outline what the Facilitator needs to do to get ready for an activity. Included are advance preparations and preparations that need to be done on the day of a program. As stated previously, advance preparation is essential if activities are to be completed in the time allotted. Advanced preparation frees the Facilitator to facilitate from Mind Warmer to Closure.

Procedure

The sections called "Procedure" outline the steps necessary for the Facilitator and the families in the implementation of an activity. The Procedure includes: instructions for the Facilitator to give the participants, suggestions for what the Facilitator might say, steps necessary for families as they assemble the art projects, etc. The Procedure lists what to do and the proper order in which to do it.

Mind Warmer

Each program begins with a "Mind Warmer," an introductory activity which each parent does together with his/her preschooler. (In educational terms, this is the "set induction.") This segment of the program serves as a transition from the car to the program. It catches people's attention and gets them focused on the holiday. It acts as a springboard on which other activities build.

Handling varying arrival times – It is a fact of life that families arrive at different times. The Mind Warmer is designed so that families can begin it whenever they arrive. If a family arrives after the Introductions and Announcements have begun, they can skip the Mind Warmer, or they can take the materials home with them and do the project at home.

Doing the Mind Warmer – The Facilitator welcomes people as they arrive. He or she then explains the Mind Warmer and gives simple instructions. It is helpful to have a sample of the project to show to families. Leave out the details so that families feel comfortable creating and individualizing their projects. For the remainder of the time, the Facilitator circulates to answer questions.

Helpful Hints for the Mind Warmer

- Have all required materials set out on the supply table(s) before participants arrive.

- Make a model of each project with the major pieces assembled. This helps to simplify and reinforce the Facilitator's verbal instructions.

- Ask those families who arrive early to help set up.

- Welcome families as they arrive. (First-timers may be better integrated into the program by working alongside a veteran family.) Show them where to sign in, obtain name tags, and hang their coats. Introduce them to the Mind Warmer and show them a sample of the finished product. Point out the supply table(s) and work area.

- Toward the end of the allotted time, alert the group as to how many minutes they have before they come together for the Introductions and Announcements segment. When appropriate, suggest that children bring the product of the Mind Warmer activity to the Introductions and Announcements area. (This is specified in the Procedure.) Children can show off their work as they parade around with the finished activity.

- Tell families what to clear off and/or clean up. Have them return leftover materials to the supply table(s) and throw out their trash.

Be sensitive to the environment and provide opportunities for recycling.

Introductions and Announcements

During this segment of the program, participants are formally welcomed. Family members are introduced and announcements are made by the Facilitator. A warm welcome helps families to feel comfortable and helps in the building of community.

The Facilitator announces all pertinent programs, celebrations, committee meetings, and ways to be involved in the sponsoring organization or institution. This information helps families find a meaningful niche in the Jewish community, in Jewish life, and in the sponsoring organization or institution.

The Facilitator makes announcements about upcoming programs. The actual pieces of publicity should be left on the sign-in table where families can pick up calendars, fliers, bulletins, brochures, and registration forms as they arrive or leave. The Facilitator introduces participants to some of the leaders of the holiday programs, those individuals who are present at each program (i.e., the president of a co-sponsoring group, greeters, etc.), and points out those people who can answer questions about the sponsoring agency.

Setting the Stage

At the end of introductions and announcements, the Facilitator has a brief opportunity to make a bridge between the Mind Warmer and the rest of the program, pointing out the connection between them. At this point, he or she outlines the remainder of the activities and introduces or reinforces any major holiday symbols, terms, and concepts. The time allotment for "Setting the Stage" is included in the time frame for Introductions and Announcements.

Helpful Hints for Introductions and Announcements

- Invite participants into a circle or form a horseshoe. They can sit on the floor or move their chairs as necessary.

- Make certain all family members (grandparents, too) are introduced. One family member, a parent or preschooler, may do the introductions.

- Have a parent or sponsor welcome everyone to the program and announce any other institutional or group programs pertinent for this audience.

- For Setting the Stage, the Facilitator may paraphrase the suggested introduction provided herein to suit his/her own style.

Story Time

Stories remain a primary form of entertainment and everyone loves them. Stories are also a Jewish form of communication and are included in each holiday program for a variety of reasons.

Most Jewish holidays and celebrations originate in a story. People create meaning and a sense of belonging as they hear and enjoy the stories of the Jewish people. Stories familiarize the listener with holiday terms, customs, symbols, foods, and actions. They transmit Jewish values, such as family, observance, and the performance of *mitzvot*.

The stories families hear at holiday programs help to raise the level of Jewish awareness, observance, and activity in the home. Encourage parents to retell the same stories at home, at bedtime, or at other times.

Some of the stories to be told at programs are outlined in this book. The Facilitator may wish to distribute copies of these outlines to parents. If desired, a list of other age appropriate holiday stories may also be distributed.

The stories for the various programs are meant to be told, not read word for word. In some cases, there are suggestions for promoting audience participation. Let creativity guide the storytelling. Puppets may be used, as well as other props and costumes. A good resource on storytelling techniques is "Storytelling: Role and Technique" by Peninnah Schram in *The Jewish Teachers Handbook*, Volume I, Chapter 8, pages 79-93 (Denver: A.R.E. Publishing, Inc., 1981).

Helpful Hints for Story Time
- Tell the story. Jazz it up with props and costumes.
- Use participatory storytelling techniques.
- Help parents to tell the story by modeling good storytelling techniques.
- Send families home with book lists, a list of bookstores or distributors, a list of books available at various local libraries. This list may include audiovisual materials on the holiday.
- Send families home with a copy of the stories in this book that are not available in any other source.

Snack

Snack time provides another opportunity for passing on Jewish customs and traditions. Foods are edible symbols. Over the three year period, families will be introduced to a wide range of food and the customs associated with them.

Snack time provides an opportunity to teach the various blessings over food. (Blessings may be found in a special section on page 487.) Wish everyone *B'tayavon* (hearty appetite).

Helpful Hints for the Snack
- Have the snack set up for easy distribution.
- Give families recipes, the names of cookbooks, names of local bakeries.
- The Facilitator may share personal anecdotes or family stories about the snack or its preparation.

Activity

Activity time is project time. The simple activities proposed for this segment of the program serve many purposes. First of all, they are designed to foster interaction between parent and child. It is intentional that preschoolers cannot do the projects alone. They are meant for parents and children to do together. Remember also that the capabilities of children ages 2 through 4 differ greatly. Encourage parents to help when necessary, but to allow children to do as much as possible. Further, each activity ties into the major themes of the day. Like the Mind Warmer, Story Time, and Snack, the Activity features aspects of selected holiday symbols, customs, terms, and concepts.

The projects outlined herein expand horizons. They are different, creative, participatory, and meaningful.

In each of the three years, no projects are repeated. However, over the three year period, certain methodologies, such as making a mobile, are repeated.

The completed projects generally go home with the families, providing a bridge between the program and the home. The projects are not only decorative, they are also useful when celebrating the holiday at home. The accomplishment of completing a project contributes to the family's link to the holiday. Encourage families to show off their projects to grandparents, other family members, and friends.

Helpful Hints for Activity Time
- Keep directions simple.
- The Facilitator provides a sample of a completed project to show how the major parts fit together. This is necessary because of the short time frame for the entire program, and it simplifies and reinforces verbal instructions. Families should always be encouraged to be creative and original.

- The Facilitator circulates from family to family, answering questions as they arise and coordinating the use of limited supplies, such as staplers.
- The Facilitator prepares all materials in advance. This will keep the program moving.
- The Facilitator instructs families as to how they can help clean up. Inform them of what they should save, throw out, collect, etc.

Closure: Music, Movement

Music is an integral part of Jewish holiday celebrations. Through music, families learn blessings, become comfortable with holiday terms, and hear about holiday practices. Music and movement go together for this age group.

Music and movement are the last scheduled activities. Therefore, during this segment the Facilitator closes out the program. Families respond to suggested sentence completions, such as "Our family enjoyed…" Completing these sentences gives families a chance to talk about the experiences of the day. The responses provide leaders with feedback. A good way to say good-bye and to teach holiday observance is to say *Chag Sameach, L'Shanah Tovah,* etc.

Choosing Songs – Each of the sessions contains suggestions for two or three holiday songs which emphasize the focus of the program. The Facilitator will need to obtain the songbooks in advance. It is useful to distribute copies of the words (even without the music) so that families can continue singing the holiday songs at home.

The Blessings – Music time presents another opportunity for teaching and reinforcing knowledge of the blessings.

Making Music – The music component can be included with or without a music specialist. Families can sing along with a cassette or a cassette may just be used as background music. Or, the cassette can be played as families make up dances, movements, or games (e.g., shake your body every time you hear the word *lulav*). Children are used to singing without accompaniment. A rhythm instrument, such as a tambourine, will help them sing together.

At the end of this final segment, the Facilitator thanks everyone for their participation. Have families do sentence completions reflecting their reaction to the experience. Wish participants a happy holiday. Remind them to take home all their projects and papers. This is a good time to distribute blessing or story sheets for use at home. Inform participants of the date of the next holiday program.

Helpful Hint for Closure: Music and Movement
- Families who need an extra few minutes to finish a project can come late to the Closure segment. (If music takes place in a different room, make sure they know where it is.)

CONCLUSION

By following the steps outlined in this book, you will be able to initiate and carry out successful holiday programs month after month. Most important, you will enable participating families to have a successful "head start" on the Jewish holidays.

Year 1

The High Holy Days Come Round Again
The High Holy Days, Year 1

Postcard and/or Flier

> To include:
> Program Title
> Sponsored by
> Audience (age group, members only or
>   general public, etc.)
> Date
> Time
> Location
> Cost (if applicable)
> RSVP or For Further Information
> Bring a small hand mirror.

Physical Set Up

> work area: tables and chairs
> tables for supplies
> table for name tags and sign-in sheet
> large trash cans
> trash bags

Holiday Symbols, Customs, Terms, and Concepts

> a time of reflection
> Jonah
> Ninevah
> the gourd or plant parable
> trying to escape from whom we are
> round *challah*
> circles and cycles
> the year as a cycle
> starting the cycle again

00:00 – 00:15
Mind Warmer: Reflection

> The High Holy Days are a time for personal
> reflection. We think about who we are and
> how we act. Each family is introduced to this
> process of self-examination as they make a
> picture of their child.

Materials

> name tags
> markers
> sign-in sheet
> 1 11" x 17" Reflection sheet per child on
>   white paper (see Directions and Patterns)
> buttons
> yarn
> cloth scraps
> felt
> ribbon
> gluesticks
> scissors
> pencils

Advance Preparation by the Facilitator

- Copy the Reflection sheet onto 8½" x 11"
  white paper. Then enlarge to 11" x 17".

- On the supply table, place these materials:
  Reflection sheets, yarn, buttons, felt, cloth
  scraps, and ribbon.

- On the supply table, place these items, each
  in a separate container: scissors, pencils,
  and gluesticks.

Procedure

- The Facilitator greets families as they
  arrive. Have them fill out a name tag for
  each family member and sign in.

- Let families know that they will be making

a picture of their child. Lead them to the supply table where they will find the materials.

- The Facilitator instructs the adults to read and explain to their child the saying on the Reflection sheet. Have each child look in a hand mirror and describe what he/she sees.

- Each family makes a picture of their child using the yarn, felt, cloth, buttons, etc. They glue these on for the child's features. (From time to time, they should stand the picture up to make certain all the parts are glued on securely.)

- Ask families to bring their pictures to the Introductions and Announcements area.

- Ask families to clean up, returning materials to the supply table.

00:15 – 00:25
Introductions and Announcements

- The Facilitator welcomes everyone on behalf of the sponsoring agency/institution.

- The Facilitator introduces himself/herself and any other official representatives of the program or the agency/institution.

- Have a member of each family introduce himself/herself and other family members.

- Announce any upcoming events for the sponsoring agency/institution that are pertinent for this group.

- Instruct people as to how they can get on the mailing list if they are not already on it.

Setting the Stage

- The Facilitator asks each child to hold up the picture of themselves.

- Say: Rosh Hashanah is a time to examine yourself closely. It is a time to look and see who and what you are and how you act. On Rosh Hashanah, we examine ourselves on the outside, and on the inside. You started by making a picture of what you are on the outside. What do you see when you look at your outsides? Can you tell me who you are or how you act? (Look for answers like: a boy or a girl, a sister or a brother, a happy person, an eager person, etc. Prompt the group as necessary.)

Now let's look at your insides. What do you like? Who do you love? What do you wish for? On Rosh Hashanah, when we look at our insides, we try to be better people. We try not to hurt anyone. We say we are sorry. We try to show our love more often. On Yom Kippur, we tell God about how we want to be a better person in the year to come.

Now we are going to hear a story about a Jew named Jonah. We will look at his insides. We will see what he liked and what he wished for. We will learn how he tried to run away from God. At the end of the story, we will understand what Jonah learned about being a better, more caring person.

00:25 – 00:45
Story: The Book of Jonah

This segment of the program features a story combined with an activity. To associate the main characters and symbols in the Book of Jonah with the story's events, families cut out the main characters and symbols and make scenes of the main events of the story. These scenes will enable families to sequence and retell the story of Jonah.

Materials

1 copy of the Do-It-Yourself Jonah Story Kit per family on bright colored paper (see Directions and Patterns)

1 copy per family of the story from The Book of Jonah (see Directions and Patterns)

1 set per child of Symbols and Characters from The Book of Jonah (see Directions and Patterns), including Jonah, a king, 2 sailors, sun, storm cloud, a plant, and a big fish on 8½" x 11" white card stock (see Directions and Patterns)

1 set per child of the following four scenes photocopied onto 8½" x 11" white card stock: A City, A Ship to Tarshish, In the Sea, A Place East of Ninevah

gluesticks

scissors

crayons

1 9" x 12" manila envelope per child

Advance Preparation by the Facilitator

- On the supply table, place these materials: the set of four scenes on card stock, the figures copied on card stock, the Book of Jonah sheets, the copies of the Do-It-Yourself Jonah Story Kit, and manila envelopes.

- On the supply table, place these items, each in a separate container: scissors, crayons, and gluesticks.

Procedure

- The Facilitator tells the story of Jonah using a set of scenes and characters and symbols. Each time one of the symbols or characters pictured on a card is mentioned, point it out.

The Book of Jonah

A long time ago, God spoke to Jonah: "Go now to Ninevah, that great city. Tell them that God knows of their wickedness, their evil and bad ways."

Jonah heard God's words. But he did not want to go to Ninevah. He did not want to tell the people of Ninevah to change their ways. So Jonah decided to run away from God. Jonah went to the city of Jaffa to catch a ship going to Tarshish.

Jonah boarded the ship. The ship set sail. Suddenly, God made the sea rough. The sky turned dark with clouds. The sea waves tossed the ship from side to side. The ship was in danger of breaking up. The sailors threw the cargo over the sides of the ship to make the ship lighter. The sailors cried out to their gods for help. Still the sea tossed the ship.

The sailors on the ship drew lots to see whose fault it was that the sea was so rough. The lot fell on Jonah. The sailors turned to Jonah: "Tell us why this bad thing has happened to us? Who are you? What is your business? Where have you come from? What is your country and who are your people?"

Jonah answered: "I am a Jew. I worship God in heaven who made the land and the sea."

The sailors looked at him and asked: "What have you done?"

Jonah told the sailors of how he was trying to run away from doing God's work. Jonah told them: "Throw me overboard into the sea. That will calm down the sea."

The sailors did as Jonah instructed. The sea became calm. The ship stopped tossing. The sailors then respected the God of Jonah, the Jew.

God provided a big fish to swallow Jonah. Jonah was in the belly of the big fish for three days and three nights. Jonah prayed to God: "Lord, you threw me into the sea. I pray that you will let me live. I was wrong to run away from You and Your work. I will do what You asked of me. Deliver me to safety."

God heard Jonah's prayer and commanded the fish to spit Jonah out onto dry land.

Jonah did what God had asked him to do. He went to Ninevah and told the people: "You have forty days to change your ways or God will destroy your city and you."

The king of Ninevah heard about Jonah's warning. The king was concerned about what God would do. He told everyone to fast and to change their evil ways.

God saw that the people of Ninevah stopped doing bad things. God was pleased. God did not destroy the city of Ninevah.

But Jonah was unhappy. He thought God was too nice and forgave the people of Ninevah too easily. Jonah went to a place above Ninevah. He sat there watching the city. God provided a plant which made shade for Jonah, giving him relief from the sun. Jonah was happy that the plant was there.

The next day, God put a worm in the plant. The worm attacked the plant which dried and shrank. The sun beat down on Jonah's head. He felt faint from the heat. Jonah was so hot that he wanted to die. He was very upset that the plant was gone.

God became angry at Jonah. "You cared so much about this plant which you did not plant and did not water. The plant came up in one day and was gone the next day." God continued, saying, "Just as you care about the plant, I care very much about Ninevah where many people live."

The Story Scenes

The families now make their own set of characters, symbols, and backdrops for the story of Jonah.

- The Facilitator explains to families that they will now be making their own Jonah Story Kit. The kit includes the main symbols, characters, and backdrops from the story of Jonah, as well as a copy of the story. The props are movable.

- Ask that one or two people from each work table collect the materials from the supply table.

- Each family cuts out the figure of Jonah from the Do-It-Yourself Jonah Story Kit instruction sheet.

- They glue the figure of Jonah onto the front of a 9" x 12" manila envelope.

- Using crayons, they color in the settings for the Jonah story.

- They color in the Jonah story characters and symbols and cut them out.

- They place the symbols, main characters, and scenes in the manila envelope.

- Ask families to clean up, returning the materials to the supply table.

- Suggest to families that they retell the story at bedtime, using their copy of the story and the scenes.

00:45 – 00:55
Snack: A High Holy Day Sampler

During this snack, families taste test some foods which are symbolic of the holidays.

Materials

round *challah*
apple juice
fish crackers
napkins
cups

Procedure

- Serve round *challah*, symbolic of the year's cycle; apple juice for a sweet new year; and fish crackers as a reminder of Jonah.

- Remember to recite *HaMotzi* together before eating the *challah* (see Blessing #3, page 487). Then recite the *Shehecheyanu*, an appropriate blessing for the new year (see Blessing #5, page 488).

00:55 – 01:10
Activity: Circles and Cycles

This activity reinforces the metaphor of circles and cycles. Families will make a collage of circles and cycles. They will attach to the collage a saying about circles and cycles which relates to Rosh Hashanah.

Materials

lots of old magazines
1 round paper plate per child
1 A Round Rosh Hashanah Collage sheet per child copied on bright colored paper (see Directions and Patterns)
gluesticks
scissors

Advance Preparation by the Facilitator

- On the supply table, place these materials: old magazines, paper plates, and the Rosh Hashanah Collage sheets.

- On the supply table, place these items, each in a separate container: gluesticks and scissors.

Procedure

- The Facilitator asks parents to read and discuss with their child the saying in the circle on the Round Rosh Hashanah Collage sheet. Say: A cycle goes around and around. It is like a circle. It does not end. Lots of Rosh Hashanah symbols are round. Apples, the *challah*, the world, the opening of the shofar. Can you think of others?

- Instruct them to be creative as they decorate a paper plate with round things they find in the magazines. They can also cut out circles.

- Ask one or two people from each work table to get the materials from the supply table.

- After finishing the collage, families cut out the pattern of the saying about circles and cycles and glue it to the middle of the plate.

- Ask families to clean up, returning materials to the supply table.

01:10 – 01:30
Closure: Hitting the High Notes —
High Holy Day Music and Movement

End the program with songs, sharing, and holiday greetings.

- Sing and move to High Holy Day music related to: circles, cycles, round *challah*, New Year, the shofar, Jonah, fish, praying to God, changing our ways, personal reflection. Include your favorite holiday tunes and greetings.

Recommended Songs:

"Apples" (*Apples on Holidays and Other Days* by Leah Abrams, Tara Publications)

"Sing Along Song: Yom Kippur" (*Especially Wonderful Days* by Steve Reuben, A.R.E. Publishing, Inc.)

"Circle" (*Seasoned With Song* by Julie Auerbach, Tara Publications)

- Have participants share their reactions to the program. Ask families to complete one of these phrases:

For Rosh Hashanah, for this New Year, we hope . . .

In the coming year, I will . . .

Our family learned . . .

Our family enjoyed . . .

Jonah is . . .

- Send everyone off with a New year greeting of *"Shanah Tovah U' metukah!"* (A Happy and Sweet New Year!)

- Remind families to take home their copy of the story, The Book of Jonah.

Reflection

Rosh Hashanah is a time to closely examine yourself, a time to look and see who and what you are. Start this process by "making" your "outsides." Use materials provided (or found at home) to add detail to this self-portrait.

Do-It-Yourself Jonah Story Kit
Instructions

Includes:
   4 Jonah story settings
   1 sheet of Jonah story symbols and characters
   1 Jonah story outline
   1 manila envelope carrying case

To make your Do-It-Yourself Jonah Story Kit:
   1. Cut out the picture of Jonah below and glue to the front of your envelope.
   2. Color in your Jonah story settings.
   3. Color in your Jonah story symbols and characters and cut them out.
   4. Use your Jonah story outline as a guide to "acting" out the Jonah story.
   5. Store the parts of your Do-It-Yourself Jonah Story Kit in your envelope.
   6. Use your Kit often and enjoy.

Symbols and Characters from the Book of Jonah

A Sailor

A Sailor

The King of Nineveh

Jonah

A Big Fish

A Plant

A Storm Cloud

The Sun

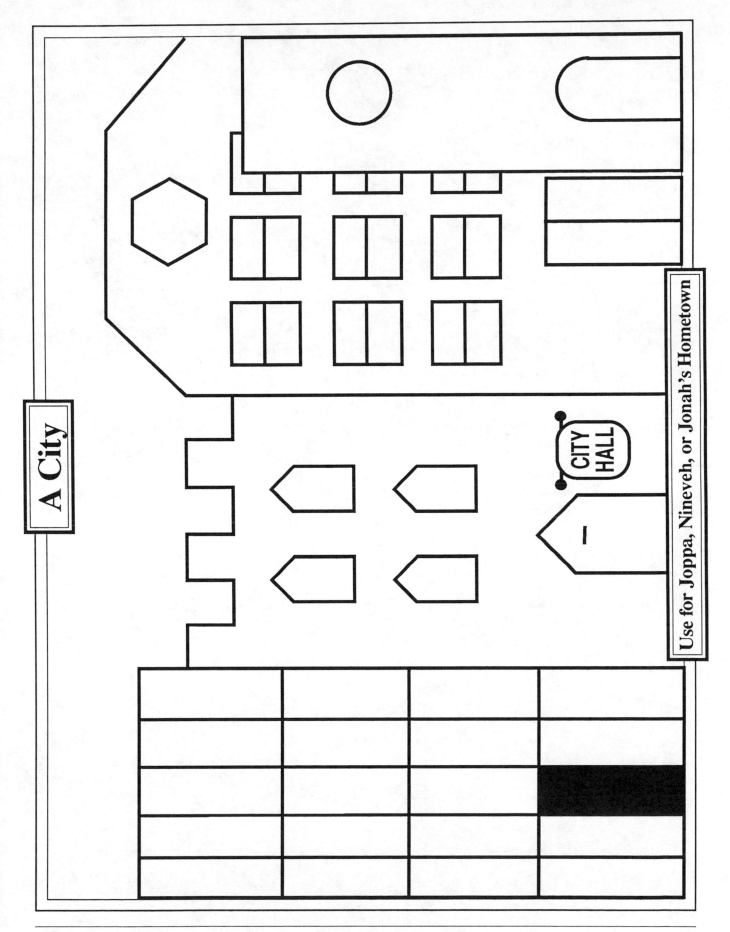

A City

CITY HALL

Use for Joppa, Nineveh, or Jonah's Hometown

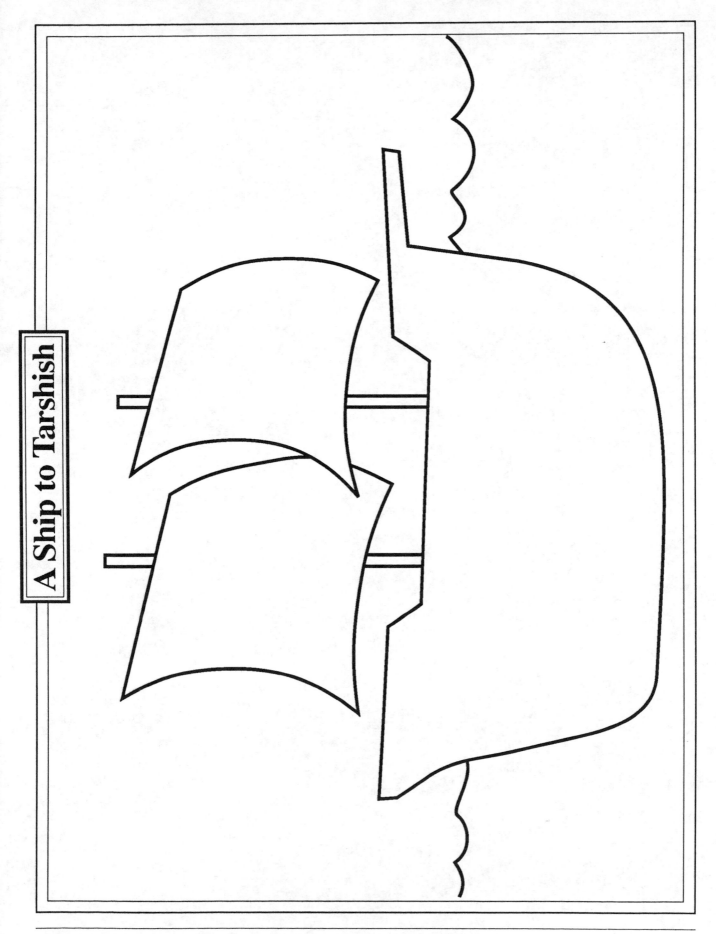

A Ship to Tarshish

In the Sea

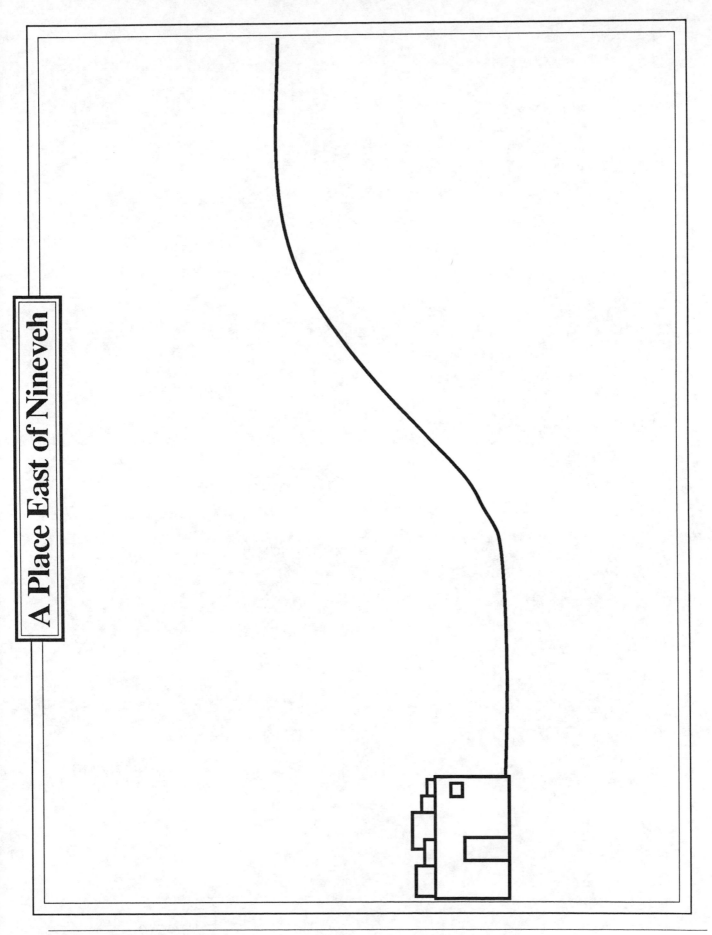

A Place East of Nineveh

Do-It-Yourself Jonah Story Kit
The Book of Jonah

A long time ago, God spoke to Jonah: "Go now to Nineveh, that great city. Tell them that God knows of their wickedness, their evil and bad ways."

Jonah heard God's words. But he did not want to go to Nineveh. He did not want to tell the people of Nineveh to change their ways. So Jonah decided to run away from God. Jonah went to the city of Jaffa to catch a ship going to Tarshish.

Jonah boarded the ship. The ship set sail. Suddenly, God made the sea rough. The sky turned dark with clouds. The sea waves tossed the ship from side to side. The ship was in danger of breaking up. The sailors threw the cargo over the sides of the ship to make the ship lighter. The sailors cried out to their gods for help. Still the sea tossed the ship.

The sailors on the ship drew lots to see whose fault it was that the sea was so rough. The lot fell on Jonah. The sailors turned to Jonah: "Tell us why this bad thing has happened to us? Who are you? What is your business? Where have you come from? What is your country and who are your people?"

Jonah answered: "I am a Jew. I worship God in heaven who made the land and the sea."

The sailors looked at him and asked: "What have you done?"

Jonah told the sailors of how he was trying to run away from doing God's work. Jonah told them: "Throw me overboard into the sea. That will calm down the sea."

The sailors did as Jonah instructed. The sea became calm. The ship stopped tossing. The sailors then respected the God of Jonah, the Jew.

God provided a big fish to swallow Jonah. Jonah was in the belly of the big fish for three days and three nights. Jonah prayed to God: "Lord, you threw me into the sea. I pray that You will let me live. I was wrong to run away from You and Your work. I will do what You asked of me. Deliver me to safety."

God heard Jonah's prayer and commanded the fish to spit Jonah out onto dry land.

Jonah did what God had asked him to do. He went to Nineveh and told the people: "You have forty days to change your ways or God will destroy your city and you."

The king of Nineveh heard about Jonah's warning. The king was concerned about what God would do. He told everyone to fast and to change their evil ways.

God saw that the people of Nineveh stopped doing bad things. God was pleased. God did not destroy the city of Nineveh.

But Jonah was unhappy. He thought God was too nice and forgave the people of Nineveh too easily. Jonah went to a place above Nineveh. He sat there watching the city. God provided a plant which made shade for Jonah, giving him relief from the sun. Jonah was happy that the plant was there.

The next day, God put a worm in the plant. The worm attacked the plant which dried and shrank. The sun beat down on Jonah's head. He felt faint from the heat. Jonah was so hot that he wanted to die. He was very upset that the plant was gone.

God became angry at Jonah. "You cared so much about this plant which you did not plant and did not water. The plant came up in one day and was gone the next day." God continued, saying, "Just as you care about the plant, I care very much about Nineveh where many people live."

A Round Rosh Hashanah Collage

Collect the following materials:
  pictures from magazines of things that are round
  a paper plate
  this pattern page

cycles and circles and

A cycle goes around and around.
It is like a circle . . . .
It does not end.
Lots of Rosh Hashanah symbols
are round . . . .
Apples, the challah, the world,
the opening of the shofar . . . .
Can you think of others?

To assemble your Collage:
  1. Glue magazine pictures of things that are round onto the paper plate.
  2. Cut out the round pattern label above.
  3. Glue the pattern label onto the middle of your collage.
  4. Use the collage as a decoration on your holiday table.
  5. Pass the collage *around* your table and have each person try to name a round thing.

Put Your Best Fruits and Best Foot Forward
Sukkot, Year 1

Postcard and/or Flier

To include:
Program Title
Sponsored by
Audience (age group, members only or
general public, etc.)
Date
Time
Location
Cost (if applicable)
RSVP or For Further Information

Physical Set Up

work area: tables and chairs
tables for supplies
table for name tags and sign-in sheet
large trash cans
trash bags
stove or microwave
large room or area for the story segment
(optional)

**Holiday Symbols, Customs, Terms,
and Concepts**

giving thanks
thanking God for food
harvest festival
Birkat HaMazon
the *mitzvah* of feeding the hungry
making a pilgrimage
One of the Three Pilgrimage Festivals
a *sukkah* as a temporary shelter
building a *sukkah*
living in a *sukkah* in the wilderness
the Temple in Jerusalem

00:00 – 00:15
Mind Warmer: Thanking God for Food

Here the connection is made between the fall
harvest and thankfulness for the food we have.
Each family makes a picture of their Sukkot
offering, gluing on cut out shapes of fruits and
vegetables.

Materials

name tags
markers
sign in sheet
1 outline per child of Thanks! sheet copied
on 11" x 17" white paper (see Directions
and Patterns)
1 copy per child of the abbreviated *Birkat
HaMazon* (Grace After Meals) copied on
back of the Thanks! sheet (see Directions
and Patterns)
copies of the Sukkot Fruit Patterns (see
Directions and Patterns); each child should
have one of every fruit as follows:
oranges on orange card stock
apples on red card stock
pears on gold or light green card stock
grapes on purple, red, or green card stock
bananas on yellow card stock
scissors
gluesticks
crayons

Advance Preparation by the Facilitator

• Enlarge the pattern Thanks! to fit onto a
piece of white paper 11" x 17". Make one
copy for each child.

- Copy the *Birkat HaMazon* onto the back of the Thanks! sheet.

- On the supply table, place these materials: Thanks! sheet with *Birkat HaMazon* on the back and the fruit patterns on card stock.

- On the supply table, place these items, each in a separate container: scissors, gluesticks, and crayons.

Procedure

- The Facilitator greets families as they arrive. Have them fill out a name tag for each family member and sign in.

- Explain that they will make a picture of their own Sukkot food offering. Lead them to the supply table where they will find the supplies and directions. The project directions are written on the outline of the child.

- Have the parents read to their child the following message which is written on the outline of the child:

Sukkot, the fall harvest festival, could be called the Jewish Thanksgiving. In ancient times, people would make a pilgrimage to the Temple in Jerusalem. They would show their thanks to God by bringing their finest fruits and vegetables from the harvest. Today we show our thanks by giving food to local food banks. As a family, take a selection of the card stock paper fruits. Write what you are thankful for this year on each fruit or vegetable. Glue it on the offering bowl below.

- Families write on each fruit something they are thankful for this year.

- They arrange the fruits and vegetables in the bowl outlined on the paper.

- They glue the fruits and vegetables in place.

- They color in their child's features: eyes, hair, etc., as desired.

- Families clean up, returning materials to the supply tables.

- Families bring their Sukkot offerings with them to the Introductions and Announcements area.

00:15 – 00:25
Introductions and Announcements

- The Facilitator welcomes everyone on behalf of the sponsoring agency/institution.

- The Facilitator introduces himself/herself and any other official representatives of the program or the agency/institution.

- Have a member of each family introduce himself/herself and other family members.

- Announce any upcoming events for the sponsoring agency/institution that are pertinent for this group.

- Instruct people as to how they can get on the mailing list if they are not already on it.

Setting the Stage

- Have the children parade around with the pictures of their Sukkot offering.

- Ask families to share one thing that they were thankful for this year.

- The Facilitator says: On Sukkot we express our thanks to God for all the newly harvested foods. (Mention some of the foods harvested in your area, such as corn or apples.) After every meal, Jewish people recite a prayer of thanks called the *"Birkat HaMazon."* The words to this prayer may be found on the back of the Thanks! sheet. As we recite this prayer, we remember people who are hungry, those who do not have enough food to eat. Saying a prayer is our way of thanking God; it is our offering.

- With the group, read and/or sing a paragraph or two from the *Birkat HaMazon*. The *Oseh Shalom* line in the *Birkat HaMazon* should be especially familiar.

- The Facilitator says: Throughout this program, we will learn about Sukkot, the fall harvest festival, the Jewish Thanksgiving.

00:25 – 00:45
Story: A Short Story About a Short-Term Shelter

This participatory story explains the function of the *sukkah* (or booth) throughout the generations. The *sukkah* was used by Jews as they wandered in the desert after leaving Egypt. Jews stayed in these booths when harvesting their crops. Today, we build a *sukkah* and eat and drink and even sleep in it in order to remember and celebrate the fall harvest festival, Sukkot.

Materials

a room or area where everyone can
   move around
1 sheet of butcher paper 6'-10' long
wallpaper scraps or wallpaper sample books
pencils
scissors
gluesticks
markers
Contact paper (optional)

Advance Preparation by the Facilitator

- On the supply table place these materials: wallpaper scraps or sample books.

- On the supply table place these items, each in a separate container: pencils, scissors, gluesticks, and markers.

Procedure

- The Facilitator tells the following story, informing families that they will participate while it is being told. (The recommended movements for families are in parentheses.)

A Sukkah

When the Jews left Egypt and were no longer slaves, they wandered all around the desert. (Wander all around.)

They stopped here and there, up the road and down the road, under a tree and beside a hill, east and west, and north and south. (Stop here and there.)

Everywhere they went, at every turn and stop on their journey, they needed a place to live. They gathered whatever they could find to make a shelter, a home that would last a few days or weeks. They built a shelter. (Gather things and build a shelter.)

They called this temporary, short-term, likely-to-fall-down-or-apart shelter, a *sukkah*.

The Jews wandered all the way from Egypt to Israel. When they arrived in Israel, there was no place for them to live. They had to build a shelter to protect themselves from the hot and cold and the wind and the sand, and to protect their cattle from the wild beasts and their food from hungry goats.

They looked and searched and gathered all the things they could find for their *sukkah*, their temporary home. (Gather things.) Then they built their *sukkah*. (Build the *sukkah*.) Then they wandered some more. (Walk.)

The Jews stayed in Israel. They planted trees, fruits, and vegetables, wheat, and barley. (Plant trees, fruits, and vegetables.) They built new homes to live in, homes that would last a long time.

A few months after they planted the fruits and vegetables, barley and wheat, they had to go to the fields to harvest all the foods. They would harvest and harvest and harvest day after day. (Do some harvesting.)

Some of the people would go out to fields that were far away from their homes. They would spend the night there. They gathered all the things they could find to make a shelter, a *sukkah*, for a night or two or three. (Gather things and build a *sukkah*.)

During the fall harvest, the Jews took part of their harvest to the Temple in Jerusalem. They walked to Jerusalem from all over Israel. They walked and walked and walked. (Walk.) Some rode on animals, but mostly they walked.

- Take time out here for families to make out of butcher paper a symbolic runner to a *sukkah* or a mural.

- The Facilitator says: We will make a display of our Sukkot pilgrimage. Each child will trace his/her feet on wallpaper using a pencil. Then cut out the two feet. Write the child's name on the feet, then glue the feet onto the sheet of butcher paper.

- Send one or two people from each table to gather the supplies from the supply table.

- Families follow the directions to make the runner.

- The Facilitator writes a heading on the runner: Our Sukkot Pilgrimage. He/she covers the runner with Contact paper (or laminates it) to waterproof it after the program.

- When finished, families clean up, returning the materials to the supply table.

- The Facilitator continues telling the story.

It was a long way to Jerusalem. There were no hotels in which the people could stay. So each night, they gathered all the things they could find, and once again they built a *sukkah*, a shelter. (Gather things and build a *sukkah*.)

When they got to Jerusalem, they offered their harvest foods to God at the Temple. So many people came to Jerusalem that they had to build a *sukkah* there, too. (Gather and build a *sukkah*.) In this way, they celebrated the fall pilgrimage holiday, Sukkot.

Today, even though we do not live in Israel, and even though we do not all grow our own food, we still celebrate Sukkot, the fall harvest festival. When we celebrate, we still gather all the things we can find, and build a *sukkah*, a temporary shelter. (Build a *sukkah*.) For eight days, we eat and sometimes even sleep in the *sukkah*. (Walk on the runner just made to a real or imaginary *sukkah*.)

Join with me as we say the blessing for the time we spend in the *sukkah* (see Blessing #10, page 488).

- The Facilitator secures the pilgrimage runner outside of a *sukkah* or tapes it to wall.

00:45 – 00:55
Snack: A Sukkot Offering

Families have an opportunity to sample some fall harvest foods and to recite *Birkat HaMazon*.

Materials

challah
small pieces of frozen corn on the cob
apple cider
cups
napkins
plates
pan for boiling corn in water or a plate for
    microwaving the corn
serving tray

Advance Preparation by the Facilitator

- During story time, have a volunteer heat up
  the corn for the snack.

Procedure

- The Facilitator introduces the fall harvest
  foods and the *challah*.

- Together with families, recite a blessing
  before eating (see Blessing #3, page 487).

- After eating, say or sing together part of
  the *Birkat HaMazon* as an offering of
  thanks to God for the food. Use the
  pictures with the *Birkat HaMazon* for
  this part of the program.

00:55 – 01:15
Activity: Good Foods from A-Z

This activity reinforces the concept of Sukkot
as a harvest festival, a time for expressing our
thankfulness to God for all the food we eat.
Each family puts together a booklet called
Good Foods from A-Z, drawing, cutting, and
pasting pictures of foods (for each letter of the
alphabet) found in magazines, or on coupons,
cans, or boxes.

Materials

1 copy per child of the *Good Foods from A-Z*

cover on harvest color card stock (see
    Directions and Patterns)
1 copy of the *Good Foods from A-Z* booklet
    per child (see Directions and Patterns)
magazines
food labels from cans or boxes
coupons
scissors
markers
pencils
gluesticks
single hole punches
yarn

Advance Preparation by the Facilitator

- Using the pattern at the end of this program,
  copy back-to-back the pages for the *Good
  Foods from A-Z* booklets on white paper.

- Copy the pattern for the cover on any
  harvest color card stock.

- Make a sample booklet (see Procedure).

- Gather magazines, coupons for discounts
  on food, and labels from cans or boxes of
  food.

- On the supply table, place these materials:
  covers of the *Good Foods from A-Z* booklet, copies of the inside pages of *Good
  Foods from A-Z*, magazines, coupons,
  labels, and yarn.

- On the supply table, place these items, each
  in a separate container: scissors, markers,
  pencils, gluesticks, and single hole punches.

Procedure

- The Facilitator tells families that they will
  be assembling a *Good Foods from A-Z*
  booklet. Because Sukkot is a harvest
  festival, we show God our thanks for all
  the food we eat.

- The Facilitator reads aloud the prayer by Edythe and Sol Scharfstein that is in the Sukkot booklet.

- Tell families that they will fill in their booklets with the name or picture of a food or foods for each letter of the alphabet.

- Let families know that they can use a middle letter for the more difficult letters like "q" and "z," or find a food that looks like the letter.

- Ask one or two people from each table to gather the materials from the supply table.

- Have families search for, cut out, glue down, or write down the names of the foods for each letter of the alphabet.

- They fold the booklet and cover in half, keeping the alphabet in order. They punch two holes near the fold. Then they thread the yarn through the holes, tying a knot at the bottom.

- Be certain that each family fills in the blank of the front page with the words "By _____" to indicate who authored the work.

- When the time is up, the Facilitator asks families to clean up, returning materials to the supply table.

- Tell families that they may complete the booklet at home.

01:15 – 01:30
Closure: Songs of Thanksgiving

End the program with songs, sharing, and holiday greetings.

- Sing and move to Sukkot music related to: thanking God, showing our thanks, food, going on a pilgrimage, the *sukkah*, and harvesting.

Recommended Songs:

"*Al Shalosh Regalim*" (*Seasoned With Song* by Julie Auerbach, Tara Publications)

"Sukkot Song" (*Especially Wonderful Days* by Steve Reuben, A.R.E. Publishing, Inc.)

"Build a Sukkah" (*Rabbi Joe Black Sings,* Temple Israel, 2324 Emerson Avenue S., Minneapolis, MN 55405)

Materials

1 copy per family of the story "A Sukkah"

Procedure

- The Facilitator leads the families in the singing of part of the *Birkat HaMazon*.

- Have participants share their reactions to the program. Ask families to complete one of these phrases:

  We are thankful for . . .

  Our family learned . . .

  Our family enjoyed . . .

  For Sukkot this year, . . .

- Send everyone off with a Sukkot greeting, *Chag Sameach*! (Happy Holiday!)

- Send everyone home with a copy of the Sukkot story.

Thanks!

Sukkot — the Fall Harvest Festival — could be called the Jewish Thanksgiving. In ancient times, people would make a pilgrimage to the Temple in Jerusalem. They would show their thanks to God by bringing the finest fruits and vegetables from the harvest.

Today we show our thanks by giving food to local food banks.

As a family, take a selection of the construction paper fruit. On each fruit, write what you are thankful for this year, and glue it onto the offering bowl below.

Birkat HaMazon

BARUCH ATAH ADONAI, ELOHEYNU MELECH HA-OLAM, HAZAN ET HA-OLAM
KULO B'TUVO B'CHAYN, B'CHESED, UV'RACHAMIM. HU NOTEN LECHEM
L'CHOL BASAR, KI L'OLAM CHASDO. UV-TUVO HA-GADOL, TAMID LO
CHASAR LANU V'AL YECHSAR LANU MAZON L'OLAM VA'ED. BA'AVUR
SH'MO HA-GADOL KI HU AYL ZAN UM'FARNAYS LA-KOL, U'MAYTIV LA-KOL,
U'MAYCHIN MAZON L'CHOL-B'RIYOTAV ASHER BARAH. BARUCH ATAH
ADONAI, HAZAN ET HA-KOL.

Blessed are You, Eternal our God, Ruler of the world, who provides food for the entire world
through your goodness, grace, kindness and mercy; God supplies bread for all living beings,
for God's goodness is everlasting. Because of God's great goodness, we have never lacked
food, nor will we ever lack it — on account of God's great name. You are God who feeds and
provides for all and is good to all. You supply food for all creatures which You have created.
Blessed are You, God, who provides food for all.

OSEH SHALOM BIMROMAV HU YA'ASEH SHALOM ALEYNU V'AL KOL
YISRAEL, V'IMRU AMEN.

May God who makes peace in the high heavens, let peace descend on us and all Israel, and let
us say, amen.

Sukkot Fruit Patterns — Oranges

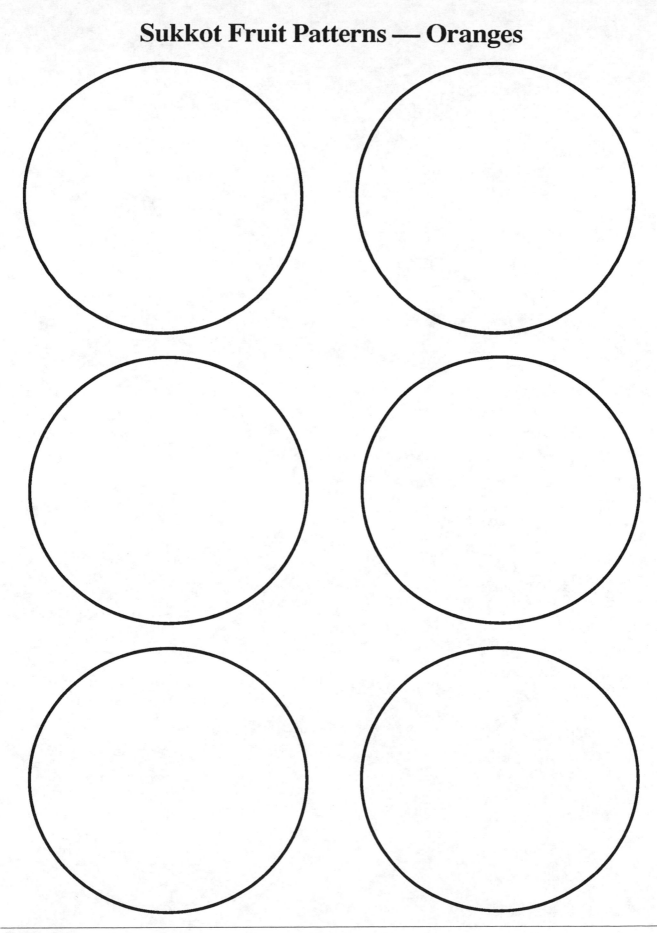

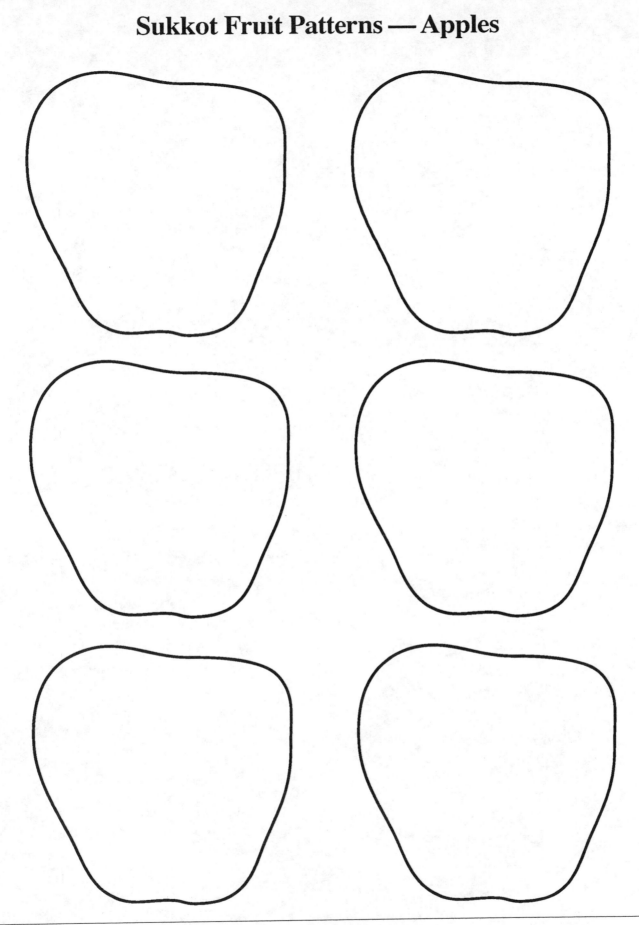

Sukkot Fruit Patterns — Pears

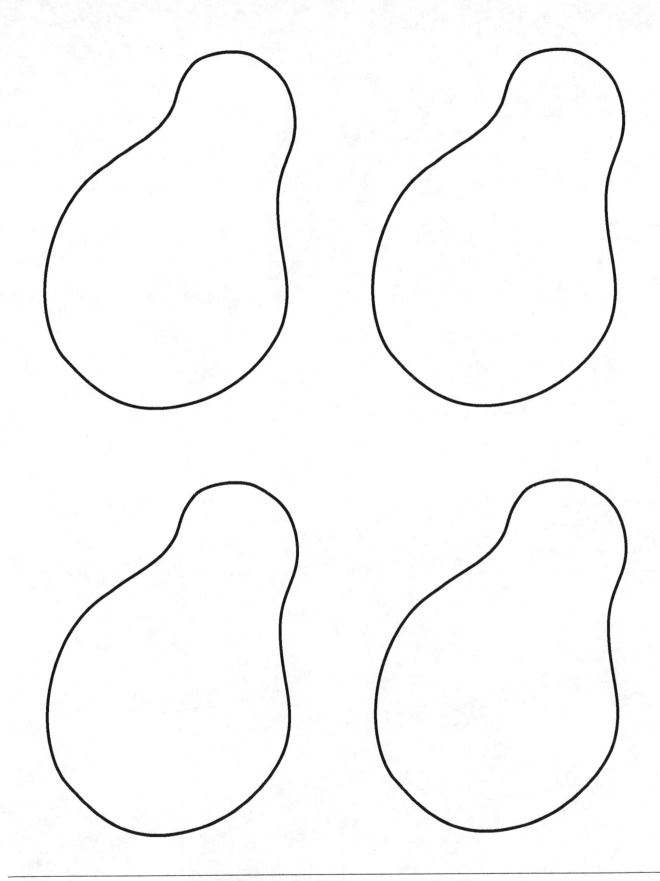

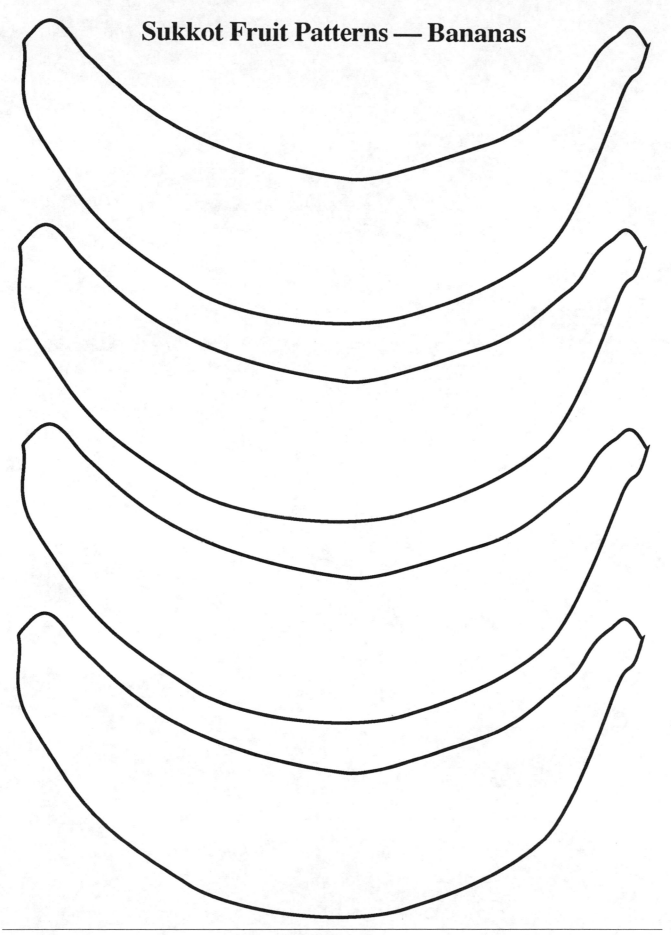

GOOD FOODS FROM A-Z

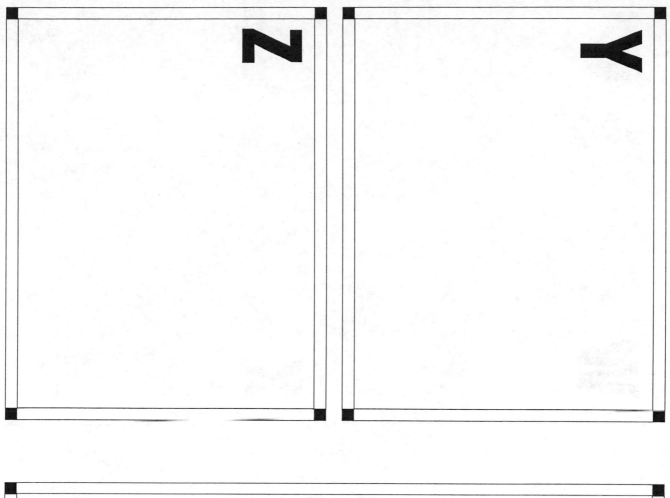

W

X

ALL FOODS THAT GROW

I thank you, dear God
For all foods that grow
In colors so bright
Just like a rainbow.

For cherries so red
For plums ripe and blue
For orange carrots
And purple grapes too.

For crisp green lettuce
And fluffy white rice
For yellow pears
And string beans so nice.

For sweet potatoes
And golden corn too
And for Your good foods
Dear God, I thank you.

From
MY FIRST BOOK OF PRAYERS
by Edythe and Sol Scharfstein

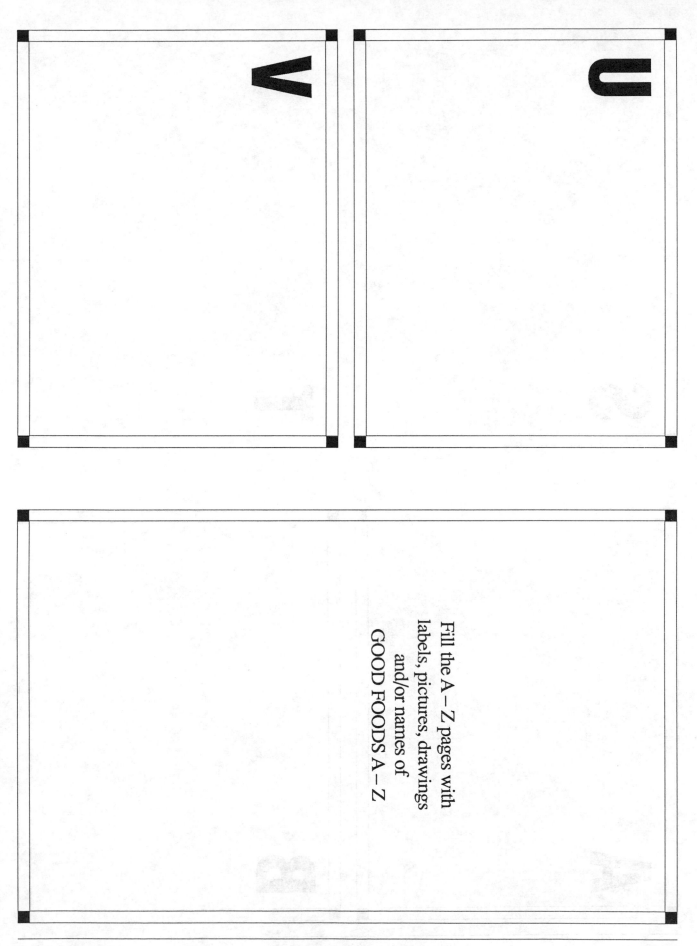

V

U

Fill the A – Z pages with
labels, pictures, drawings
and/or names of
GOOD FOODS A – Z

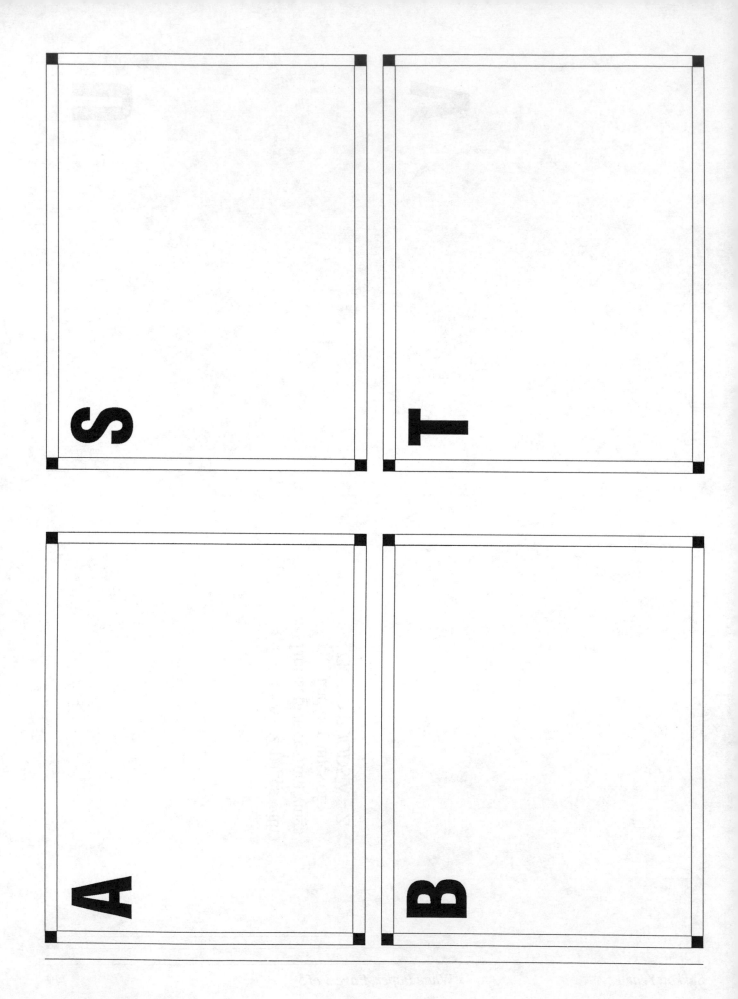

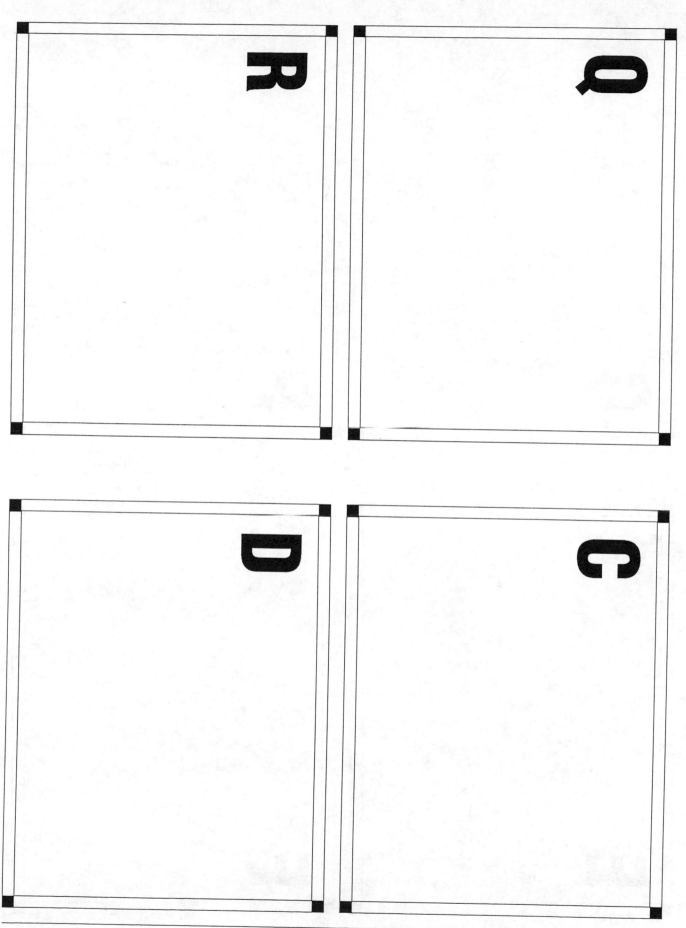

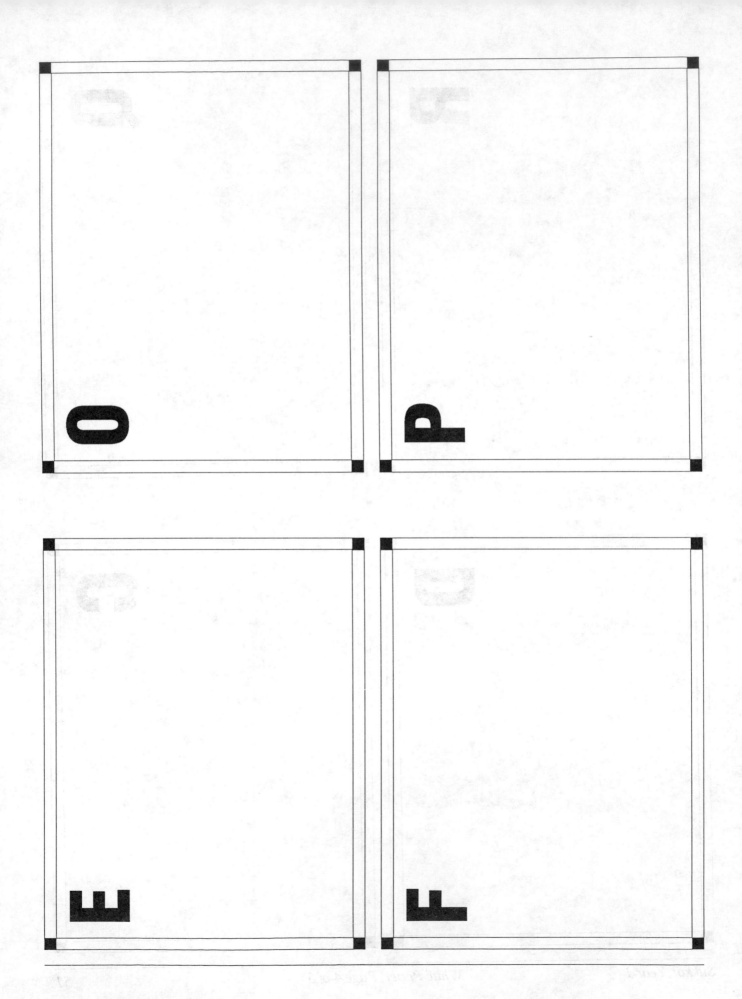

O

P

E

F

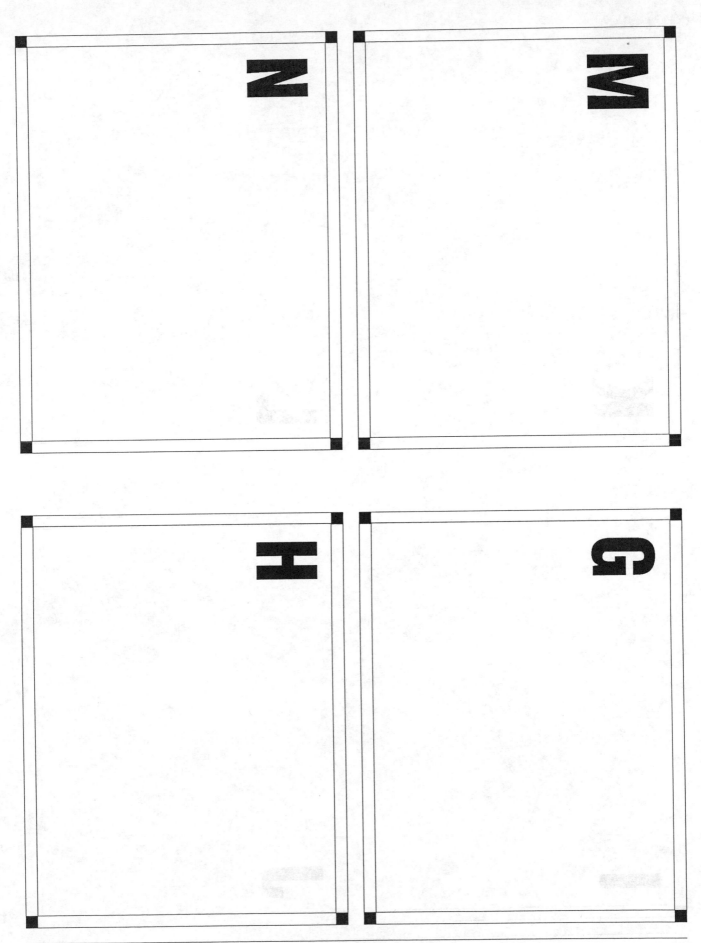

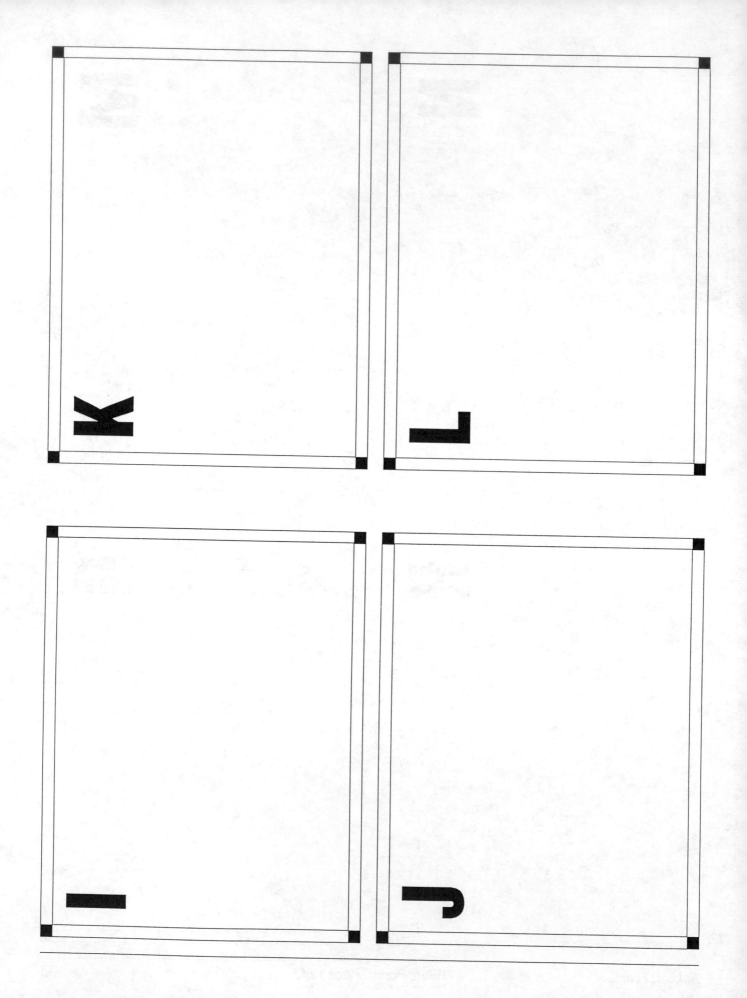

Shabbat Shalom!
Shabbat, Year 1

Postcard and/or Flier

To include:
Program Title
Sponsored by
Audience (age group, members only or
    general public, etc.)
Date
Time
Location
Cost (if applicable)
RSVP or For Further Information

Physical Set Up

work area: tables and chairs
tables for supplies
table for name tags and sign-in sheet
table to be set for Shabbat
large trash cans
trash bags
extra table set up with white tablecloth
    and the Shabbat Feelie Bags

Holiday Symbols, Customs, Terms, and Concepts

Shabbat candlesticks
Kiddush cup
challah
flowers
Shabbat symbols in the home and synagogue
blessings for lighting candles, drinking wine,
    and eating *challah*
making Shabbat holy, a special day
a special time with family
preparation
blessing
telling Shabbat stories
singing Shabbat songs

00:00 – 00:15
Mind Warmer: Getting a Feel for Shabbat

The Shabbat symbols are an important aspect of Shabbat. During this activity, the children will reach into "Shabbat Feelie Bags." They will touch the various Shabbat symbols without looking at them. Afterward, they will answer questions about where each of these Shabbat symbols is found and how each is used.

Materials

name tags
markers
sign-in sheet
1 white tablecloth
challah cover
flowers (real, paper, plastic, or silk)
2 Shabbat candles
Kiddush cup
2 Shabbat candlesticks
challah
5 grocery or shopping bags
1 copy per child of the sheet titled Jewish
    Symbols on white paper (see Directions
    and Patterns)
1 9" x 12" sheet of construction paper or
    posterboard
crayons
1 copy on any bright colored paper of the
    Shabbat Mind Warmer Sign (see Directions
    and Patterns)

Preparation

• Assemble a Shabbat Feelie Bag for each of the items that follow. Draw a question mark on each bag. In each of the five grocery or shopping bags, place one of the following five Shabbat symbols:

> *challah* cover
> flower
> *Kiddush* cup
> Shabbat candlesticks and candles
> *challah*

- On the supply table, place copies of the sheet titled Jewish Symbols.

- On the supply table, place crayons in a container.

- Make a Shabbat Mind Warmer Sign. Cut out the outline of the sign from the bright colored sheet of paper.

- Glue the sign on one half of the piece of construction paper or poster board.

- Fold the paper in half so that it will stand on the table.

- Cover the table with the white tablecloth.

- Place the five Shabbat Feelie Bags and the sign on a table.

Procedure

- The Facilitator greets families as they arrive. Have them fill out a name tag for each family member and sign in.

- Explain that the first thing they will be doing is to feel some Shabbat symbols in a Shabbat Feelie Bag. Parents and children should all touch the symbols without peeking into the bag.

- Direct participants to the table where they will find the Shabbat Feelie Bags.

- After they feel the Shabbat symbols, ask families to go to the supply table to get the Jewish Symbols sheet and three crayons.

- Parents should have their child point out on the Jewish Symbol sheet the five Shabbat symbols found in the Shabbat Feelie Bags.

- Parents then read the directions to the child. As a family, they decide which Jewish objects are found only in the home, which are found only in the synagogue, and which are found in both the home and in the synagogue.

- The child records his/her answers with crayons in three different colors.

- The child may finish coloring in the Jewish symbols on the sheet. Or, as time permits, he/she may go back to feeling and identifying the Shabbat symbols in the Shabbat Feelie Bag.

00:15 – 00:25
Introductions and Announcements

Materials

the 5 Shabbat Feelie Bags from the Mind Warmer

Procedure

- The Facilitator welcomes everyone on behalf of the sponsoring agency/institution.

- The Facilitator introduces himself/herself and any other official representatives of the program or the agency/institution.

- Have a member of each family introduce himself/herself and other family members.

- Announce any upcoming events for the sponsoring agency/institution that are pertinent for this group.

- Instruct people as to how they can get on the mailing list if they are not already on it.

Setting the Stage

- The Facilitator asks: Who can tell me one of the things that they felt inside the Shabbat Feelie Bag? (Be certain families name all the objects — candlesticks and candles, *Kiddush* cup, flowers, *challah,* and *challah* cover. As the children volunteer responses, take the object out of the corresponding Shabbat Feelie Bag.)

- The Facilitator says: On Shabbat, we use special objects and do special things. (Hold up an object.) What do we do with this? (Encourage more than one response for each item. For example, regarding candlesticks and candles: we polish them, we set them on the Shabbat table, we light them, we say or sing a blessing over them, we look at them.)

  Continue: During this program on Shabbat, we are going to focus on what we can do to make Shabbat holy (special), and different from our ordinary weekday activities. We will think about what we can do at home and in the synagogue to make Shabbat holy.

00:25 – 00:40
Story: Tales of Shabbat

To make Shabbat special, we tell and share stories from our heritage and our own lives. From today's fanciful Shabbat story, we learn about the symbols and rituals surrounding Shabbat.

Materials

- 1 copy of *Mrs. Moskowitz and the Sabbath Candlesticks* by Amy Schwartz (Philadelphia: Jewish Publication Society, 1983)
- 1 piece per child of colored 12" x 18" construction paper
- 1 rectangular doily per child as close to 12" x 18" as possible
- 1 file folder or sheet of tagboard 9" x 12"
- 1 *Kiddush* cup per child on silver or gold paper
- 2 Shabbat candles per child on white construction paper
- 1 vase per child on textured paper or wallpaper
- 1 *challah* plate per child on any color of construction paper
- 2 *challot* per child on brown construction paper
- 2 candlesticks per child on silver or gold paper
- sesame or poppy seeds in cups, one cup per table
- scraps of cloth (velvet if possible)
- tissue paper in flower petal colors
- crayons
- gluesticks
- scissors
- 1 copy of the Shabbat Texture Picture Directions and Shabbat Texture Picture Patterns (see Directions and Patterns)

Advance Preparation by the Facilitator

- Cut out the 6 Shabbat symbols from Shabbat Texture Picture Patterns.

- Trace these 6 Shabbat symbols onto a file folder or tagboard. (Stronger material is better, as you will be tracing the symbols so many times.)

- Trace the file folder or tagboard symbols for each child as follows:
  1 *Kiddush* cup on gold or silver paper
  2 candles on white construction paper
  1 vase on textured paper or wallpaper
  2 *challot* on brown paper
  2 candlesticks on gold or silver paper
  1 *challah* plate on any color construction paper

- The Facilitator makes a sample Shabbat texture picture (see Procedure).

- On the supply table, place the following materials: Shabbat Texture Picture Directions sheet, 12" x 18" construction paper, doilies, the pre-cut Shabbat symbols (*Kiddush* cups, candles, vases, *challot*, candlesticks, and *challah* plates), tissue paper, scraps of velvet or other cloth, and cups of poppy or sesame seeds.

- On the supply table, place these items, each in its own container: scissors, gluesticks, and crayons.

Procedure

- The Facilitator reads *Mrs. Moskowitz and the Sabbath Candlesticks*.

- Participants identify the symbols and actions related to Shabbat that are mentioned in the story. Ask the children to raise a hand the first time they hear a Shabbat object or action mentioned in the story.

- After reading the story, the Facilitator says: Now we will set our own Shabbat table to be as nice as Mrs. Moskowitz's table. We will make a Shabbat texture picture of a Shabbat table.

- The Facilitator instructs one or two members from each work table to pick up from the supply table the materials for everyone in their group.

- Families glue the doily tablecloth onto the construction paper.

- They set the table. They place and glue onto the top of the doily tablecloth: the *Kiddush* cup, candlesticks, *challah* plate, and vase.

- Each family glues *challot* onto the *challah* plate and candles onto the candlesticks.

- They add details by gluing sesame or poppy seeds onto the *challah* and crumpled tissue paper "flowers" above the mouth of the vase. They cut and glue a flap made of velvet (or other cloth) as a *challah* cover over the *challah* plate. (They should glue just one edge of the cloth so that it can be lifted to reveal the *challah*.) They draw flames for the candles, and leaves and stems for the flowers.

- Ask families to clean up, returning materials to the supply table.

00:40 – 00:50
Snack: Shabbat Munchies at Home and in the Synagogue

During this snack, families have an opportunity to practice the Shabbat blessings recited in the home and in synagogue.

Materials

1 table for the Shabbat ritual objects
1 white table cloth
flowers
vase
2 Shabbat candlesticks
2 Shabbat candles
matches
Kiddush cup
grape juice
challah
challah cover
challah plate
cups
napkins

Advance Preparation by the Facilitator

- Make copies for each family of the blessings over candles, wine, and bread.

- On the table with the white tablecloth, place

the Shabbat symbols and snack: the *challah* on a *challah* plate under a *challah* cover, the grape juice, napkins, cups, and copies of the sheet with the blessings.

Procedure

- The Facilitator says: Now that you have heard about Mrs. Moskowitz's Shabbat, we will do what she did. We will recite the Friday evening Shabbat blessings and snack on Shabbat foods.

- Recite together the blessings over candles, wine, and bread using the ritual objects on the table (see Blessings #1, 2, 3, page 487).

00:55 – 01:10
Activity: Setting a Place for Shabbat in Our Home

As a conclusion to the theme of celebrating Shabbat in the home, families will decorate their own Shabbat tablecloth.

Materials

1 9' white paper tablecloth with plastic back for every two families

1 copy per family of A Stenciled Tablecloth for Shabbat Directions (see Directions and Patterns)

1 set of Shabbat Stencils I-V for every 3-4 families made of poster board (see Directions and Patterns)

crayons or markers

Advance Preparation by the Facilitator

- Pre-cut the 9' long white paper tablecloths into two pieces, each of which are 4½' long.

- Copy and cut out of poster board the Shabbat stencils, one set for each group of three or four families.

- On the supply table, place the 4½' long white paper tablecloths, Shabbat stencils, and A Stenciled Tablecloth for Shabbat Directions sheet.

- On the supply table, place the crayons in a container.

Procedure

- The Facilitator explains that each family will make a Shabbat tablecloth for use in their home. They will do this by tracing the stencils of the Shabbat symbols onto a 4½' long piece of white paper tablecloth using crayons or markers.

- Families may also make a border of Shabbat symbols. Or, they can stencil the symbols in any pattern or way they wish. (It is recommended that this step be done on the floor.)

- Ask one person from each table to get the materials for their table.

- Families make the patterned tablecloths.

- Ask families to clean up, returning materials to the supply table.

01:10 – 01:30
Closure: Sweet Shabbat Melodies

End the program with songs, movement, sharing, and Shabbat greetings.

Materials

1 copy per family of the Shabbat blessings for Friday evening (see Blessings #1, 2, 3, page 487).

Procedure

- Sing and move to Shabbat songs related to: Shabbat blessings; Shabbat symbols; work and rest; family; creation; God resting on Shabbat and admiring the work of creation; being holy.

  Recommended Songs:

  "*L'cha Dodi*" (*Especially Wonderful Days* by Steve Reuben, A.R.E. Publishing, Inc.)

  "*Shabbat Shalom*" (*To See the World Through Jewish Eyes,* Volume I, Union of American Hebrew Congregations)

- Have participants share their reactions to the program. Go around the room asking each family to complete one of these phrases:

  Our favorite Shabbat symbol is . . .

  Our family enjoyed . . .

  Shabbat is . . .

  Next Shabbat, we . . .

- Send everyone off with a Shabbat greeting of "*Shabbat Shalom*!" (A Sabbath of Peace).

- Distribute to each family a copy of the Friday evening Shabbat blessings.

Jewish Symbols

Circle the object you think you felt in the mystery bags.

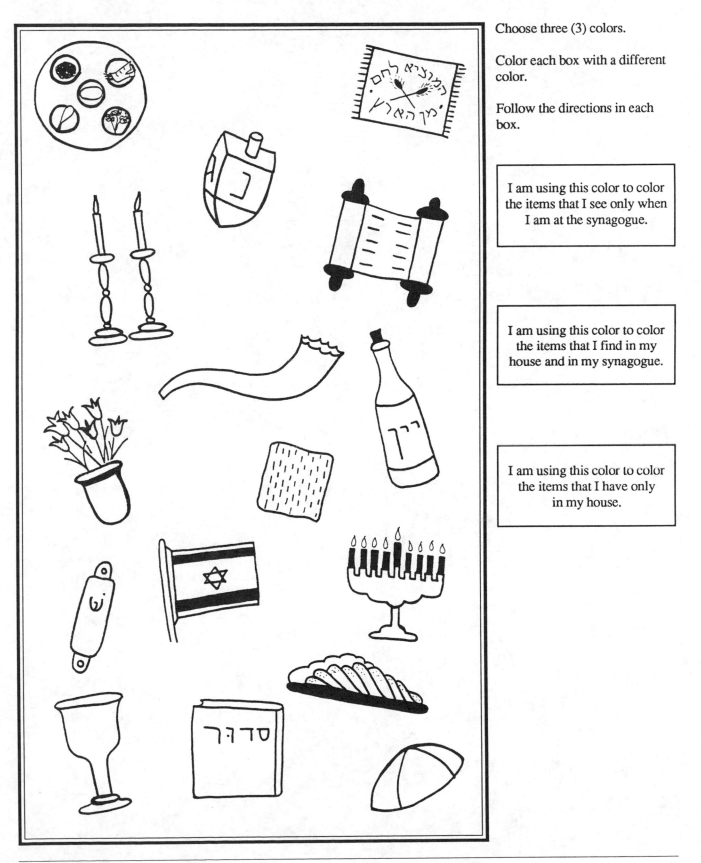

Choose three (3) colors.

Color each box with a different color.

Follow the directions in each box.

I am using this color to color the items that I see only when I am at the synagogue.

I am using this color to color the items that I find in my house and in my synagogue.

I am using this color to color the items that I have only in my house.

Shabbat Mind Warmer Sign

Cut out the sign below. Mount it on a piece of 9" x 12" construction paper or poster board folded into a 6" x 9" book. Stand the sign in front of the Shabbat Feelie Bags. You might want to make more than one.

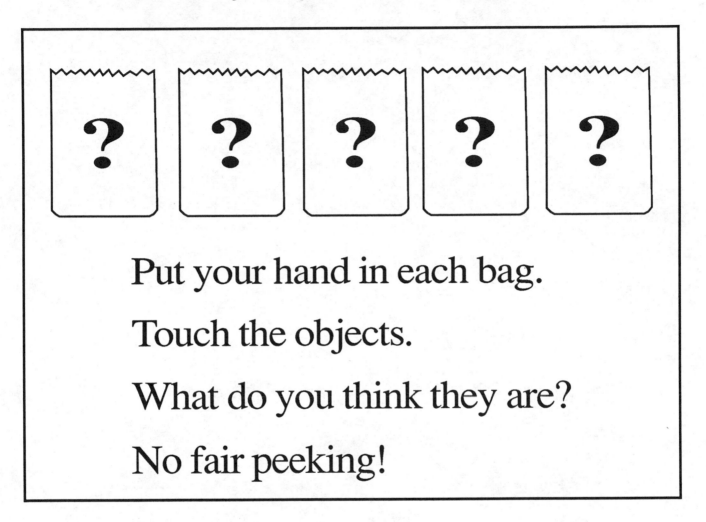

Put your hand in each bag.

Touch the objects.

What do you think they are?

No fair peeking!

Shabbat Texture Picture
(Directions)

For each textured picture, you will need the following materials:

    1 piece of 12" x 18" construction paper

    1 rectangular doily for a tablecloth

    1 small piece of velvet for a *challah* cover

    colored tissue paper to make flowers

    sesame or poppy seeds for the challah

    a set of pre-cut shapes from Shabbat Texture Picture Patterns

To Assemble:

1. Glue the doily tablecloth onto the construction paper

2. Set the table. Glue onto the tablecloth: the *Kiddush* cup, the candlesticks, the *challah* plate, and the vase.

3. Glue the *challot* onto the *challah* plate and the candles onto the candlesticks.

4. Add details. Glue sesame seeds or poppy seeds onto the *challah* and crumpled tissue "flowers" above the mouth of the vase. Cut and glue a velvet flap (*challah* cover) over the *challah* plate. Draw flames for the candles, and leaves and stems for the flowers.

Shabbat Texture Picture Patterns

Challah Plate
any color construction paper

Challah (Make 2)
brown paper

**Candlestick
(Make 2)**
silver or gold paper

Kiddush Cup
silver or gold paper

Candle (Make 2)
white construction paper

Vase
textured wall paper

A Stenciled Tablecloth for Shabbat
(Directions)

1. Spread half of a 54" x 108" plastic-backed white paper tablecloth on the floor.

2. Select pre-cut poster board patterns and lay them on the tablecloth.

3. Trace the patterns with a crayon.

4. Repeat the process until the tablecloth is pleasingly patterned. (Remember, it's nice to share the stencil patterns with others!)

5. Add other details or drawings to the tablecloth.

6. Take your tablecloth home and use it at a Shabbat meal.

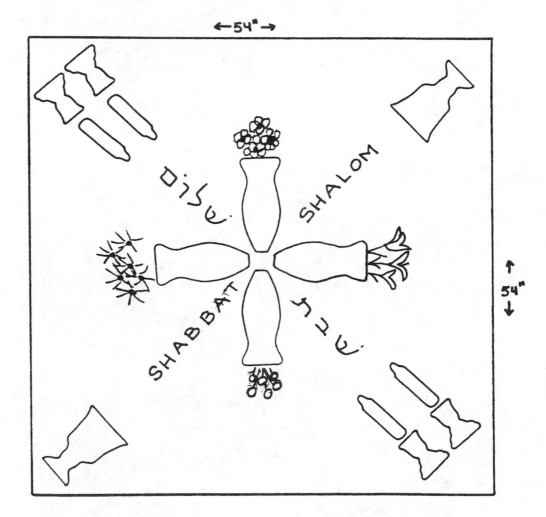

Shabbat Stencil I

Cut candles and candlesticks from poster board, one for every 3-4 families.

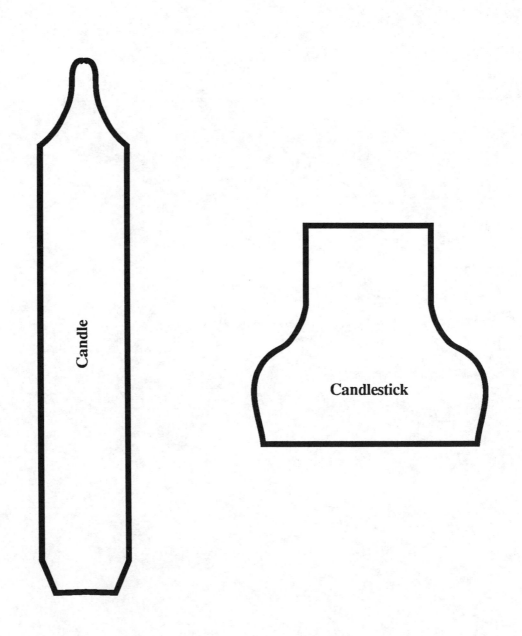

Candle

Candlestick

Shabbat Stencil II

Cut *Kiddush* cup and wine bottle from poster board, one for every 3-4 families.

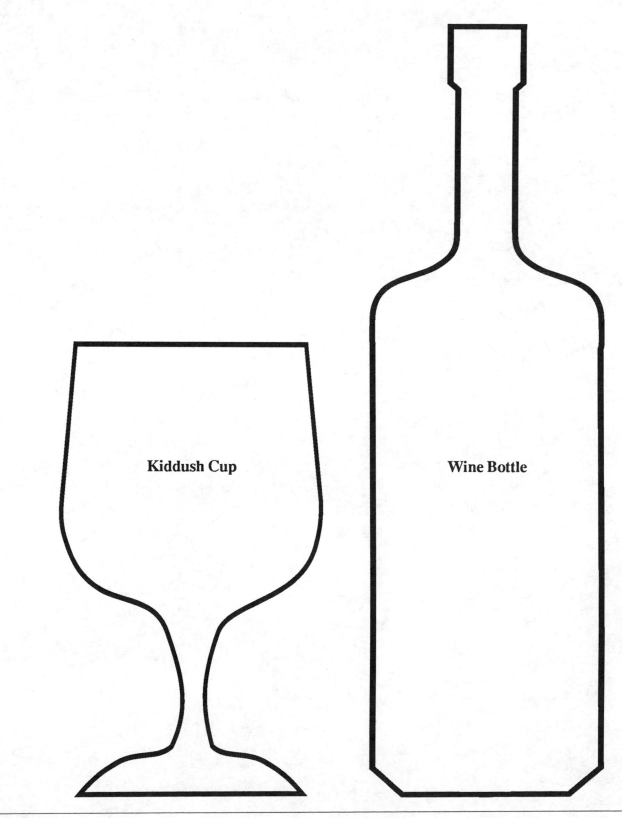

Kiddush Cup

Wine Bottle

Shabbat Stencil III

Cut *challah* knife and *challah* from poster board, one for every 3-4 families.

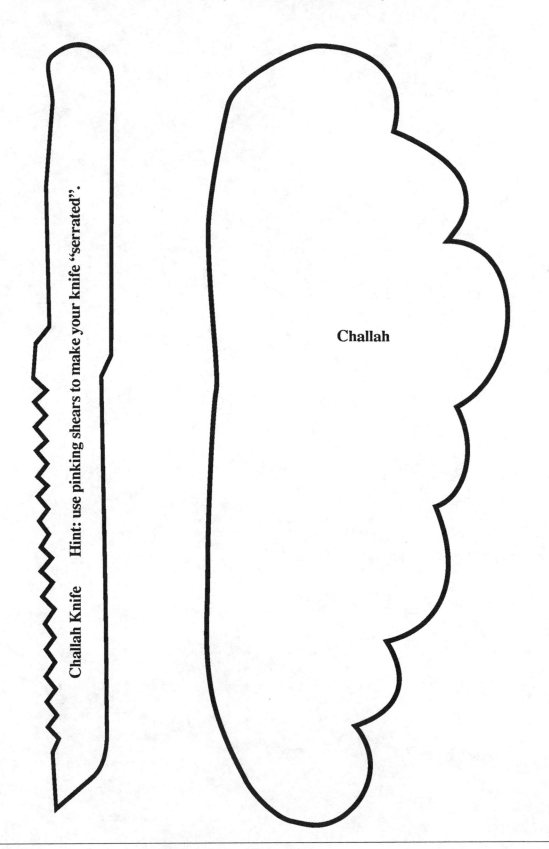

Hint: use pinking shears to make your knife "serrated".

Challah Knife

Challah

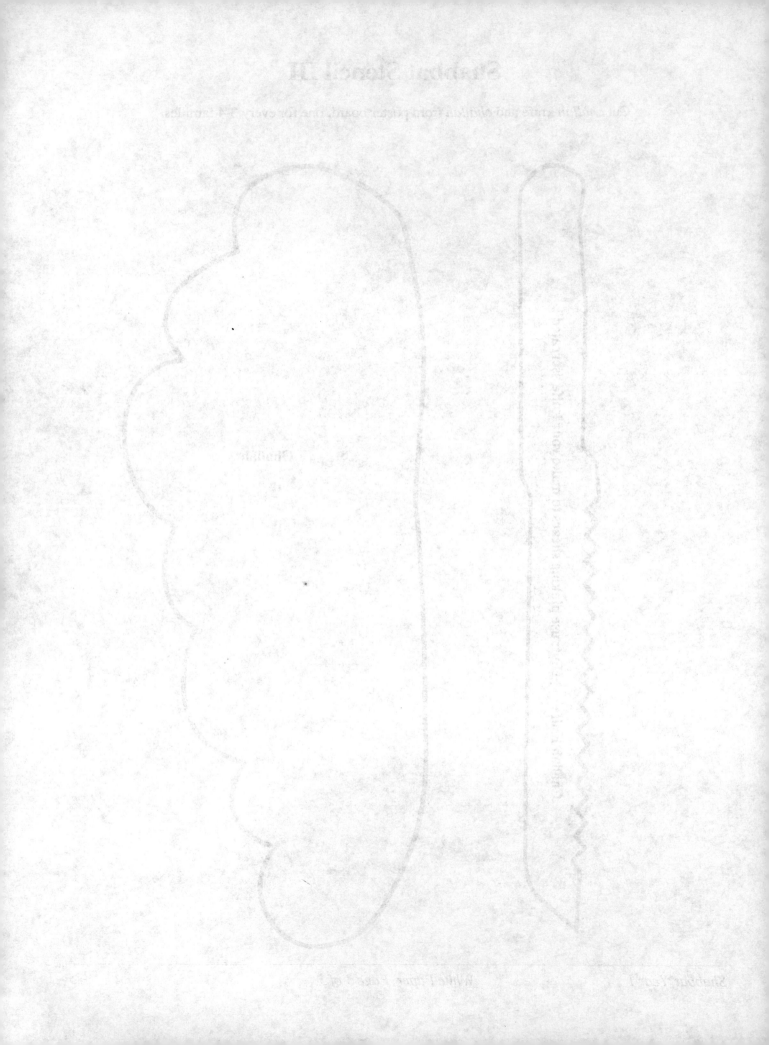

Shabbat Stencil IV

Cut the vase from poster board, one for every 3-4 families.

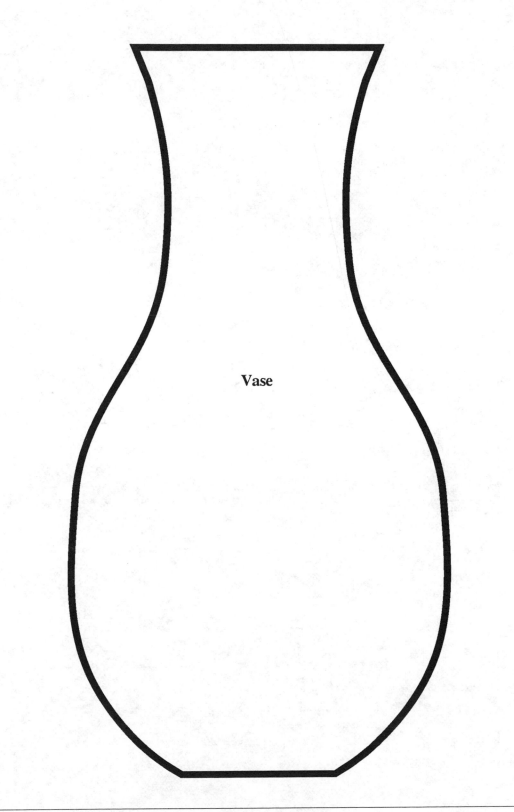

Vase

Shabbat Stencil V

Cut the dinner plate from poster board, one for every 3-4 families.

Dinner Plate

A Celebration of Rededication
Chanukah, Year 1

Postcard and/or Flier

To include:
Program Title
Sponsored by
Audience (age group, members only or
   general public, etc.)
Date
Time
Location
Cost (if applicable)
RSVP or For Further Information

Physical Set Up

work area: tables and chairs
tables for supplies
table for name tags and sign-in sheet
trash cans
trash bags
tray for snack
sanctuary or additional room (if possible)

Holiday Symbols, Customs, Terms, and Concepts

Chanukah means "dedication"
the Temple in Jerusalem
the desecration of the Temple in Jerusalem
the rededication of the Temple in Jerusalem
the synagogue as a modern-day Temple
idols versus God
the Maccabees stand up for God
the fight and victory of the Maccabees
oil for the *Ner Tamid* (the Eternal Light)
light
chanukiah, nine branched *menorah*
three blessings for Chanukah: candles,
   miracles, and *Shehecheyanu*

00:00 – 00:10
Mind Warmer: The Scene of the Miracle, the Temple in Jerusalem

Families first reconstruct the Temple by putting together a puzzle. Then, alongside the puzzle of the Temple in Jerusalem, they put together a puzzle of a modern-day synagogue.

Materials

name tags
markers
sign-in sheet
1 copy per child of the picture of The Temple
   in Jerusalem on any color card stock
   (see Directions and Patterns)
1 copy per child of A Modern-Day Synagogue
   on a different color of card stock (see
   Directions and Patterns or use a picture of
   your own synagogue)
1 Ziplock sandwich size bag per child
1 piece of black construction paper 12" x 18"
gluesticks
recycle container

Advance Preparation by the Facilitator

- A picture of a modern-day synagogue is provided in the patterns. However, if possible, use a picture of your synagogue. Either draw a picture of it or use a photograph of the outside of the building or the sanctuary. Copy the drawing or photograph onto card stock.

- Pre-cut the picture of the Temple in Jerusalem and the picture of the modern-day synagogue into 8-10 big puzzle pieces.

- For each family, place one set of puzzle pieces of the Temple in Jerusalem and one set of puzzle pieces of the modern-day synagogue together in a single Ziplock bag. (Since the Temple and the synagogue have been copied on two different colors of card stock, families will be able to separate the two puzzles with ease.)

- On the supply table, place these supplies: Ziplock bags of puzzle pieces and the construction paper.

- On the supply table, place a container of gluesticks.

Procedure

- The Facilitator greets families as they arrive. Have them fill out a name tag for each family member and sign in.

- Inform families that they will be putting together two puzzles. When they are finished, they will be asked what the puzzles are about and what they have to do with Chanukah.

- Send families to the supply table to pick up their materials and supplies.

- Have families sort the puzzle pieces into the two different colors.

- Families put the puzzles together one at a time on the black construction paper. With a long edge closest to them, they do one puzzle on one half of the page and the other puzzle on the other half. (It may be helpful to fold the paper in half, using the crease as a dividing line.)

- When they complete each puzzle, they glue it down on the construction paper.

- Families guess what the puzzles show and what they have to do with Chanukah.

- Ask families to clean up, returning materials to the supply table. Remind them to put plastic bags in the recycle container.

00:10 – 00:20
Introductions and Announcements

Materials
1 picture of the Western Wall (optional)

Procedure

- The Facilitator welcomes everyone on behalf of the sponsoring agency/institution.

- The Facilitator introduces himself/herself and any other official representatives of the program or the agency/institution.

- Have a member of each family introduce himself/herself and other family members.

- Announce any upcoming events for the sponsoring agency/institution that are pertinent for this group.

- Instruct people as to how they can get on the mailing list if they are not already on it.

Setting the Stage

- The Facilitator holds up an example of the completed puzzle pictures. Ask the families to share what they think the puzzle pictures show. Then have them share their ideas on what the puzzle pictures have to do with Chanukah.

- Emphasize that the Maccabees rededicated the Temple in Jerusalem. The Western Wall, which still stands today, was a supporting wall around that very Temple mount. Chanukah means "dedication."

- The Facilitator says: In a modern-day synagogue, just as in the Temple in Jerusalem, we keep a light burning all the time. We call that light the *Ner Tamid* (the Eternal Light). Most Eternal Lights today contain light bulbs, but some use oil as the Temple in Jerusalem did in the days of the Maccabees. With oil, the Maccabees rededicated the Temple. Chanukah means "dedication."

- Explain that families will now reenact the story of Chanukah.

00:20 – 00:40
Chanukah: A Participatory Story

This participatory story involves movement, audience response, play acting, and even a hunt for olive oil.

Materials

    a few "idols" (use statues or dolls or
       stuffed animals)
    a bottle of olive oil
    1 paper towel per person
    a few pieces of Chanukah *gelt*
    1 oil burning *chanukiah*
    oil
    wick
    piece of aluminum foil

Advance Preparation by the Facilitator

- Set up the sanctuary or a different room. If it is necessary to use the same room as for the rest of the program, set it up in front of the participants. (Ask participants to turn toward a wall or cover their eyes as you set it up.) Hide the bottle of olive oil. Put things out of order: turn over a few chairs, take the Prayerbooks out of the racks, add some crumpled papers, etc. Place the "idols" on the pulpit or in the room.

Procedure

- The Facilitator tells the Chanukah story. (Actions for families to role play are in parentheses.)

A Book About the Maccabees

A long time ago, most of the Jews lived in Judea. Today we call that land Israel. Every day, the Jews walked around the streets of Jerusalem going about their business. (Everyone walks around.) Some of the Jews took care of sheep. Others made clothes from wool and leather. Some sold food at the market, others bought food at the market. (Everyone demonstrates one of these tasks.)

At that time, the mean king Antiochus and the Syrians ruled in Jerusalem. The mean Syrians practiced their Greek ways. They bowed down to idols. (Hold up sample idols.) They prayed to these statues instead of to God. The Syrians were mean to the Jews. They put idols in the Temple in Jerusalem, in God's house. They wanted the Jews to worship these idols instead of God.

The Syrians said to the Jews: "Hey, you, all of you, bow down to our idols." (Families respond verbally.) "What if we give you pieces of gold (use Chanukah *gelt*), will you bow down to our idols?" (Again, families respond verbally.)

The Syrians did not like the Jews. The Jews did not like the Syrians.

In Modi'in, there was a family of brave, strong, and faithful people called the

Maccabees. (Everyone look brave, strong, and faithful.) The Maccabees were very angry at the Syrians. (Participants state why they are angry. For example: "We want to pray to God." "They have made a mess of our Temple.")

The Maccabees decided to fight the Syrians so that they could be free to remain Jews. And so this very small group of Jews shot arrows and threw stones (act out these things) at the big Syrian army. They attacked and ran to the hills to hide in caves. (Everyone runs and hides.)

They did this for so long and they did this so well that the Syrians finally gave up. The Jews once again ruled Israel. All the Jews cheered. (Cheer, make up cheers, wave banners.)

The Maccabees fought this war because they cared about God and God's Temple. After the fighting, they rushed to the Temple to clean it up. (Pass out paper towels. Using the towels, dust and polish. Straighten up.)

Now the Temple was clean. But something was still not right. The *Ner Tamid* was not burning. A cruse of oil was needed for the rededication ceremony. The Jews looked for a cruse of special olive oil that wasn't broken. (Search!) At last, they found one, but it held enough oil for one day only. Yet, when they lit the oil, it lasted for (Count!) one, two, three, four, five, six, seven, eight days. That was a miracle!

Today, we light our *chanukiah* in memory of this rededication of the Temple. We burn candles in most *chanukiot,* but in some of them, we burn oil. (Set up the oil burning *chanukiah*. Use the bottle of oil that the families found.) We start with one candle,

and every night add another. Our lights remind us of why the Maccabees fought: to be able to pray to God and to remain as Jews.

00:40 – 00:50
Snack: A Little Light Frosting

Enjoy a Chanukah treat in the shape of a Chanukah symbol.

Materials

cake in the shape of a *chanukiah* or with
    Chanukah designs on top
punch
plates
forks
napkins
cups

Advance Preparation by the Facilitator

- Order the cake from a bakery in the shape of a *chanukiah* or other Chanukah design, or with the words "Happy Chanukah" written on it. Or, make a cake in the shape of a *chanukiah* out of a rectangular sheet cake. Cut the cake in strips. Out of the strips, make the branches, base, and candles of a *chanukiah*.

Procedure

- Enjoy a snack of cake and punch. Recite a blessing before eating (see Blessing #8, page 488).

00:50 – 01:10
Activity: Chanukah Candle Wax Catcher

Families make a candle wax catcher for the family *chanukiah*. On each wax catcher are

the Chanukah blessings and directions for
lighting the Chanukah candles.

Materials

1 12" x 18" sheet of construction paper
   per child
enough Contact paper to provide each child
   with a piece just a bit larger than 12" x 18"
1 Chanukah Candle Wax Catcher direction
   sheet per family (see Directions and
   Patterns)
1 Chanukah Blessings sheet per child on 8½"
   x 14" paper (see Directions and Patterns)
assorted Chanukah wrapping paper
gluesticks
scissors

Advance Preparation by the Facilitator

- Enlarge the Chanukah Blessings sheet onto
  8½" x 14" paper. Make one copy for each
  child.

- On the supply table, place these materials:
  construction paper, blessing sheets, Contact
  paper, wrapping paper, and Chanukah
  Candle Wax Catcher sheets.

- On the supply table, place these items,
  each in a separate container: scissors and
  gluesticks.

Procedure

- Families glue the Chanukah Blessings sheet
  onto the construction paper.

- They cut out the Chanukah symbols from
  the Chanukah Candle Wax Catcher. They
  trace these symbols onto the wrapping
  paper, then cut out the shapes. They glue
  the shapes to the drip catcher. (Or, they just
  cut out the designs on the Chanukah
  wrapping paper.)

- They cut the Contact paper so that it is just
  a bit larger than the construction paper.

- They cover the construction paper design
  with clear Contact paper and fold over the
  edges.

- Happy candle lighting and drip catching!

01:10 – 01:30
Closure: Rock for All Ages

End the program with songs, sharing, and
holiday greetings.

Materials

1 copy of the Chanukah story per family

Procedure

- Sing and move to Chanukah music
  related to: the Temple in Jerusalem, the
  Maccabees, miracles, the miracle of the oil,
  eight days of Chanukah, the *shamash,*
  heroism, standing up for one's beliefs,
  religious freedom, freedom.

  Recommended Songs:

  > "Nu in the Middle" (*Apples on Holidays
  > and Other Days* by Leah Abrams,
  > Tara Publications)

  > "Hanukah Means Freedom" (*Especially
  > Wonderful Days* by Steve Reuben,
  > A.R.E. Publishing, Inc.)

- Recite the Chanukah blessings. Have the
  families follow the words on their new
  Chanukah candle drip catchers. Be certain
  to sing at least one verse of "Rock of
  Ages."

- Have participants share their reactions to
  the program. Ask each family to complete
  one of these phrases:

Chanukah is . . .
Our family learned . . .
Our family enjoyed . . .
One thing we will try at home . . .

- Send people off with Chanukah greetings of *"Chag Sameach!"* (Happy Holiday!)

- Send home with families a copy of the Chanukah story A Book About the Maccabees.

The Temple in Jerusalem

The Temple in Jerusalem probably looked like this:

A Modern-day Synagogue

A modern-day synagogue looks like this:

Chanukah Candle Wax Catcher

Collect:
   1 piece of 12" x 18" construction paper
   1 8½" x 14" Chanukah Blessing sheet
   1 length of clear Contact paper
   Chanukah wrapping paper

To Assemble:
   1. Glue the Chanukah Blessings sheet to the center of the construction paper.

   2. Using the patterns below, trace and cut symbol shapes out of Chanukah wrapping paper.

   3. Carefully cover your Chanukah candle wax catcher with a length of clear Contact paper.

   4. Take your wax catcher home and use under your *chanukiah* to catch your Chanukah candle drips.

Chanukah Blessings

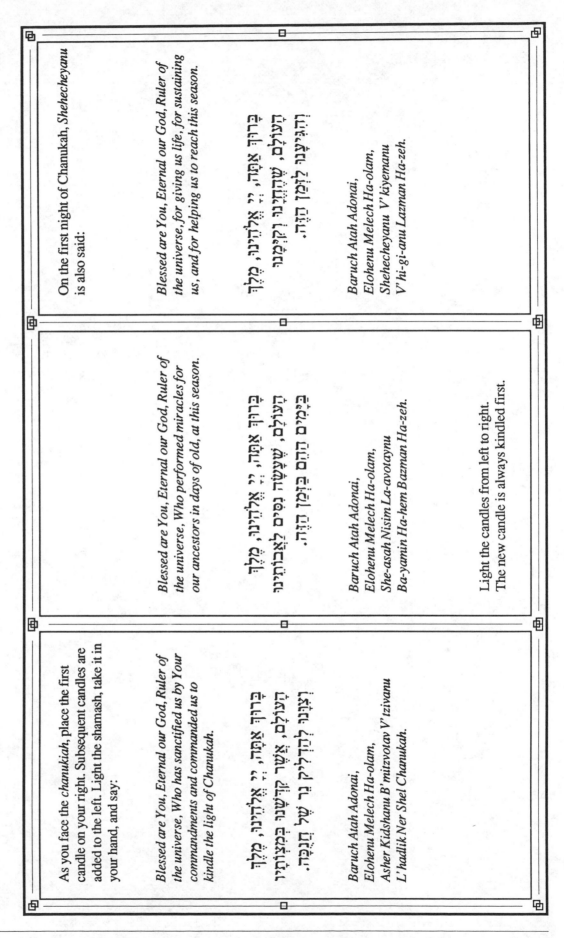

As you face the *chanukiah*, place the first candle on your right. Subsequent candles are added to the left. Light the shamash, take it in your hand, and say:

Blessed are You, Eternal our God, Ruler of the universe, Who has sanctified us by Your commandments and commanded us to kindle the light of Chanukah.

בָּרוּךְ אַתָּה יְיָ, אֱלֹהֵינוּ מֶלֶךְ הָעוֹלָם, אֲשֶׁר קִדְּשָׁנוּ בְּמִצְוֹתָיו וְצִוָּנוּ לְהַדְלִיק נֵר שֶׁל חֲנֻכָּה.

Baruch Atah Adonai,
Eloheinu Melech Ha-olam,
Asher Kidshanu B'mitzvotav V'tzivanu
L'hadlik Ner Shel Chanukah.

Blessed are You, Eternal our God, Ruler of the universe, Who performed miracles for our ancestors in days of old, at this season.

בָּרוּךְ אַתָּה יְיָ, אֱלֹהֵינוּ מֶלֶךְ הָעוֹלָם, שֶׁעָשָׂה נִסִּים לַאֲבוֹתֵינוּ בַּיָּמִים הָהֵם בַּזְּמַן הַזֶּה.

Baruch Atah Adonai,
Eloheinu Melech Ha-olam,
She-asah Nisim La-avotaynu
Ba-yamin Ha-hem Bazman Ha-zeh.

Light the candles from left to right.
The new candle is always kindled first.

On the first night of Chanukah, *Shehecheyanu* is also said:

Blessed are You, Eternal our God, Ruler of the universe, for giving us life, for sustaining us, and for helping us to reach this season.

בָּרוּךְ אַתָּה יְיָ, אֱלֹהֵינוּ מֶלֶךְ הָעוֹלָם, שֶׁהֶחֱיָנוּ וְקִיְּמָנוּ וְהִגִּיעָנוּ לַזְּמַן הַזֶּה.

Baruch Atah Adonai,
Elohenu Melech Ha-olam,
Shehecheyanu V'kiyemanu
V'hi-gi-anu Lazman Ha-zeh.

It's a Tu B'Shevat Seder
Tu B'Shevat, Year 1

Postcard and/or Flier

To include:
Program Title
Sponsored by
Audience (age group, members only or
    general public, etc.)
Date
Time
Location
Cost (if applicable)
RSVP or For Further Information
Ask families to bring a fruit or vegetable
    and some used netting from a sack of
    onions, potatoes, or citrus fruit.

Physical Set Up

work area: tables and chairs
tables for supplies
table for name tags and sign-in sheet
large trash cans
trash bags

Holiday Symbols, Customs, Terms, and Concepts

trees and plants
the New Year of the Trees
taking care of trees and the earth
Tu B'Shevat *Seder*
"Tu" stands for 15
Shevat as a month in the Jewish calendar
thanking God for trees and plants
uses of trees
produce of trees
products of trees
the giving tree
growing
planting seeds
seasons
blessings over tree and plant produce
recycling

00:00 – 00:15
Mind Warmer: A Present for Your Tree

Tu B'Shevat is the New Year of the Trees.
Families make a bird feeder — a gift for the
tree and for the birds that live in trees.

Materials

name tags
markers
sign-in sheet
twine
birdseed
peanut butter
1 stale or oven dried bagel per child
knives or spoons for spreading
Pam (cooking oil substitute)
baby wipes
1 paper lunch bag per child
1 copy per work table of A Present for a
    Tree: A Bird Feeder (see Directions
    and Patterns)
bowls
pencils
scissors

Advance Preparation by the Facilitator

- Make a sample bird feeder to show
  families. (See Procedure for detailed
  instructions.)

- On the supply table, place these materials: birdseed in bowls, peanut butter, knives or spreaders, Pam, baby wipes, paper lunch bags, bagels, twine, and A Present for a Tree: A Bird Feeder sheets.

- On the supply table, place these items, each in its own container: scissors and pencils.

Procedure

- The Facilitator greets families as they arrive. Have them fill out a name tag for each family member and sign in.

- Tell families that for Tu B'Shevat, the New Year of the Trees, they will be making a present for a tree and for the birds that live in trees — a bird feeder.

- Show them the sample bird feeder.

- Send families to the supply table for their materials.

- Families cut a piece of twine about 2' long.

- They spray Pam (or pour some oil) on their hands.

- They cover a bagel with peanut butter using a knife, spoon, or spreader.

- They roll the bagel with peanut butter in the bowl with the bird seed.

- They tie the twine though the bagel. (The twine will be used to attach the feeder to a tree branch.)

- Everyone wipes their hands clean with the baby wipes.

- Each family places their bird feeder in a paper lunch bag for transporting it safely home. With a pencil, they write their last name on the outside of the bag.

- Ask families to clean up, returning materials to the supply table.

00:15 – 00:25
Introductions and Announcements

- The Facilitator welcomes everyone on behalf of the sponsoring agency/institution.

- The Facilitator introduces himself/herself and any other official representatives of the program or the agency/institution.

- Have a member of each family introduce himself/herself and other family members.

- Announce any upcoming events for the sponsoring agency/institution that are pertinent for this group.

- Instruct people as to how they can get on the mailing list if they are not already on it.

Setting the Stage

- The Facilitator says: Tu B'Shevat is the New Year of the Trees. Trees are important to us for many reasons. For example, we use trees to make things, we eat fruits that grow on trees, trees provide us with shade in the summer, trees keep the soil healthy and in place.

  During this Tu B'Shevat program, we are going to have a *Seder*. Usually, we think of a *Seder* for Passover. But we can have a special *Seder* on Tu B'Shevat. Just as on Passover, we will drink four cups of juice and ask four questions. Yet, because it is all about trees, this special Tu B'Shevat *Seder* is different from a Passover *Seder*.

00:25 – 00:50
The Tu B'Shevat Seder

The Tu B'Shevat *Seder* has become popular in many communities in recent years. Just as for a Passover *Seder*, there is an order to the Tu B'Shevat *Seder*: blessings are said, questions asked, and special foods eaten.

Materials

small clear plastic cups, 1 per person

plates

napkins

white, pink, red, and dark grape juice (mix the colors to make the lighter shades)

bread or rolls

pencils

1 copy per table of the sheet Fifteen Things Trees Give, Do, or Provide (see Directions and Patterns)

1 copy of *The Giving Tree* by Shel Silverstein (New York: Harper and Row, 1964)

container or bag for recycling the plastic cups

fruit protected on the outside, such as oranges, walnuts, pecans, or other nuts with a shell

fruit with pits, such as whole dates, olives, or cherries (pits are needed, so don't use the pitless variety)

fruit that is entirely edible, such as raisins and figs

Advance Preparation by the Facilitator

- Prepare fruits and nuts in small bite size pieces; peel and cut oranges; chop walnuts, pecans, and figs. Leave one sample of each food whole.

- Prepare a sampling of the following foods on a plate, one per work table: oranges, walnuts, pecans, dates, olives, cherries, figs, and raisins. Add the bread or rolls to the plate.

- On the supply table, place these materials: small clear plastic cups; plates; napkins; 4 grape drinks in different colors; the sheet Fifteen Things Trees Give, Do, or Provide; and the plates with samples of food.

- On the supply table, place a container filled with pencils.

Procedure

- As the Leader of the *Seder*, the Facilitator introduces the Tu B'Shevat *Seder* to the group. Let families know that they will sample many tasty food products that come from trees. In this case, they will also drink four cups of grape juice in four different colors. Ask families to watch for other customs, blessings, and rituals they recognize.

- Send one or two representatives from each work table to gather the materials from the supply tables.

- The families fill the first cup with the white grape juice.

- The Facilitator says: This *Seder* is like a trip through the seasons. What season does the color of your grape juice represent? (Answer: winter.) Winter is the season when the ground can become white with snow.

- Together recite the blessing over the white grape juice, the fruit of the vine (see Blessing #2, page 487).

- Drink the grape juice.

- The Facilitator says: Tu B'Shevat falls on the 15th of the month of Shevat in the Jewish calendar. The "Tu" in Tu B'Shevat stands for the number 15.

- Explain that there are worksheets at each table. On the sheet, each table group makes a list of 15 things trees give, do, or provide. (Examples: provide shade, are made into paper, grow apples and peaches.)

- Ask families to share some of their answers about what trees give, do, and provide.

- The Facilitator says: The first kind of fruit we are going to eat is protected on the outside. What can you find on your tray that is protected on the outside? (Answer: oranges and nuts.) Choose the one you like best.

- Together recite the appropriate blessing (see Blessing #7, page 488). Go over the ending of the blessing first.

- Everyone eats the fruit and nuts.

- The families fill the cups a second time with pink grape juice (or combine the dark and light grape juices to make pink).

- The Facilitator says: What season is most like this color of juice? (Answer: spring.) In Israel, in the spring, a flower called cyclamen comes out in pink. In other places, pink cherry blossoms, pink dogwood, and pink azaleas begin to bloom.

- Together recite the blessing for the fruit of the vine (see Blessing #2, page 487).

- Everyone drinks the grape juice.

- The Facilitator says: Spring is a time to plant. Parents, you get to plant "child seeds" for this activity. Get off your chairs, children, you are now a seed. Everyone act out the story of a seed.

First, we dig the dirt. Then we plant the tiny seeds. Cover the seeds with dirt and water. Then we wait for the plant to grow and blossom. Sometimes the sun shines. Other times, the clouds bring rain to water the plants. Little by little, our plants grow bigger and bigger. We dig out all the weeds around the plant. Finally, a flower blossoms, or a vegetable begins to grow.

Plants, tell your parent and caretaker what kind of plant you are. (Each child shares what kind of plant he/she is.) Now, in our garden, we have flowers that make the world beautiful and vegetables to eat that

make us healthy. You may return to your chairs.

- The Facilitator continues: The second kind of fruit from trees that we will eat is the opposite of the first. We can eat the outside of this fruit, but not the inside. What can you find on your tray that fits this description? (Have children answer: cherries, olives, whole dates.) Choose the fruit of this kind that you like best.

- Together recite the appropriate blessing (see Blessing #7, page 488). Go over the ending of the blessing first.

- Everyone eats the fruit. Be careful not to eat the seeds!

- The families fill the cups with red grape juice (or mix the dark and light grape juices to make red).

- The Facilitator asks: What season does this juice represent? (Answer: summer.) Summer in Israel is poppy season. Poppies are bright red.

- Together recite the blessing over the fruit of the vine (see Blessing #2, page 487).

- Everyone drinks the grape juice.

- The Facilitator tells the story *The Giving Tree* by Shel Silverstein. The story is about a boy who recognizes a tree only for what it gives him. Finally, when the tree is almost gone, the tree reminds him that he must take care of trees and not just use them.

- The Facilitator says: You may eat the inside and the outside of the third sort of fruit. It comes from plants. What kind of fruit do you see on the tray that fits this description? (Answer: figs and raisins.) Pick the one that you like best.

- Together recite the appropriate blessing (see Blessing #7, page 488).

- Everyone eats the fruit.

- The Facilitator fills the cups with the dark grape juice.

- The Facilitator asks: What season does this "wine" represent? (Answer: Fall.)

- Together recite the blessing over the fruit of the vine (see Blessing #2, page 487).

- Everyone drinks the grape juice.

- The Facilitator says: We've been doing a lot of thanking. Here is a story about being thankful.

Giving Thanks for Bread

Once upon a time, a boy actually thanked his mom for a sandwich because the bread was so delicious. This is what happened:

The mother said, "Thank the baker who baked the bread."

The boy went to the baker.

The baker said: "Thank the miller who ground up the wheat so that I could bake the bread."

So the boy went to the miller. The miller said: "Son, better that you thank the farmer who grew the wheat. Without the farmer, there would be no wheat to grind."

The boy found the farmer. The farmer said, "Don't thank me. Thank the sun and rain, without them, the seeds would not grow."

The boy turned to the sun and rain to thank them. They said to the boy: "Do not thank us. Thank God who put us here. Thank God who brings forth bread from the earth."

- The Facilitator says: Let's all take some bread from the earth.

- Together recite *HaMotzi*, the blessing over bread (see Blessing #3, page 487), then eat the bread.

- The Facilitator says: This year, let us promise to take care of all trees and to recycle as much as we can. Trees give us shade, food, paper, books, and much more. Trees help protect the soil and the air. May it be a good year for the trees.

- Ask families to clean up, returning materials to the supply table. Make a point of separating the plastic cups and any other recyclable items into a special bag or receptacle.

00:55 – 01:10
Activity: Tu B'Shevat Playing Cards

Families get to put together their own set of Tu B'Shevat playing cards all about growing trees and plants and Tu B'Shevat.

Materials

3 sheets per child of Tu B'Shevat Playing Cards I copied on card stock (see Directions and Patterns)

4 sheets per child of Tu B'Shevat Playing Cards II copied on card stock (see Directions and Patterns)

1 sheet per child of Tu B'Shevat Playing Cards III copied on card stock (see Directions and Patterns)

scissors

pencils

1 sandwich size Ziplock bag per child (use bags recycled from Chanukah program)

crayons

Advance Preparation by the Facilitator

- When copying the playing cards onto card

stock, use the same color of card stock for the three sheets.

- On the supply table, place these materials: Tu B'Shevat Playing Cards I, II, III and the Ziplock sandwich bags.

- On the supply table, place these items, each in a separate container: scissors, pencils, and crayons.

Procedure

- The Facilitator tells families that they will be making their own set of Tu B'Shevat playing cards.

- Tell families that they will need eight sheets of the Tu B'Shevat Playing Cards: three of I, four of II, and one of III. Point out to the families the slight variation in the cards.

- Send one or two people from each work table to pick up the materials from the supply table.

- Have parents review with their children what is pictured on the playing cards. Children color in the pictures.

- Families cut out the cards and at least one set of directions.

- They write their last name on the back of one set of directions.

- They play one of the games: *Go Fish, Memory* or *Concentration*, or *Old Maid*.

- Each family puts their cards in a Ziplock

bag, making certain that their last name shows through.

- Ask families to clean up, returning the materials to the supply table.

01:10 – 01:30
Closure: A Musical Tribute to Trees

End the program with songs, sharing, and holiday greetings.

- Sing and move to Tu B'Shevat music related to: trees, products of trees, produce from trees, the number 15, taking care of plants, growing, planting seeds.

  Recommended Songs:

  "Planting" (*Apples on Holidays and Other Days* by Leah Abrams, Tara Publications)

  "Pitter Patter" (*Seasoned With Song* by Julie Auerbach, Tara Publications)

- Have people share their reactions to the program. Ask each family to complete one of these phrases:

  Trees are . . .

  Our family learned . . .

  Our family enjoyed . . .

  On this Tu B'Shevat, the New Year of the Trees, we . . .

- Send everyone off with a Tu B'Shevat greeting of "*Shanah Tovah L'ilanot!*" (Happy New Year, Trees!)

A Present for a Tree: A Bird Feeder

Collect the following materials:
    1 stale or oven-dried bagel
    1 18" length of twine
    1 paper sandwich bag
    pan or bowl of birdseed
    jar of peanut butter
    spoon or spreader
    Pam (or other cooking oil substitute)

To Assemble:

1. Take a stale bagel and coat it totally with peanut butter. (Hint: Coating hands with a bit of cooking spray or vegetable oil keeps peanut butter from sticking to fingers.)

2. Dip the peanut butter coated bagel into a pan or bowl of birdseed and dredge it as if coating chicken to be fried. (The bagel should be completely encrusted with birdseed.)

3. Thread the twine through the hole in the bagel and knot the ends together.

4. Place the bird feeder in a paper sandwich bag to transport it home.

5. At home, hang the bird feeder on a favorite tree.

6. Recycle the paper sandwich bag. Tu B'Shevat is a "green" holiday.

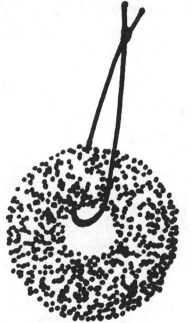

Fifteen Things That Trees Give, Do, or Provide

Tu B'Shevat means the 15th of the Hebrew month of Shevat.
List 15 things trees give, do, or provide:

1. _____

2. _____

3. _____

4. _____

5. _____

6. _____

7. _____

8. _____

9. _____

10. _____

11. _____

12. _____

13. _____

14. _____

15. _____

Tu B'Shevat Playing Cards I (You need 3 of this page)

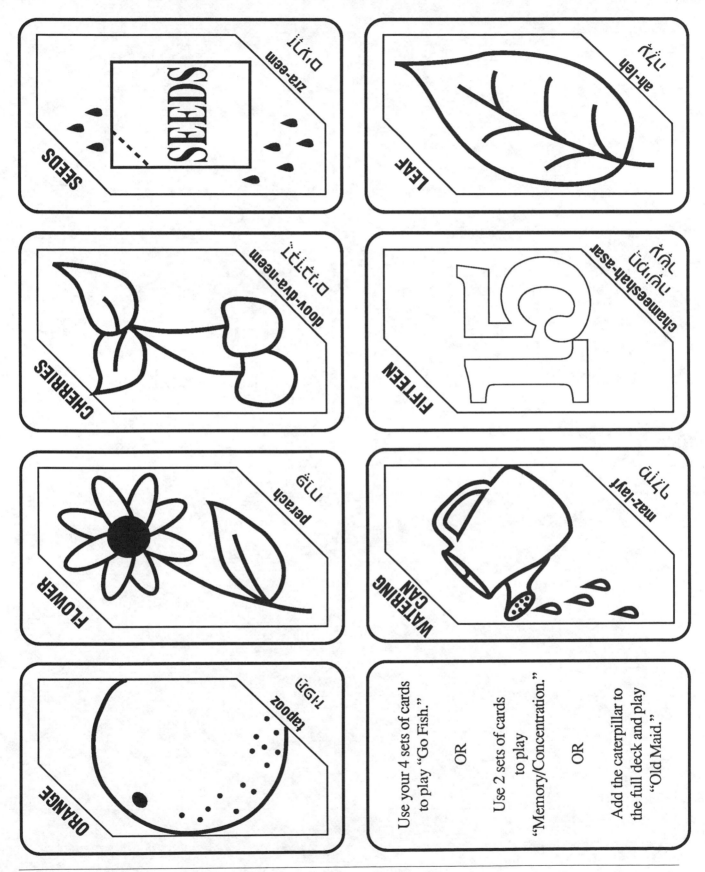

SEEDS — zra-eem — זְרָעִים

LEAF — ah-leh — עָלֶה

CHERRIES — door-dva-neem — דֻבְדְּבָנִים

FIFTEEN — chameeshah-asar — חֲמִשָּׁה עָשָׂר

FLOWER — perach — פֶּרַח

WATERING CAN — maz-layf — מַזְלֵף

ORANGE — tapooz — תַּפּוּז

Use your 4 sets of cards to play "Go Fish."

OR

Use 2 sets of cards to play "Memory/Concentration."

OR

Add the caterpillar to the full deck and play "Old Maid."

Tu B'Shevat Playing Cards II (You need 4 of this page)

A Purim Send-Off
Purim, Year 1

Postcard and/or Flier

To include:
Program Title
Sponsored by
Audience (age group, members only or
  general public, etc.)
Date
Time
Location
Cost (if applicable)
RSVP or For Further Information
Bring an apron and something to roll dough.

Physical Set Up

work area: tables and chairs
tables for supplies
table for name tags and sign-in sheet
large trash cans
extra trash bags
use of an oven
access to sink for washing hands

**Holiday Symbols, Customs, Terms
and Concepts**

hamantaschen
preparation
the masks Jews and others wear
Purim characters: King Ahasuerus, Queen
  Esther, Mordecai, Haman
good and evil
pride in being Jewish
standing up for Jews
Megillat Esther (Scroll of Esther)
listening and reacting to the reading of
  Megillat Esther
a festive celebration

gifts for someone in need: making Purim
  cards for someone in the hospital or in a
  group home, a shut-in, or a new Russian
  immigrant

00:00 – 00:15
**Mind Warmer: Noshin' on Your
Own Hamantaschen**

Families will roll their own dough, fill and
fold the *hamantaschen*, and eat the goodies
that they make.

Materials

Materials and ingredients for dough for each
  3-4 dozen *hamantaschen* (needed in advance of the program):
  ½ cup of margarine
  1 teaspoon grated orange rind
  1 cup of sugar
  1 egg
  2 tablespoons orange juice
  2 cups of flour
  2 teaspoons baking powder
  ¼ teaspoon salt
  appropriate mixing equipment and spoons

Materials and ingredients needed at the Purim
  program:
  pre-prepared *hamantaschen* dough
  filling (use pie filling in cherry or apricot
    and/or orange marmalade and/or
    pre-made poppy seed filling)
  1 can opener
  1 round cookie cutter or drinking glass
  about 2" round for every three to four
    preschoolers

flour
wax paper (to cover table if necessary)
masking tape (optional)
spoons
cookie sheets
spatula
1 copy of the Very Delicious Hamantaschen Dough recipe per family (see
Directions and Patterns)
extra rolling pins
extra aprons
dish rags and towels
bowls with flour

Advance Preparation by the Facilitator Before the Day of the Program

Note: This *hamantaschen* recipe makes enough dough for 3-4 dozen *hamantaschen*. The Facilitator should prepare the dough a day in advance. Here is how:

- Cream margarine with the orange rind and sugar.

- Add the egg and orange juice.

- Slowly and thoroughly mix in the dry ingredients.

- Dust with flour and chill until very firm.

- Freeze overnight, as chilled dough is easier to roll.

Advance Preparation by the Facilitator on the Day of the Program

- Arrange for a parent or other person to watch the *hamantaschen* while they bake in the oven.

- Open cans of filling.

- If necessary, spread wax paper on the table tops. Secure the wax paper with masking tape.

- Dust table tops with flour for easy rolling.

- Preheat oven to 375 degrees.

Procedure

- The Facilitator greets families as they arrive. Have them fill out a name tag for each family member and sign in.

- Tell families that during this Mind Warmer they will be making *hamantaschen*.

- Give each family a copy of the recipe for Very Delicious Hamantaschen Dough. Point out the steps that they will follow (steps 5-7): rolling out the dough, cutting out a circle using a cookie cutter or glass, placing a spoonful of filling in the middle of their dough circle, folding and pinching three corners.

- Point out the tables where the families will be making the *hamantaschen*.

- Wearing the aprons they brought, families do steps 5-7, then place the filled *hamantaschen* on cookie sheets. They may make as many *hamantaschen* as time and dough allow.

- Bake the *hamantaschen* at 375 degrees for 12 minutes. They will be ready to eat for snack. (Let families know that they will not necessarily get to eat the same *hamantaschen* that they made.)

- The Facilitator asks families to help with clean up, including wiping down the table tops.

- Allow time for families to wash their hands.

00:15 – 00:25
Introductions and Announcements

- The Facilitator welcomes everyone on behalf of the sponsoring agency/institution.

- The Facilitator introduces himself/herself and any other official representatives of the program or the agency/institution.

- Have a member of each family introduce himself/herself and other family members.

- Announce any upcoming events for the sponsoring agency/institution that are pertinent for this group.

- Instruct people as to how they can get on the mailing list if they are not already on it.

Setting the Stage

- The Facilitator asks: What is it that we have all just made, other than a mess? (Answer: *hamantaschen*.) Raise your hand if you like eating *hamantaschen*. Let's see what the group's favorite *hamantaschen* filling is. Raise your hand when you hear your favorite filling called out: Cherry? Chocolate chip? Apricot? Peanut butter? Spinach? Poppy Seed? Prune? Other? (Tally the number of votes for each filling and share with the group. This will add a little Purim fun.)

  Continue: One of the best parts of celebrating any holiday, whether it is Sukkot, Chanukah, Purim, or Pesach, is the preparation for it. The more we prepare, the more we look forward to the holiday and the more special the holiday becomes. Today, you prepared for Purim by coming to this program, and by making *hamantaschen*.

  Hamantaschen are eaten especially on Purim. Which Purim character's name do you hear in the word, "*hamantaschen*"? (Answer: Haman.) *Hamantaschen* means "Haman's pocket." When it is snack time, we will all be able to munch on the goodies you made.

00:25 – 00:45
Story: The Masks of Purim

The story for this program is the story of Esther, as found in *Megillat Esther* (literally the Scroll of Esther). Before the story, everyone will cut out a mask of a favorite Purim character. During the story, they will wear their masks, and will stand up every time their character's name is mentioned.

Materials

1 copy of *Megillat Esther*, the Scroll of Esther (see Directions and Patterns for Purim, Year 3)

1 copy per child of the Mordecai Mask on bright blue card stock (see Directions and Patterns)

1 copy per child of the Haman Mask on green card stock (see Directions and Patterns)

1 copy per child of the Esther Mask on red card stock (see Directions and Patterns)

1 copy per child of the King Ahasuerus Mask on gold card stock (see Directions and Patterns)

scissors

1 wire hanger

glitter, curly ribbon, wiggle eyes, feathers, etc.

1 large paper grocery bag

wrapped pieces of candy, 1 or 2 pieces per child

stapler

staples

markers

Advance Preparation by the Facilitator

- Copy the four masks on the four different colors of card stock as indicated.

- Make a Haman Purim piñata for this portion of the program. Here is how:

- Fill the brown paper grocery bag with the candy.

- Close the bag. With the blank side of the bag facing you, fold the top of the bag through the opening of the hanger as if it were a pair of pants. There should be a blank side, and a side with an overlap and a store logo or printed message.

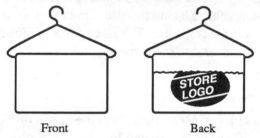

Front   Back

- Staple. (Put the stapler over the wire hanger and staple through all the layers of the bag.)

- Decorate the blank side of the piñata with an outrageous face and make it truly garish, using all sorts of fun items, such as curly ribbon, glitter, wiggle eyes, and feathers.

- On the supply table, place the various mask outlines.

- On the supply table, place a container filled with scissors.

Procedure

- Explain that every family member present, including adults, will make a mask of their favorite Purim figure. Encourage the family members to make a different mask. The masks will be worn during the reading of *Megillat Esther*.

- Go over the four characters:

Queen Esther – Brave Jewess who stands up for her people, and risks her life in a time of need.

Mordecai – The very loving uncle who guides and cares for his niece Esther. He is both a good citizen and a good Jew. He tells King Ahasuerus about a plan to get rid of him. He is proud of being a Jew. He asks Esther to save the Jewish people.

King Ahasuerus – A kind king whose advisor, Haman, takes advantage of his kindness.

Haman – The bad guy who plans to destroy the Jewish people.

- On Purim, it is a custom to dress up, wearing hats, masks, and other costume items. Each family member chooses his/her favorite Purim character, then obtains a mask outline and pair of scissors from the supply table.

- With scissors, an adult family member cuts a place for the face in a mask.

- Next have them cut a mask for each adult family member present.

- All bring their masks to the area where *Megillat Esther* will be read.

- The Facilitator reads *Megillat Esther*, abbreviating it as necessary.

- During the reading, whenever one of the four characters is mentioned, all children and adults holding a mask of that character in front of their faces stand up.

- After reading *Megillat Esther*, show families the Haman piñata. Ask two strong parents to hold the hanger. The children try breaking the piñata by punching it with their fists. If the piñata does not break after sufficient punches have been thrown, the Facilitator or a parent breaks it (cuts it). Make certain every child gets some candy.

00:45 – 00:55
Snack: Homemade Nosh of Hamantaschen

Families eat the *hamantaschen* made during the Mind Warmer.

Materials

hamantaschen
juice
cups
napkins

Procedure

- Everyone takes *hamantaschen* and some juice.

- Together recite a blessing before noshing (see Blessing #8, page 488).

00:55 – 01:15
Activity: Performing a Purim Deed — Sending a Purim Greeting to Someone in Need

Each family will make two mask cards, one of which will be sent to someone in need.

Materials

crepe paper streamers in yellow, brown, black, and red
1 Purim Mask Card Pattern per child on 8 ½" x 11" white paper (see Directions and Patterns)
1 Inside of Card sheets per child on colored paper (see Directions and Patterns)
2 sheets per child of 9" x 12" bright color construction paper
metallic or bright colored ribbon that a scissor can curl
4 wiggly eyes per child
metallic pieces or sequins that can be used for eyes, noses, ends of a smile
feathers
crayons
scissors
gluesticks
pens

Advance Preparation by the Facilitator

- The Facilitator makes a sample card (see Procedure).

- The Facilitator provides the names and addresses of Jewish people in need, or places with Jewish people in need, to whom the families can send their Purim mask card. Examples are patients in a hospital, residents of a home for the aged, people who receive meals on wheels, a new Soviet immigrant, etc.

- On the supply table, place the construction paper, Purim Mask Card Pattern sheets, the sheets with the *Megillah*-shaped card inserts, crepe paper, streamers, ribbon, wiggly eyes, metallic pieces (or sequins), and feathers.

- On the supply table, place each of these items in a separate container: scissors, crayons, gluesticks, and pens.

Procedure

- The Facilitator says: There are two *mitzvot* associated with Purim. One is the sending of gifts to someone we know (a friend, a relative, a teacher). This is called *Mishloach Manot*. The other is sending a gift to someone in need, such as someone in the hospital; an elderly person living in a home for the aged; a person, elderly or handicapped, who has difficulty getting out of the house; a new Soviet Jewish immigrant; etc. This is called *Matanot L'evyonim*.

- The Facilitator tells families that they will have the opportunity to make two cards, one to send to someone in need, and one to share with a relative or friend. The cards will be in the shape of a mask since, on Purim, we dress up in costumes with masks.

- The Facilitator tells families that they may make and send their Purim mask cards to someone in need whom they know, or to someone whose name is on the list provided for them. Before they start making the cards, they should decide who will receive them.

- The Facilitator shows a sample Purim Mask Card, then sends families to the tables to work.

- The Facilitator asks one or two people from each work table to gather the materials from the supply table.

- Families cut the mask shapes out of the sheet entitled Purim Mask Card Pattern.

- Families fold the construction paper in half, trace the mask pattern, and cut out the mask.

- They cut out the *Megillah*-shaped "Happy Purim! _____ made this card for you at _____ ."

- They fill out the *Megillah*-shaped insert. They write in the child's name, then glue the insert on the inside of the construction paper mask-shaped card.

- They write in the recipient's name, add a special note to the person, and add whatever other message they wish before making the cover.

- To make their colorful Purim mask card cover, families do the following:

  - They make hair out of crepe paper.

  - They decorate the hair with ribbons and curl them with a scissors, feathers, and sparkles as desired.

  - They make a face using the metallic shapes, wiggly eyes, etc., for eyes, nose, smile, ends of lips.

  - They draw in the remaining details with crayons.

- Families make a second card to take home or to give as *Mishloach Manot*, a gift to someone they know.

- The Facilitator collects the cards designated for someone in need. He/she appoints individuals to be responsible for distributing them to the Jewish home, hospital, or the like.

- Ask families to clean up, returning the materials to the supply table.

01:15 – 01:30
Closure: The Rash, Rash, Rash of Purim

End the program with songs, sharing, and holiday greetings.

- Sing and move to Purim music related to: *hamantaschen*, masks, dressing up, giving gifts to the needy, the Purim characters, and Jewish pride.

Recommended Songs:

"Purim's a Time" (*Seasoned with Song* by Julie Auerbach, Tara Publications)

"*Al Ha-Neeseem*" (*Especially Wonderful Days* by Steve Reuben, A.R.E. Publishing, Inc.)

- Have people share their reactions to the program. Ask families to complete one of these phrases:

Our favorite Purim character is _____ because . . .

Our family learned . . .

Our family enjoyed . . .

For this Purim, we . . .

- Send everyone off with *"Chag Sameach!"* (Happy Purim!)

Very Delicious Hamantaschen Dough
(Makes about 3-4 dozen)

Ingredients:
    1/2 cup margarine
    1 teaspoon grated orange rind
    1 cup sugar
    1 egg
    2 tablespoons orange juice
    2 cups flour
    2 teaspoons baking powder
    1/4 teaspoon salt

1. Cream the margarine with the rind and sugar.

2. Add the egg and orange juice. Mix well.

3. Slowly and thoroughly mix in the dry ingredients.

4. Dust with flour and chill until very firm.

5. Roll dough on a floured board and cut into circles
   with a round cookie cutter or glass.

6. Fill with your favorite filling and fold into a triangle.
   Pinch the corners together firmly.

7. Bake for about 12 minutes in a 375 degree oven.

Mordecai Mask

Your Face
Can Replace
This Blank Space
If You Cut It Out Post-Haste!

Esther Mask

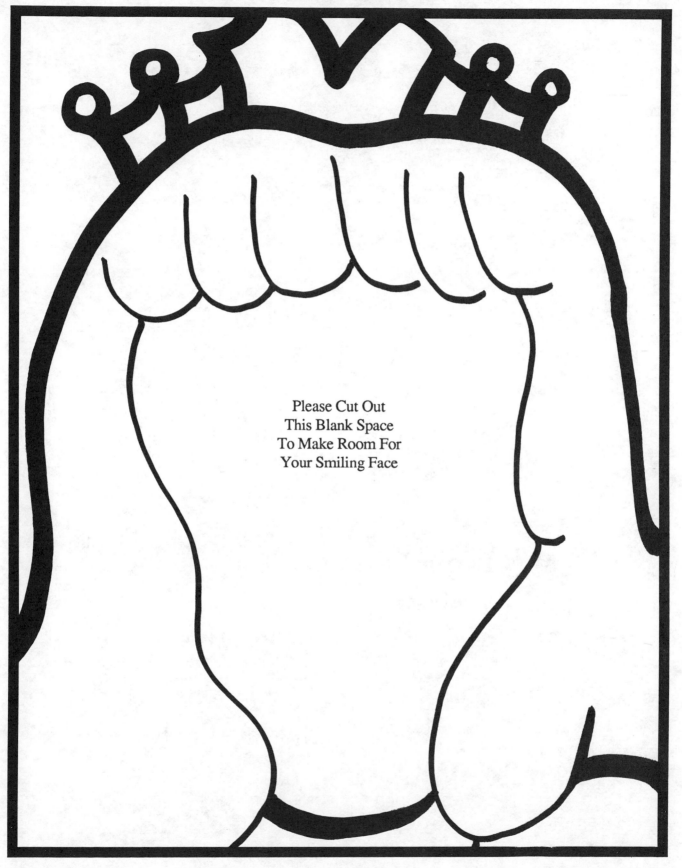

Please Cut Out
This Blank Space
To Make Room For
Your Smiling Face

Haman Mask

Please Cut Out
This Space
To Make Room For
Your Face

King Ahasuerus Mask

If You Cut Out
This Blank Space,
Ahasuerus Can Have
Your Face!

Purim Mask Card Pattern

1. Take one copy of this sheet for your family.

2. Fold a piece of 9" x 12" construction paper in half to make a 6" x 9" rectangle.

3. Then place the pattern below on the fold.

4. Place the pattern over the construction paper and cut.

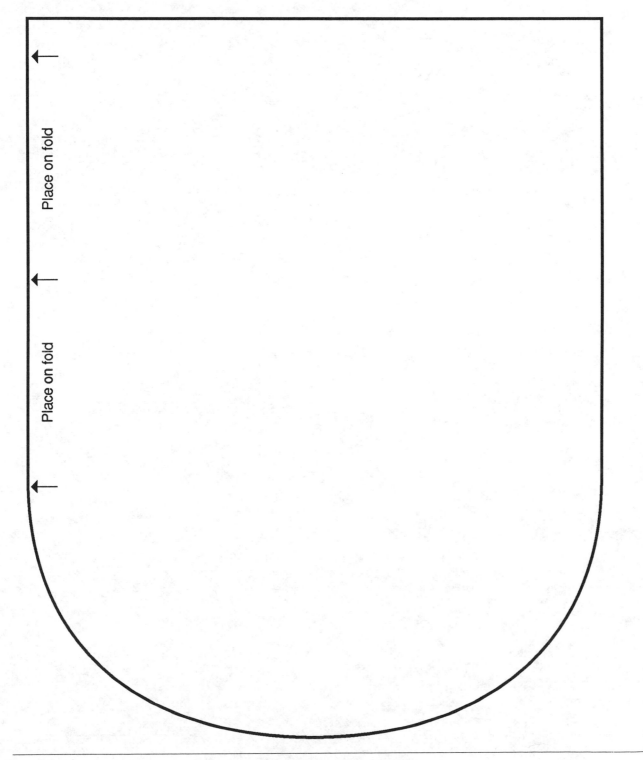

Inside of Card

1. Take a blank Purim Mask Card Pattern.

2. Use the assorted, assembled fun stuff — wiggle eyes, sequins, feathers, ribbon, etc. — to create a fabulous mask for the front of your card.

3. Cut out the message below, sign your name on the line, and glue it onto the inside of your card.

My Wilderness Experience
Passover, Year 1

Postcard and/or Flier

To include:
Program Title
Sponsored by
Audience (age group, members only or
  general public, etc.)
Date
Time
Location
Cost (if applicable)
RSVP or For Further Information
Bring a fly swatter.

Physical Set Up

work area: tables and chairs
tables for supplies
table for Wilderness Kit components
table for sign-in sheet
large trash cans
trash bags
empty room or room with empty space for
  telling the story

Holiday Symbols, Customs, Terms, and Concepts

the Haggadah
living and reliving a Jewish story
Shemot — being counted
the Passover *Seder*
journey through the wilderness
faithfulness versus faithlessness to God: all
  that glitters is not gold
slavery: building storehouses
choosing freedom
splitting of the Reed Sea
the Ten Plagues
surviving

00:00 – 00:15
Mind Warmer: Building the Storehouses

Families simulate the experience of slavery
and the building of storehouses for Pharaoh.
They will make pseudo-tile murals of the
storehouses.

Materials

name tags
markers
sign-in sheet
1 enlarged or large picture of one of the
  Storage City sheets for every 5 families
  (see Directions and Patterns)
assorted construction paper
magazines
gluesticks

Advance Preparation by the Facilitator

- Enlarge the patterns of Storage Cities I and
  II on a copy machine. Or, draw storage
  cities freehand on butcher paper or poster
  board large enough for several families to
  be able to work on the same storehouse
  outline.

- Place the outline(s) of the storehouse on the
  floor or on the work tables.

- On the supply table, place these materials:
  construction paper and magazines.

- On the supply table, place a container filled
  with gluesticks.

Procedure

- The Facilitator greets families as they

arrive. Have them fill out a name tag for each family member and sign in.

- Instruct families to work on building one of the storehouses, Pithom or Raamses, for the Pharaoh.

- Show them where the outlines of the storehouses are. Instruct them on how to "build" the storehouse, making "bricks" from scraps of construction paper or magazines. They are not to use scissors, but must tear each scrap and glue it on.

- Some families "make" the bricks (by tearing the paper); others "build" (by gluing the storehouses brick by brick).

- When there are five minutes left, tell the families that the Pharaoh will be angry if the storehouses are not finished in the next five minutes.

- Have each family bring their storehouses to the Introductions and Announcements area.

00:15 – 00:25
Introductions and Announcements

Materials
masking tape

Procedure
- The Facilitator welcomes everyone on behalf of the sponsoring agency/institution.

- The Facilitator introduces himself/herself and any other official representatives of the program or the agency/institution.

- Have a member of each family introduce himself/herself and other family members.

- Announce any upcoming events for the sponsoring agency/institution that are

pertinent for this group.

- Instruct people as to how they can get on the mailing list if they are not already on it.

Setting the Stage

- To display the storehouses, tape them to a wall. The Facilitator asks for comments on how well or how poorly they were made. Are the bricks even? Do they look secure? Is everything covered? How do you think Pharaoh would feel about your work? Remind the families that they just spent time as "slaves" building the storehouses for Pharaoh. Then ask: Did you enjoy your work? If you had to do it every day in the hot, hot sun for hours and hours, would you enjoy the work? How would it feel to be a slave?

- Say: The Jews who built Pharaoh's storehouses out of bricks they made from straw did not like being slaves. The work was hard. Pharaoh's taskmasters were mean. During Passover, we remember and relive the Exodus experience — our slavery in Egypt, our wandering in the desert, and the time when we received the Ten Commandments and the Torah at Mount Sinai. At the *Seder*, we read in the Haggadah that each person must experience the Exodus as if he or she were there. That is what we are going to do today. We are going to relive that experience.

00:25 – 00:45
Story Time: Making the Exodus Story
My Story
The story for this program is a reenactment of the Exodus from Egypt. The Facilitator reads a modified passage from the Torah, then asks the families to do a task. For this segment of the

program, you will need an empty room or a room with a space large enough to relive the Exodus story.

Materials

2 belts (the type people wear)
1 copy per child of the tablets of the Ten Commandments on any dull color paper (see Directions and Patterns)
1 copy per child of The Golden Calf pattern on gold metallic paper (see Directions and Patterns)
shofar

Advance Preparation by the Facilitator

- Outline and cut out of metallic paper one copy of The Golden Calf pattern for every child.

- Copy the outline of the Ten Commandments on dull color paper. Make one copy for every child, and cut each out.

Procedure

- The Facilitator tells the following simplified version of Exodus 1:1-1:7:

The Exodus from Egypt

These are the names of the children of Israel who came to Egypt: Reuben, Simeon, Levi, Judah, Issachar, Zebulun, Benjamin, Dan, Naphtali, Gad, Asher, and Joseph. Now we will say the names of the children of Israel of *this* generation who are reliving the Exodus from Egypt. (Have children and adults shout out their own names.)

The Pharaoh, the ruler of Egypt, was scared of the children of Israel, the Jews. There were many children of Israel — too many, thought Pharaoh. So Pharaoh forced the Israelites to build store cities called Pithom and Raamses. (Point to the storehouse murals they made.) The Hebrews, another name for the Jews, did not like being slaves. It was very hard work, and the taskmasters were mean. So they moaned and groaned. (Moan and groan loudly.)

Who do you think heard the Hebrews moaning? (Ask for responses.) God did. God listened to all their complaints. (Give families a minute to come up with a complaint. Ask them to share their complaints with the group.)

God sent Moses and Aaron to help the Hebrew slaves join together and make a plan for leaving Egypt. (Ask: Who here wants to leave slavery and leave Egypt? Get all the families together, eager to leave Egypt.)

- The Facilitator says: To leave Egypt we must cross through the Sea of Reeds. We could get wet. It is the only way to go. (Go to a space where you have room to play the game *Belts*. Use two long belts. Ask for four adult volunteers to move the belts back and forth to create the two sides of a flowing river.)

- The Facilitator says: Moses held out his arm over the Sea of Reeds. God split the waters with a strong wind during the night. In the middle of the sea was dry ground. The Hebrews went into the sea on dry ground, the waters forming a wall on their right and on their left. The Israelites began crossing the sea.

- As the children start "crossing the sea," recite or sing the line from Exodus 15:11, the *Mi Chamocha* prayer:

Mi Chamocha Ba'aylim Adonai.
Mi Kamocha Ne'dar Bakodesh.
Norah Tehillot Oseh Feleh.

Who is like You, O Eternal, among the mighty? Who is like You, majestic in holiness, awesome in splendor, working wonders!

- The Jews were tired, but safe. They went to sleep. (Have each person put hands together and rest head on hands.)

- (Blow the shofar. Continue the story.) Moses was on the top of Mount Sinai. All the children of Israel stood at the foot of the mountain. They heard the thunder and the shofar. These were the Ten Commandments that God gave to Moses on two tablets of stone:

#1 – God is One.

#2 – Worship only God.

#3 – Do not worship idols.

#4 – Remember and observe Shabbat.

#5 – Honor your parents.

#6 – Do not murder.

#7 – Be faithful to your husband or wife.

#8 – Do not steal.

#9 – Do not gossip.

#10 – Do not be jealous of others, wanting what they have.

For many days the Jews wandered (wander around) in the wilderness. They collected manna (collect manna) to eat (eat) and slept (sleep). Then they wandered some more (wander again), collected manna (collect more manna), and slept (sleep some more; this time, while families are sleeping, the Facilitator scatters the outlines of all the golden calves and about a third of the Ten Commandment tablets.)

- The Facilitator says: Wake up. While you were sleeping, something happened. Find something that looks interesting to you. Come and sit near me when you find that interesting thing.

- Families search. As soon as they find something interesting, a golden calf or tablets of the Ten Commandments, they sit near the Facilitator.

- The Facilitator says: Tell me what you found. Why do you like it? (Let participants respond.)

- The Facilitator explains: While in the wilderness, some of the Jews lost their trust in Moses and God. They did not like walking so far, or there was not enough food to eat. They felt that life was worse in the wilderness than in Egypt. So they built a golden calf, an idol, and they prayed to it instead of to God.

The Ten Commandments is a list of rules which make our lives special. These rules tell us how to treat other people and how we should care for others, especially our parents. They tell us what it means to be a Jew, to pray to the one and only God and to celebrate Shabbat.

- The Facilitator asks: Who would like to turn in their golden calf for the Ten Commandments? (Make the exchanges.) Now you have all relived and experienced the Exodus from Egypt. You are a free Jew, free to worship God! Let's all cheer for God and our freedom. (Shout: Yeah, we are free! Go, God!)

00:45 – 00:55
Snack: The Daily Feeding of Manna

This is a simple but appropriate snack. For the daily ration of manna, serve Fig Newtons or coconut cookies (wilderness foods!). Because the group is "in the wilderness," serve water or Gatorade to help prevent dehydration.

Materials

Fig Newtons and/or coconut cookies
Gatorade or water
cups

Procedure

- The Facilitator says: Every day, God provided manna in the wilderness for the Israelites. On Shabbat, they received a double portion. Your daily feeding of manna is cookies and water (or Gatorade).

- Together recite a blessing before eating the snack (see Blessing #8, page 488).

00:55 – 01:15
Activity: Assembling an Official Wilderness Kit

Every Passover *Seder* is a recreation, or reliving, of the Exodus experience. During this activity, each family will assemble an Official Wilderness Kit to help them through the Exodus experience.

Materials

1 copy per family of the Official Wilderness Kit Directions I, II, and III (see Patterns and Directions)
1 brown grocery bag per child
1 copy per child of the Official Wilderness Kit Label with contents on colored paper (see Directions and Patterns)
1 copy per child of A Swatter on light colored card stock (see Directions and Patterns)
1 copy per child of the Sun Visor outline on light colored card stock (see Directions and Patterns)

elastic string (available at costume stores)
1 travel brochure per child about Israel (obtain from El Al, a travel agent, Israeli consulate, or *sheliach*)
1 box of facial tissues
1 packet of salt per child (obtain from distributor, local hot dog stand, or fast food restaurant)
1 copy per child of Map on white paper (see Directions and Patterns)
1 paint stir stick per child
1 sandwich size plastic bag per child
1 Dayenu Sign per child copied on white card stock (see Directions and Patterns)
1 copy back-to-back of The Fan I and The Fan II on 8 ½" x 11" white paper (see Directions and Patterns)
scissors
crayons
gluesticks
stapler
staples
matzah
matzah crackers

Advance Preparation by the Facilitator

- Staple together the three pages of the Official Wilderness Kit.

- Make a sample Official Wilderness Kit.

- On the supply table, place the following items:

  matzah
  matzah crackers
  brown grocery bags
  Official Wilderness Kit label with contents
  Official Wilderness Kit Directions
  Sun Visor Directions
  copies of A Swatter
  Israel travel brochure
  packets of salt
  Dayenu Signs

paint stir sticks
sandwich size plastic bags
The Fan I and II sheets
Maps of the Exodus route
box of facial tissue
elastic string

- On the supply table, place these items, each in a separate container: scissors, crayons, gluesticks, staplers, and staples.

Procedure

- To introduce the activity, the Facilitator shows the items in the sample Kit and says: Every Passover *Seder* is meant to be a recreation or a reliving of the Exodus experience. The making of a Wilderness Kit will help to prepare you for your *Seder* and will help you during your *Seder*. Remember to bring your Wilderness Kit with you to your *Seder*.

- Tell the families to pick up a copy of the Official Wilderness Kit Directions and to collect their materials from the supply tables.

To make a satchel for the Official Wilderness Kit:

- Families make handles in the brown grocery bag. They cut ovals out of the top of the bag.

- They glue the Official Wilderness Kit Label onto the front of the satchel.

To make A Swatter for wilderness creatures:

- Families cut out a copy of the ten plagues from the sheet called A Swatter.

- They glue it to a fly swatter.

To make a Sun Visor:

- Each family chooses or creates their own saying or design to put on their visor. Since the visor is reversible, a second saying or design can be written on the other side.

- Participants cut out the Sun Visor pattern.

- They cut a piece of elastic string and staple it to the two ends of the visor at the "x's".

To plot a route through the wilderness:

- Families plot a course through the wilderness by tracing the route on the map with a favorite color.

To make a Dayenu Sign:

- Families color in the word "*Dayenu*" in Hebrew and English.

- They fold the *Dayenu* sign in half so that one side shows Hebrew and the other English.

- They put the paint stir stick between the two layers and staple in place.

To make unleavened trail mix:

- Families put some *matzah* crackers and *matzah* pieces in a plastic bag.

To make The Fan:

- Families color the pictures on both sides of the fan.

- Starting with a short 8½" side, they pleat the fan.

- They staple the bottom of the fan.

To finish the Official Wilderness Kit:

- Each family completes this project by putting all the items they made into their bag. They finish packing, adding an Israel brochure, handkerchief (tissue), and salt to their Official Wilderness Kit.

- They write their family's last name on the bag.

- Ask families to clean up, returning materials to the supply tables.

- Remind the families to take their Official Wilderness Kits to their Passover *Seder*.

01:15 – 01:30
Closure: Let My People Go!

End the program with singing, sharing, and holiday greetings.

- Sing and move to Passover music related to: slavery, freedom, *Dayenu, Mi Chamocha*, survival, wandering in the wilderness, receiving the Ten Commandments, worshiping God, the Passover *Seder*, names, being counted as a Jew.

Recommended Songs:

"Pesach Is Here Today" (*Especially Wonderful Days* by Steve Reuben, A.R.E. Publishing, Inc.)

"Out of Egypt" (*Apples on Holidays and Other Days* by Leah Abrams, A.R.E. Publishing, Inc.)

- Have participants share their reactions to the program. Ask families to complete one of these phrases:

Going through the wilderness . . .

Our family enjoyed . . .

Our family learned . . .

For our Passover *Seder*, we . . .

- Send everyone off with a Passover greeting, *"Chag Sameach*!" (Happy Holiday!)

Storage Cities I

1. Enlarge the pictures of Pithom and Raamses onto paper the size you want your mural to be.

2. Have some people be brickmakers. They have the tedious task of tearing magazines and/or construction paper into small paper "bricks."

3. Have the rest of the people be bricklayers. They have the tedious task of gluing the paper "bricks" onto the mural to "build" the storage cities of Pithom and Raamses.

4. As Facilitator, you have the thankless task of being the overseer.

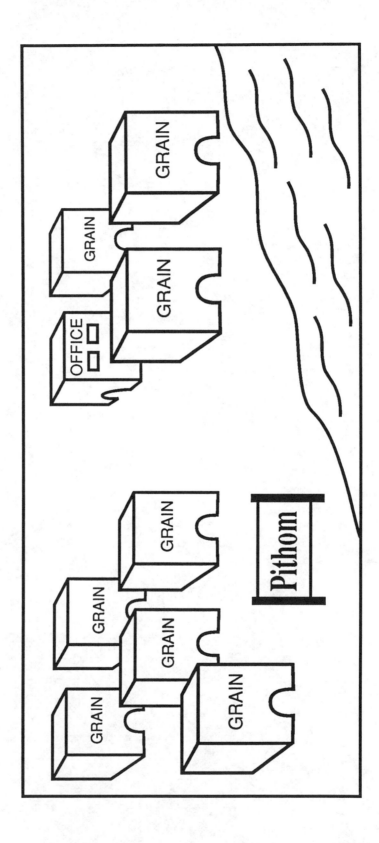

Storage Cities II

When completed, these murals will make good communal *Seder* decorations or a bulletin board which promotes the holiday party program.

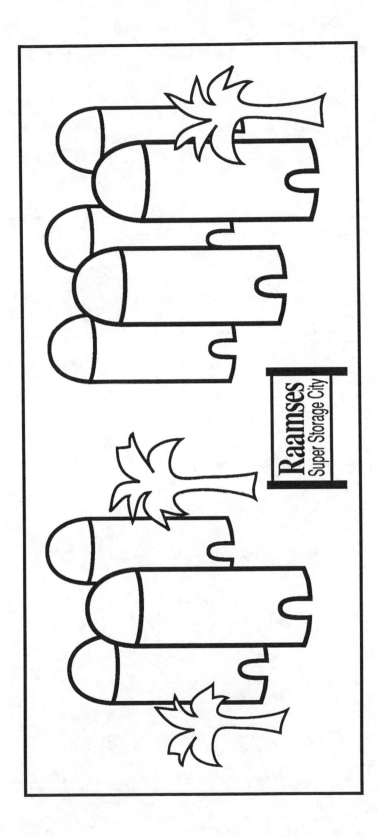

Raamses
Super Storage City

The Golden Calf

Use this pattern to cut calves out of gold paper. You will need a golden calf for each child at the party.

Ten Commandments

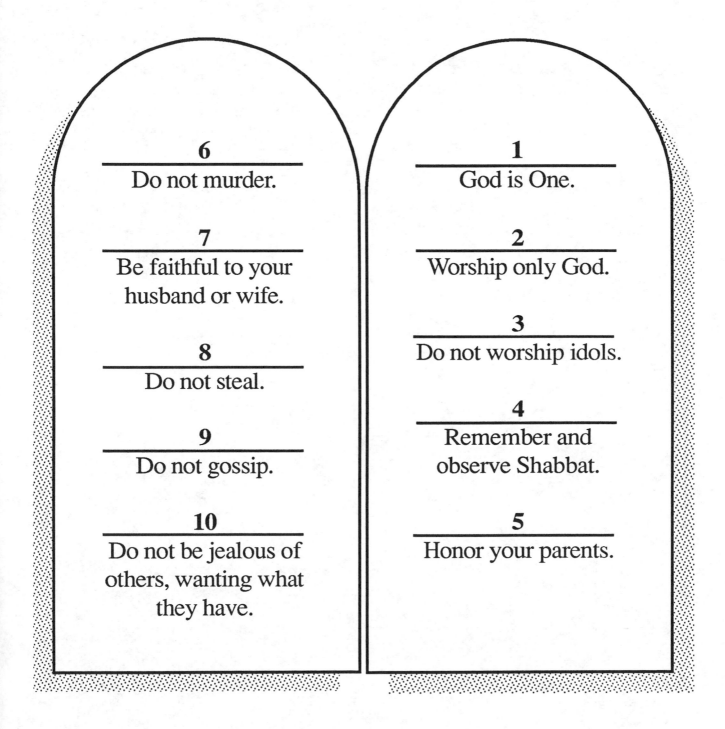

6	**1**
Do not murder.	God is One.
7	**2**
Be faithful to your husband or wife.	Worship only God.
8	**3**
Do not steal.	Do not worship idols.
9	**4**
Do not gossip.	Remember and observe Shabbat.
10	**5**
Do not be jealous of others, wanting what they have.	Honor your parents.

The Official Wilderness Kit I
(Directions)

Collect the following materials and supplies:

1 brown grocery bag   *matzah* or *matzah* crackers
elastic string   scissors
1 paint stick   stapler
1 sandwich bag   gluestick
1 Israel brochure   crayons
1 paper tissue   all 6 pages of the Official Wilderness Kit
1 salt packet   Patterns

To assemble the Official Wilderness Kit:

1. Make a satchel for the Official Wilderness Kit.

     a. Make handles. Cut ovals out of the top of the brown grocery bag.

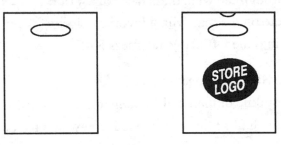

     b. Glue the Official Wilderness Kit Label (see page 1 of 6) onto the front of the satchel.

2. Make A Swatter (see page 2 of 6).

     a. Cut out the rectangle with the 10 plagues.

     b. (optional) Use stickers and variety store items — plastic flies, fake blood — to decorate the swatter.

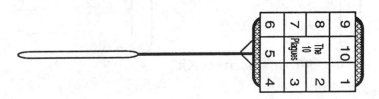

     c. Glue the ten plagues to the back of the swatter part of the fly swatter.

     d. Put the swatter in the Official Wilderness Kit.

The Official Wilderness Kit II
(Directions)

3. Make a visor (see page 3 of 6).
   a. Decorate the visor. (See the pattern for some suggestions.)
   b. Cut out the visor.
   c. Attach the elastic string at the X's.

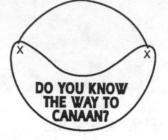

   d. Put the visor into the Official Wilderness Kit.

4. Plot a course through the wilderness (see page 4 of 6).
   a. Trace the route on the map with a favorite color.
   b. Put the map into the Official Wilderness Kit.

5. Make a Dayenu Sign (see page 5 of 6).
   a. Color in the outline of the word *Dayenu* in Hebrew and English.
   b. Fold the sign in half so that one side is Hebrew and the other side English.

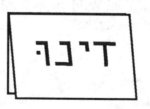

   c. Put the paint stir stick between the two layers and staple in place.

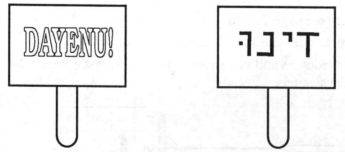

   d. Place the sign into the Official Wilderness Kit.

6. Pack some unleavened trail mix.
   a. Fill the sandwich bag with pieces of *matzah* or *matzah* crackers.
   b. Put this snack into the Official Wilderness Kit.

The Official Wilderness Kit III
(Directions)

7. Make a fan (see page 6 of 6).

   a. Color both sides of the fan.

   b. Starting with the short 8½" side, pleat the fan.

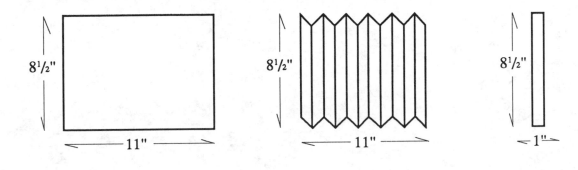

   c. Staple the bottom of the fan.

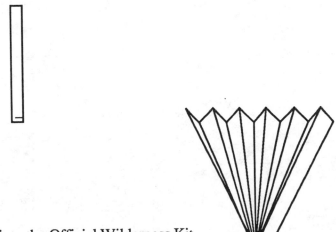

   d. Put the fan into the Official Wilderness Kit.

8. Finish packing. Add the Israel Brochure, the handkerchief, and the salt package to the Official Wilderness Kit.

The Official Wilderness Kit Label

Contents:

1. A Swatter
(For wilderness creatures)

2. Sun Visor
(To protect you from the hot sun)

3. Map
(To help you find your way)

4. Travel Brochure
(Information about the land that flows with milk and honey)

5. Dayenu Sign
(Use at your own discretion)

6. Unleavened Trail Mix
(A snack to enjoy between servings of manna)

7. Handkerchief
(For wiping eyes when eating maror or to protect eyes during sandstorms)

8. Salt
(For dipping karpas and/or for dehydration)

9. Fan
(To cool you in the burning hot wilderness)

Hillel says:

If I am not for myself, who will be for me?

A Swatter

Cut out the ten plagues. Then color and/or further embellish this before attaching to your fly swatter.

9 Darkness *Choshech*	**10** Death of Firstborn *Makkat B'chorot*	**1** Blood *Dam*
8 Locusts *Arbeh*	***The 10 Plagues***	**2** Frogs *Tzefardayah*
7 Hail *Barad*		**3** Lice *Kinnim*
6 Boils *Sh'chin*	**5** Cattle Disease *Dever*	**4** Swarming Things *Arov*

Use this during your *Seder* to help you remember all 10 of the plagues.

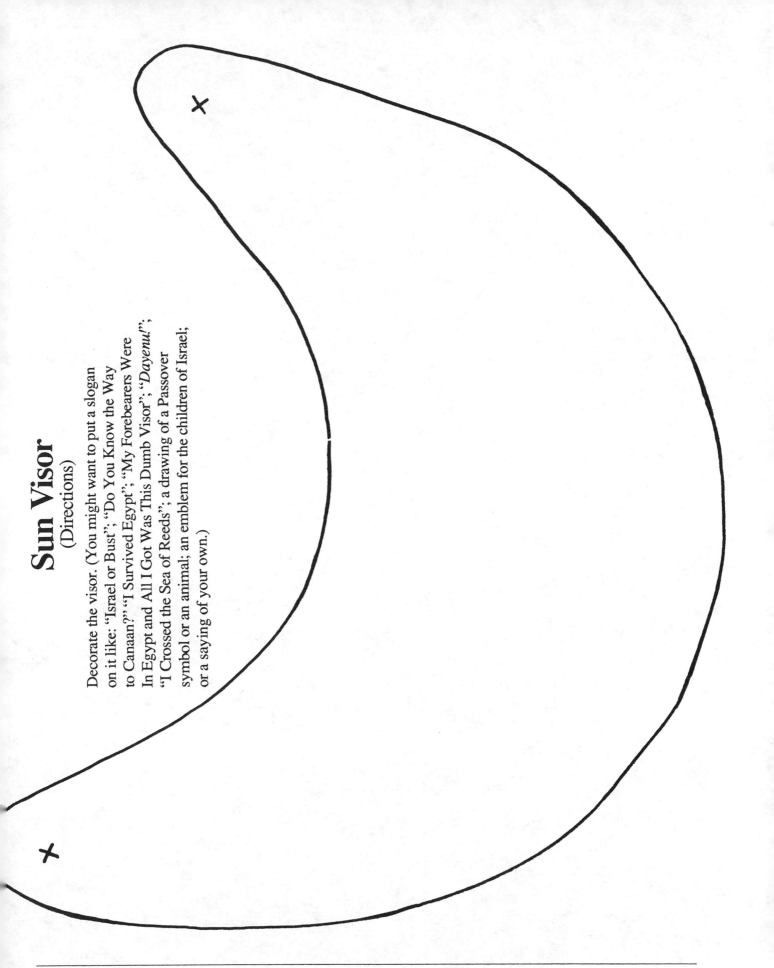

Sun Visor
(Directions)

Decorate the visor. (You might want to put a slogan on it like: "Israel or Bust"; "Do You Know the Way to Canaan?" "I Survived Egypt"; "My Forebearers Were In Egypt and All I Got Was This Dumb Visor"; *"Dayenu!"*; "I Crossed the Sea of Reeds"; a drawing of a Passover symbol or an animal; an emblem for the children of Israel; or a saying of your own.)

Map

Use your favorite color to trace the route on the map.

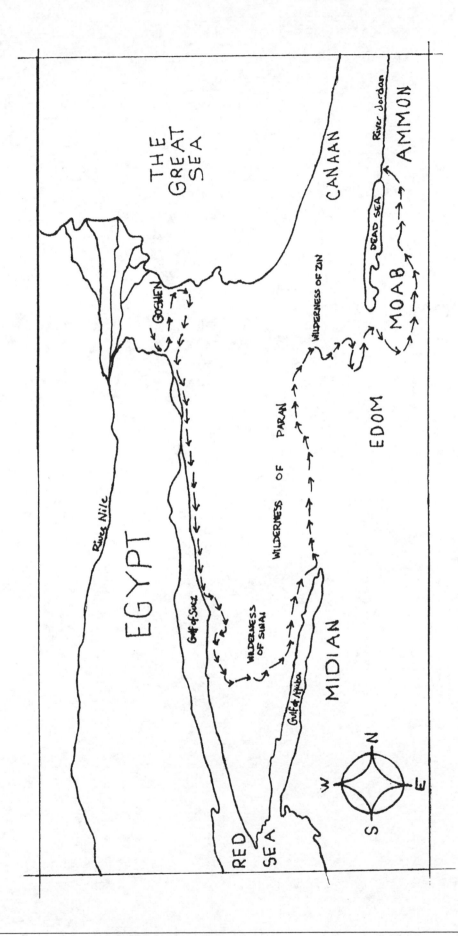

דַּיֵּנוּ

DAYENU!

The Fan I

Color both sides of this fan. Fold it accordian style and staple it at the bottom.

The Fan II

Color both sides of this fan. Fold it accordian style and staple it at the bottom.

The 33rd Day of the Omer Is Fun
Lag B'Omer, Year 1

Postcard and/or Flier

To include:
Program Title
Sponsored by
Audience (age group, members only or
   general public, etc.)
Date
Time
Location
Cost (if applicable)
RSVP or For Further Information
Come dressed in play clothes.

Physical Set Up

work area: tables and chairs
tables for supplies
table for name tags and sign-in sheet
large trash cans
trash bags
fire place or camp fire (optional)
empty room or space for games
Note: As setting permits, parts of this program
   can be done outside.

Holiday Symbols, Customs, Terms, and Concepts

Lag B'Omer — the 33rd day of the counting
   of the Omer
a holiday between Passover and Shavuot
special holiday honoring scholars
Pirke Avot (Sayings of Our Ancestors)
playing games
Simeon Bar Yochai
Bar Kochba
bows and arrows
camp fire, outdoors experience
keshet is a bow, a rainbow

00:00 – 00:10
Mind Warmer: Pirke Parents — Things My Parents Say

Lag B'Omer is a celebration that honors
Jewish scholars. *Pirke Avot* (Sayings of Our
Ancestors) is wisdom literature found in the
Talmud. For this Mind Warmer, children will
extract wisdom from their local scholars —
their parents. They will make this wisdom into
a booklet, called *Pirke Parents: Things My
Parents Say*.

Materials

name tags
markers
sign-in sheet
1 copy per child of Pirke Parents: Things
   My Parents Say sheets photocopied front
   and back on white paper 11" x 17" (see
   Directions and Patterns)
crayons
pens or pencils

Advanced Preparation by Facilitator

- Put together the *Pirke Parents* booklet.
  Copy the two patterns for this program
  enlarged onto 11" x 17" white paper. Then,
  copy the pattern front and back to make a
  one page booklet.

- On the supply table, place copies of the
  Pirke Parents booklets.

- On the supply table, place these items, each
  in a separate container: crayons, pens or
  pencils.

Procedure

- The Facilitator greets families as they arrive. Have them fill out a name tag for each family member and sign in.

- Tell the families that they will be making a booklet called *Pirke Parents: Things My Parents Say* in honor of Lag B'Omer.

- Instruct families to pick up the materials with directions for this project at the supply table.

- Families fold the sheet of 11" x 17" paper in half to form a booklet.

- Parents read the inside front page and back page of the booklet about *Pirke Avot*.

- Parents read to their children the phrases near the diagrams, for example, "This is my dad. He always says . . ." Children complete the phrases and parents write down the child's words.

- Families finish drawing in the details of the two diagrams to look like the parents. Families can add "bubbles" as in cartoons to indicate the "things my parents say."

- Ask families to clean up, returning materials to the supply table.

00:10 – 00:20
Introductions and Announcements

- The Facilitator welcomes everyone on behalf of the sponsoring agency/institution.

- The Facilitator introduces himself/herself and any other official representatives of the program or the agency/institution.

- Have a member of each family introduce himself/herself and other family members.

- Announce any upcoming events for the sponsoring agency/institution that are pertinent for this group.

- Instruct people as to how they can get on the mailing list if they are not already on it.

Setting the Stage

The Facilitator says: The "Lag" in Lag B'Omer stands for the number 33. Lag B'Omer is the 33rd day of the counting of the Omer, the fifty days from Passover to Shavuot. Each Shabbat during the fifty days, part of *Pirke Avot* (Sayings of our Ancestors) is read. Today, you have made your own book, *Pirke Parents: Things My Parents Say.*

Lag B'Omer is a day honoring some of Judaism's wisest people. It is a day of rejoicing. It is a day celebrated with picnics, games, music.

Later, we will hear a story about Lag B'Omer. First, let's play some games in honor of Lag B'Omer.

00:20 – 00:35
Activity: Let the Games Begin

One Lag B'Omer custom is to celebrate with games. Families will play Jewish games.

Materials

1 *gragger* per 6 -10 people
masking tape or sticks

Advance Preparation by the Facilitator

- These games can be played outdoors or indoors. Mark a starting line and a finish line. Use masking tape for indoor games and sticks for outdoor games.

Procedure

- These games require teams of no less than six. Teams of 8-10 are ideal. Divide the families into teams.

Leap Frog (for the Second Plague)

- All the children line up one behind the other. The children are to leap like frogs down on all fours. The last child in line leaps over all the other teammates. When that child gets to the front, the child at the end of the line leaps over all the other teammates. Do this until the front child reaches the finish line. (The parents can be a "ribbit" chorus cheering on their team.)

Honor Ma and Pa

- Children stand on the starting line. Parents stand on the finish line. Children run to their parent(s), hug them, and the whole family runs back. As soon as the one family crosses the line, the next child goes. This continues until one team finishes.

Rush, Rush with a Purim Rash, Rash

- In this game, players run while twirling a Purim *gragger* over their head.

- The Facilitator divides each team into half, one half at the starting line and the other half behind the finish line. One player begins by running and twirling the *gragger* over his/her head. Once the player reaches the other side, then he/she passes the *gragger* to the next player. The first team to finish wins.

From Slavery to Freedom

- Each player runs to the finish line like a slave and walks back to the starting line like a free person. The first team to cross the finish line wins.

The Spinning Dreidel

- Parent(s) and children do this *dreidel* spin race together. The child is the *dreidel*. Have the child hold his/her hands over his/her head. Parents grab hold of the arms and spin the child down to the finish line. The first team to spin all its families across the finish line wins.

00:35 – 00:50
Story and Snack by the Camp Fire

It is a Lag B'Omer custom to build a camp fire or bonfire. Families will eat some traditional North American camp fire foods and hear a story while sitting around a real or imaginary camp fire.

Materials

$\frac{1}{2}$ baked potato per family
little hot dogs, 2 per person
popcorn
marshmallows (if you have a real camp fire)
skewers (if you have a real camp fire)
margarine
juice
cups
microwave or stove
popcorn popper (optional)
cooking pans
serving plates
serving bowls
serving forks
wood, matches, tinder, and bucket of water for outdoor camp fire option
twigs, flame colored tissue paper, and newspaper for indoor simulated camp fire option
plates
forks
napkins

Advance Preparation by Facilitator

- Arrange for someone to prepare the baked potatoes, hot dogs, and popcorn.

- For indoor use, make a mock camp fire out of twigs, tissue paper, and newspaper. Place the twigs in a tepee shape on the newspaper. Crumple up tissue paper to look like a flame.

- For outdoor use, arrange for a volunteer to prepare and put out the camp fire.

- Place foods and serving items on the supply table.

Procedure

- The Facilitator lets the families know that they will be continuing their Lag B'Omer celebration with a traditional camp fire. What goes with a camp fire? Food and stories. They will have both.

- Together recite the appropriate blessing (see Blessing #9, page 488).

- Ask families to collect their snacks of camp fire food from the supply table and come to the camp fire for a story.

- Tell this story:

A Lag B'Omer Tale

A long time ago in Israel, the Jews were ruled by the Romans. The Romans were mean rulers. They made up lots of rules about what the Jews could and could not do.

Just because the Romans made the rules, the Jews did not always obey. There were two ways that the Jews tried to get back at the Roman rulers. One was the way of a famous leader, Bar Kochba.

Bar Kochba was a hero. He was good with shooting bow and arrows. Many families sent their children to train with Bar Kochba in order to fight against the Romans. Do you think the Romans allowed Bar Kochba

to train an army? No! The clever parents said "We are training our children to hunt."

The Jews became good at using bows and arrows. But they were not good enough to beat the Romans. After a battle led by Bar Kochba, the Romans made a rule that the Jews did not like at all.

Some people would have been angry if music, dancing, and merrymaking were forbidden. Still others would have been unhappy if they were asked to pay the rulers lots of money. But these were not the rules that made the Jews so unhappy.

The rule that made the Jews angry was the rule forbidding them from studying. No more classes. No more school. No more lectures by Rabbis. That was the Roman rule that made the Jews so upset.

The second way that the Jews fought the Romans was the way of the leader Simeon Bar Yochai. He was a great and wise person. His way of fighting was through study, study of the Torah and Jewish law. This was his way of keeping Judaism alive. He had many, many students.

Like Bar Kochba, Simeon Bar Yochai was a brave man. The Romans did not want the Jews to study. So Simeon Bar Yochai had to hide in a cave for twelve years. Our tradition tells us that by a miracle, he stayed alive those twelve years living off the fruit of a carob tree.

In the end, it was not the bows and arrows of our hero Bar Kochba that kept the Jewish people alive. It was the words, ideas, and wisdom of Simeon Bar Yochai that won out over the Romans. There are no more Romans. But we Jews are still here. Today, we still study the Torah and Jewish law. We go to school. We listen to Rabbis teach.

We read books. It was study that kept the Jewish people alive then and study that keeps us alive today.

On Lag B'Omer, we celebrate the wisdom and bravery of these Jewish heroes, scholars like Simeon Bar Yochai. He died on Lag B'Omer. It is said that he was such a wise and kind and righteous person that no rainbows appeared during his lifetime. For the rainbow is a reminder of God's promise to Noah not to destroy the world no matter how many wicked people lived on earth.

Today, we say "yes" to study. So, to honor Simeon Bar Yochai, we will draw rainbows. This will be our promise to God to follow Jewish laws and traditions. We will always try to be good, not wicked people.

- Ask families to clean up, returning materials to the supply table.

Note: At this time, you may choose to have a real *kumsitz*, singing and playing music around the camp fire.

00:50 – 01:10 Activity:
The Rainbow of Promise

Keshet is the Hebrew word meaning both "bow," as in bow and arrow, and "rainbow." The bow reminds us of Bar Kochba's way of trying to save the Jews. The rainbow reminds us of people like Simeon Bar Yochai who remember the promises God made to the Jewish people. In recognition of our continuing commitment to that promise, families will draw rainbows.

Indoors, this activity can be done on bulletin board paper with colored chalk. Outdoors, families may do sidewalk sketching.

Materials

colored chalk
long sheets of bulletin board paper (for indoor or rainy weather use)
sidewalks (for outdoor sketching)
masking tape (for indoor or rainy weather use)

Advance Preparation by Facilitator

- Cut the bulletin board paper into sheets 10' to 12' long. Allow for a 2' x 2' segment for each family.

- Use masking tape to secure the bulletin board paper to the floor to keep it flat.

- On the supply table, place a container of colored chalk.

Procedure

- The Facilitator says: The Hebrew word *keshet* has a double meaning. It means both "bow" and "rainbow." Both of these are symbols of Lag B'Omer. To show our continued commitment to God to keep our promises, our part of the deal, we will draw rainbows. Be creative. Rainbows of color can come in many different forms. You may outline your name in black and color in each letter with a different color of the rainbow.

- Instruct families that they should claim a segment of the bulletin board paper (if inside) or sidewalk (if outside) and draw a rainbow or rainbows.

- Every 3-4 families located on the same segment of paper or portion of sidewalk should send a representative to the supply table for chalk.

- Families draw their rainbows.

- Ask families to clean up, returning chalk to the supply table and washing their hands.

- Allow time for admiring each rainbow.

01:10 – 01:30
Closure: Somewhere Over the Rainbow

Close out the program with songs, sharing, and holiday greetings.

- Sing and move to Lag B'Omer music and movement related to: parents, wise people, Jewish scholars, games, studying, bows and arrows, rainbows, harvesting, counting, Shavuot.

  Recommended Songs:

  "Somewhere Over the Rainbow" *(The Wizard of Oz)*

"The Alef-Bet Song" *(Musical Curriculum for Hebrew and Heritage* by Debbie Friedman, Behrman House)

Your favorite Jewish songs

- Have people share their reactions to the program. Ask families to complete one of these phrases:

  Lag B'Omer is . . .

  Our family enjoyed . . .

  Our family learned . . .

- Send everyone home with a Lag B'Omer greeting of "Happy Lag B'Omer." Shavuot will soon be here!

PIRKE PARENTS
THINGS MY PARENTS SAY

Pirke Avot is a small book that is part of the Talmud. It begins like this:

Moses received the Torah at Mount Sinai, and he passed it on to Joshua, Joshua to the elders, the elders to the prophets, and the prophets handed it down . . . .

Pirke Avot contains many statements by famous Jewish teachers. These teachers had lots of advice about how to behave — just like parents.

Directions: Add details to the outlines of people so that they look like your parents. You can even make them talk like your parents.

"*. . . be a tail to lions, don't be a head to foxes.*"
Pirke Avot 4:20

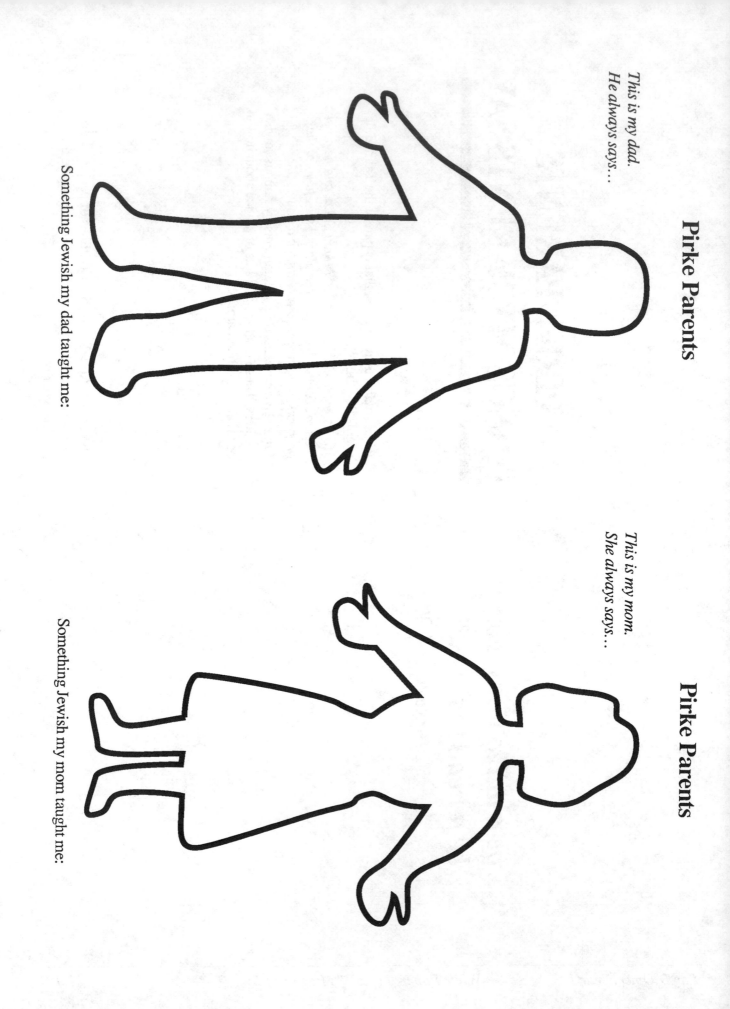

This is my dad.
He always says…

Something Jewish my dad taught me:

This is my mom.
She always says…

Something Jewish my mom taught me:

The Giving of the Torah on Mount Sinai
Shavuot, Year 1

Postcard and/or Flier

To include:
Program Title
Sponsored by
Audience (age group, members only or
general public, etc.)
Date
Time
Location
Cost (if applicable)
RSVP or For Further Information

Physical Set Up

work area: tables and chairs
tables for supplies
table for name tags and sign in sheet
large trash cans
trash bags
sanctuary (preferable but optional)

Holiday Symbols, Customs, Terms and Concepts

the giving and receiving of the Torah
the Ten Commandments
positive commandment: should do
negative commandment: should not do
staying up all night to study
learning the *alef-bet* as a form of study
the Torah service
the Torah service as a recreation of the giving
of the Torah on Mount Sinai
eating white foods representing the clouds
engulfing Mount Sinai

00:00 – 00:15
Mind Warmer: An Alef-bet Sampler

Historically, Shavuot is the day on which the Torah was given at Mount Sinai. On this holiday, people spend the entire night studying. During this Mind Warmer, families study the first ten letters of the Hebrew *alef-bet*.

Materials

name tags
markers
sign-in sheet
1 copy per child of the Alef-bet Sampler
enlarged onto 11" x 17" white paper (see
Directions and Patterns)
crayons
pencils (or pens)
1 ink pad for 6-8 families
baby wipes

Advance Preparation by Facilitator

- On the supply table, place these materials: copies of the Alef-bet Sampler on white paper and ink pads.

- On the supply table, place these items, each in a separate container: crayons and pens or pencils.

Procedure

- The Facilitator greets families as they arrive. Have them fill out a name tag for each family member and sign in.

- Tell the families that they will be making an Alef-bet Sampler.

- Instruct each family to pick up a copy of the Alef-bet Sampler sheet and crayons, pencils (or pens) at the supply table.

- Parents read the name of the Hebrew letters and children color them in.

- Parents pronounce each of the Hebrew words, then read the sentence that goes with the Hebrew word. The child completes the sentence. Parents write down the child's responses.

- Use the ink pads for the child to make his/her thumb print for the letter *Alef* which begins the word *etzbah* (finger).

- Ask families to clean up, returning materials to the supply table.

- Use baby wipes for cleaning fingers.

00:15 – 00:25
Introductions and Announcements

Materials
squeeze bottle of honey

Procedure
- The Facilitator welcomes everyone on behalf of the sponsoring agency/institution.

- The Facilitator introduces himself/herself and any other official representatives of the program or the agency/institution.

- Have a member of each family introduce himself/herself and other family members.

- Announce any upcoming events for the sponsoring agency/institution that are pertinent for this group.

- Instruct people as to how they can get on the mailing list if they are not already on it.

Setting the Stage

- Say: During the Mind Warmer, you made an Alef-bet Sampler of the first ten letters of the Hebrew alphabet. Those first ten letters represent the numbers one through ten. Shavuot is the day on which we read about how God gave the Ten Commandments to the Jewish People. Tradition teaches that not only were the Ten Commandments given on Shavuot, but that the entire Torah was given at Mount Sinai.

  In recognition of the giving of the Torah, it is a custom to spend the night studying. You have begun this Shavuot program studying the Hebrew *alef-bet*. In honor of that occasion, all the children should come forward to get a taste of honey on their finger. The honey symbolizes the sweetness of studying our Jewish heritage. (All the children come forward. The Facilitator puts honey on a finger.)

- The Facilitator continues: We will spend the remainder of this program focusing on that Shavuot gift from God, the Torah. It was a gift that we Jews were eager and willing to accept.

00:25 – 00:45
A Real Torah Story

In many ways, the Torah service mirrors the giving of the Torah at Mount Sinai. This combined story and activity draws the connection between the two. The families will go through a Torah service and a participation story about the giving of the Torah at Mount Sinai. (It would be helpful to have the music specialist available for the musical portions of the service.)

Materials

Torah or miniature Torah
an Ark (preferable but optional)
sanctuary (preferable but optional)

Advance Preparation by the Facilitator

- Practice dressing and undressing the Torah.

Procedure

- (Optional) The Facilitator leads the group to the sanctuary or to a place where there is an Ark.

- Explain to families that today's Torah service is very much like the giving of the Torah on Mount Sinai and that they will now participate in a Torah service.

Torah Service

- The Facilitator says: We will now begin our Torah service. Just as the Israelites stood at Mount Sinai, we, too, will stand when the Torah is taken out. (Take the Torah out of the Ark. Ask all to rise.)

- All Sing:

  Ki Mitzion Taytzay Torah. (2x)
  U' devar Adonai Merushalayim.

  The Facilitator translates: For out of Zion (Israel) shall go forth Torah, and the word of the Lord from Jerusalem.

- All Sing:

  Shema Yisrael Adonai Eloheynu Adonai Echad.

  Translate: Hear, O Israel, the Eternal is our God, the Eternal is One.

- All Sing:

  Echad Eloheynu Gadol Adoneynu Kadosh Sh'mo.

Translate: Our God is One; our Lord is great; holy is God's name.

- Facilitator says: Now we will march around with the Torah. It is a custom to kiss a Torah touching it with a *tallit* (prayer shawl), prayerbook, or one's hand. This shows our love for God. God gave us the Torah because God loves us. (The Facilitator or a parent marches around with the Torah. Children may follow behind. Sing or hum "*L'cha Adonai Hagedulah*" or the *Shema* or another Jewish melody.)

- (The Facilitator undresses the Torah, passing around the ornaments and garments for all to see and touch.) The Facilitator says: Please be seated. The Israelites prepared to receive the Torah on Mount Sinai for three days. Today, the Torah reader prepares the Torah portion. The Torah was given with one voice on Mount Sinai. One person at a time reads the Torah portion. While one person reads the Torah, two other people watch and help the Torah reader. These three are like the three parties who were present at Mount Sinai — God, Moses and the Israelites. (Ask for two volunteers to stand beside the Facilitator and follow along.)

- All who can, chant the Torah blessing before the reading of the Torah:

Leader: *Barchu Et Adonai Ham' vorach.*

Congregation: *Baruch Adonai Ham' vorach L'olam Va-ed.*

Leader: *Baruch Adonai Ham' vorach L'olam Va-ed.*

Together: *Baruch Atah Adonai Eloheynu Melech Ha-olam Asher Bachar Banu Mekol Ha' amim V' natan Lanu Et Torato. Baruch Atah Adonai Notayn Hatorah.*

Praise the Eternal to Whom all praise is due. Praised be the Eternal to Whom our praise is due, now and for ever!

Blessed is the Eternal our God, Ruler of the universe, Who has chosen us from among all peoples by giving us the Torah. Blessed is the Eternal, Giver of the Torah.

- The Facilitator tells this participation story. Instructions for the congregation are in the parentheses.

God told the Israelite people to prepare for three days. (Wash. Prepare a special meal. Dress in nice clothes.) For in three days you are to go and stand beneath the mountain of the Lord.

On the third day, the mountain was covered with a cloud. There was lightning and thunder. (Put hands over ears.) There was a very loud blast of a horn. (Everyone does the Bronx cheer.) The people were afraid. (Shake and look afraid.)

God told the people, "Stand at the foot of the mountain. Only Moses shall come up the mountain." The people went to the foot of the mountain. (Walk to where the Torah is.)

Moses brought these Ten Commandments to the people from God, the Eternal:

God is One.

Worship only God.

Do not worship idols.

Remember and observe Shabbat.

Honor your parents.

Do not murder.

Be faithful to your husband or wife.

Do not steal.

Do not gossip.

Do not be jealous of others, wanting what they have.

These were the words that God spoke to Moses. The Israelites stepped back in fear (Take three steps backwards.)

- All who can, chant the blessing after the reading of the Torah:

Baruch Atah Adonai, Eloheynu Melech Ha-olam, Asher Natan Lanu Torat Emet V'chayay Olam Natah B'tochaynu. Baruch Atah Adonai Notayn Hatorah.

Blessed is the Eternal our God, Ruler of the universe, Who has given us a Torah of truth, implanting within us everlasting life. Blessed is the Eternal, Giver of the Torah.

- (The Facilitator raises the Torah high so that all can see the printed words. This is called *Hagbah*.) Sing or say in Hebrew (optional) and English:

V'zot Hatorah Asher Sahm Mosheh Lifnay B'nai Yisrael Al Pi Adonai B'yad Moshe.

This is the Torah that Moses placed before the people of Israel to fulfill the word of God.

- (Dress the Torah.) Together sing either "*Eytz Chaim Hee*" or "It is a Tree of Life."

Eytz Chaim Hee La'machazikim Bah V'tomchehah M'ushar. D'rachehah Darchay-noam, V'chol N'tivotechah Shalom.

It is a tree of life to those who hold fast to it, and all who cling to it find happiness. Its ways are ways of pleasantness, and all its paths are peace.

(Return the Torah to the Ark.)

00:45 – 00:55
Snack: It's Light and Fluffy Like the Clouds on Mount Sinai

It is a custom to serve white foods on Shavuot. These white foods are symbolic of the cloud that covered Mount Sinai during the giving of the Ten Commandments.

Materials

frozen vanilla yogurt or vanilla ice cream cups
spoons
bowls for the frozen yogurt
juice
cups

Procedure

- The Faciliator explains the symbolism of eating a white food on Shavuot. It represents the cloud covering Mount Sinai.

- Together recite the appropriate blessing (see Blessing #9, page 488).

- Enjoy the fluffy white snack.

00:55 – 01:10
Activity: We Are the World Collage

During this activity, families complete a collage of Ways To Make the World a Better Place. The possibilities are separated into two categories: things we do want to happen and things we don't want to happen. As with the Ten Commandments, these things are placed on two tablets.

Materials

1 copy per child of Ways To Make the World a Better Place enlarged onto 11" x 17" white paper (see Directions and Patterns)
magazines
catalogues
newspapers
other printed material
gluesticks
scissors

Advance Preparation by the Facilitator

- On the supply table, place the following materials: Ways To Make the World a Better Place sheets, magazines, catalogues, newspapers, and other printed material.

- On the supply table, place these items, each in its own container: scissors and gluesticks.

Procedure

- The Facilitator introduces the project to the families.

- Ask that one person from each work table pick up the materials from the supply table.

- Have parents read to their children the explanation and directions at the top of the Ways To Make the World a Better Place sheet. This explanation relates the Ten Commandments to the task at hand.

- Have families search through the printed matter to find pictures that fit in the two categories — things we do want to happen, and things we don't want to happen.

- Ask families to clean up, returning materials to the supply table.

01:10 – 01:30
Closure: On Top of Mount Sinai All Covered with Clouds

End the program with singing, blessings, sharing, and holiday greetings.

Procedure

- Sing and move to Shavuot music related to: the Torah, the Ten Commandments, Mount Sinai, Moses, rules and commandments, clouds and thunder, the giving and the receiving of the Torah.

Recommended Songs:

"The Torah" (*Especially Jewish Symbols* by Jeff Klepper, A.R.E. Publishing, Inc.)

"Hands Hold the Torah" (*To See the World Through Jewish Eyes*, Volume I – Early Childhood, Union of American Hebrew Congregations)

"Ten Commandments" (*Bible People Songs* by Jeff Klepper and Jeff Salkin, A.R.E. Publishing, Inc.)

"Torah" (*Apples on Holidays and Other Days* by Leah Abrams, Tara Publications.)

"*Al Shalosh Regalim*" (*Seasoned with Song* by Julie Auerbach, Tara Publications)

- Practice some of the songs from the Torah service.

- Have participants share their reactions to the program. Ask families to complete one of these phrases:

To make the world a better place, we . . .

The Torah . . .

Learning . . .

Our family enjoyed . . .

- Send everyone off with a Shavuot greeting, "*Chag Sameach*!" (Happy Holiday!)

Alef-bet Sampler

Color in the Hebrew letters. Then complete the sentences in each box.

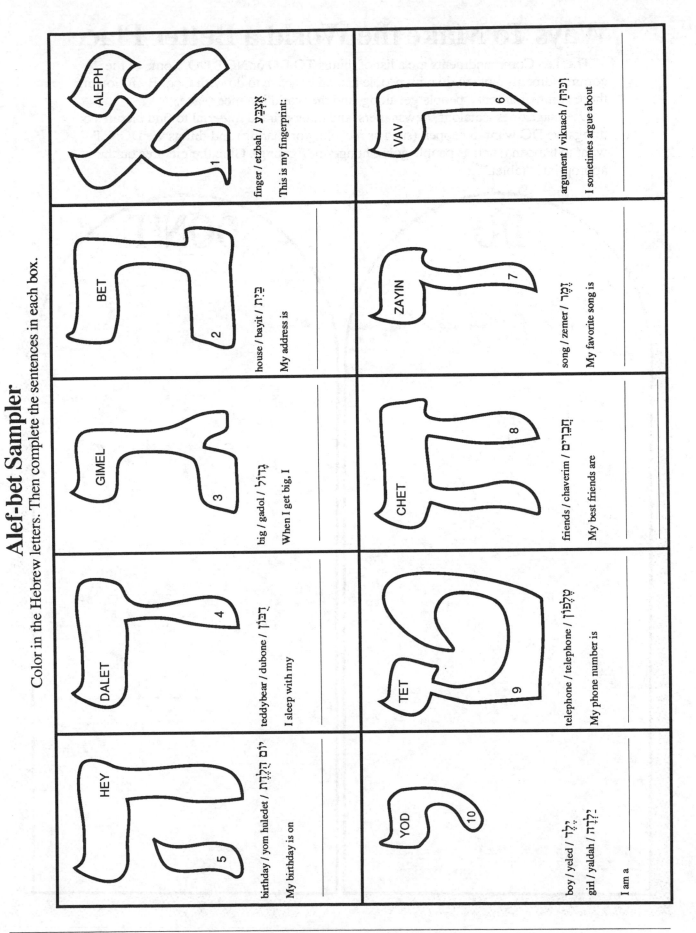

ALEPH 1
finger / etzbah / אֶצְבַּע
This is my fingerprint:

BET 2
house / bayit / בַּיִת
My address is

GIMEL 3
big / gadol / גָּדוֹל
When I get big, I

DALET 4
teddybear / dubone / דֻּבּוֹן
I sleep with my

HEY 5
birthday / yom huledet / יוֹם הֻלֶּדֶת
My birthday is on

VAV 6
argument / vikuach / וִכּוּחַ
I sometimes argue about

ZAYIN 7
song / zemer / זֶמֶר
My favorite song is

CHET 8
friends / chaverim / חֲבֵרִים
My best friends are

TET 9
telephone / telephone / טֶלֶפוֹן
My phone number is

YOD 10
boy / yeled / יֶלֶד
girl / yaldah / יַלְדָה
I am a

Ways To Make the World a Better Place

The Ten Commandments are a list of things TO DO or NOT DO. Some of the commandments have to do with people and others have to do with God. By following these commandments, people get along, and the world is a nice place.

Use magazines, catalogs, newspapers, and other printed material to find pictures of things we DO want to happen (such as recycling or sharing) and things we DON'T want to happen (such as people going hungry or fighting). Glue the pictures on the appropriate "tablet."

Year 2

Wave the "Layv" — Simchat Torah Is Here
Simchat Torah, Year 2

Postcard and/or Flier

To include:
Program Title
Sponsored by
Audience (age group, members only or
 general public, etc.)
Date
Time
Location
Cost (if applicable)
RSVP or For Further Information

Physical Set Up

work area: tables and chairs
tables for supplies
table for name tags and sign-in sheet
large trash cans
trash bags

**Holiday Symbols, Customs, Terms,
and Concepts**

Yisrael, the last word in the Torah
Lamed, the last Hebrew letter in the Torah
Beresheet, the first word in the Torah
Bet, the first Hebrew letter in the Torah
Lamed and *Bet* spell *layv*, meaning "heart"
ending and beginning the reading of the Torah
the Torah cycle
Five Books of the Torah
Chumash (the Five Books of the Torah)
the joy of the Torah
dancing with the Torah
The Jewish People as the Heart of the Torah
The Torah as the Heart of the Jewish People
honey
sweetness of learning

rolling the Torah
undressing and dressing the Torah
the Torah ornaments

**00:00 – 00:15
Mind Warmer: Wave the "Layv"**

Simchat Torah is a time for dancing with the
Torah, waving flags, and carrying banners. On
Simchat Torah, we read the last part of the
Torah and the first part of the Torah. Families
will make a unique Simchat Torah flag out of
the last and first letters in the Torah, *Lamed*
and *Bet*.

Materials

name tags
markers
sign-in sheet
1 Simchat Torah Letter Flag Pattern I per
 two children copied on white paper (see
 Directions and Patterns)
1 Simchat Torah Letter Flag Pattern II per
 two children copied on white paper (see
 Directions and Patterns)
1 6" x 11" piece of poster board per child
1 paint stir stick per child
wiggle eyes
feathers
ribbon
sequins
gluesticks
staplers
staples
scissors

Advance Preparation by the Facilitator

- Make sample *Lamed* and *Bet* flags.

- On the supply table, place these supplies: *Lamed* and *Bet* letters on white paper, poster board, paint sticks, wiggle eyes, sequins, feathers, and ribbon.

- On the supply table, place each of these items in a separate container: gluesticks, staplers, staples, and scissors.

Procedure

- The Facilitator greets families as they arrive. Have them fill out a name tag for each family member and sign in.

- The Facilitator shows each family the sample flags and asks them to collect their materials for this project from the supply table.

- Families go to the work tables where they will be making a *Lamed* or a *Bet* flag for Simchat Torah.

- Have the families cut out a piece of poster board. Staple a *Lamed* or *Bet* Hebrew letter to the poster board, cut out the Hebrew letter, then decorate it with the wiggle eyes, feathers, sequins, ribbon, etc.

- Using a stapler, attach the Hebrew letter to the paint stick. Families may want to glue the letter on the stick first and then staple it. Make certain the letter does not flop around too much.

00:15 – 00:20
Introductions and Announcements

- The Facilitator welcomes everyone on behalf of the sponsoring agency/institution.

- The Facilitator introduces himself/herself and any other official representatives of the program or the agency/institution.

- Have a member of each family introduce himself/herself and other family members.

- Announce any upcoming events for the sponsoring agency/institution that are pertinent for this group.

- Instruct people as to how they can get on the mailing list if they are not already on it.

Setting the Stage

- Have the children hold up their unique Simchat Torah flags.

- Say: On Simchat Torah, we dance with the Torah, waving flags. On Simchat Torah, we celebrate the reading of the end of the Torah and then the beginning of the Torah.

  It is traditional for the Torah reader to read the last line of the Torah and the first line of the Torah. The last word of the Torah is *Yisrael*. (Have the families repeat the word.) *Yisrael* ends with an "l" sound. That sound is represented by the Hebrew letter *Lamed,* which is on many of your flags. (Point out the *Lamed*. Say "*Lamed*" and "l" together as a group.)

  The first word of the Torah is *Beresheet*. (Practice saying "*Beresheet*" together.) *Beresheet* begins with a "b" sound. That is the sound of the Hebrew letter *Bet* which is also on many of your flags. Point out the Hebrew letter *Bet*. Say "*Bet*" and "b" together as a group.)

  Now stand up and find a person whose flag has the other Hebrew letter. Hug the person.

  Together, the *Lamed* and *Bet* make the Hebrew word "*layv*," which means heart. The Torah is the heart of the Jewish people. This Simchat Torah, you will be able to march and dance with the Torah and with your very special and unique flags.

00:20 – 00:40:
The Original Jewish Storybook: The Torah

Usually, this portion of the program involves the telling of a story. This time, you will introduce the families to the Torah, the original Jewish storybook.

Materials

Torah (or a miniature Torah with Hebrew letters or a *Tikkun*)
access to the Ark in a sanctuary or a room with an Ark

Advance Preparation by the Facilitator

For this part of the session, a Torah is needed. If possible, do this segment in a sanctuary or in a room where there is an Ark. If a Torah is not accessible, use a miniature Torah that has Hebrew letters or a *Tikkun* (the book used to practice Torah reading) or the book *The Torah* in English.

- Familiarize yourself with the ornamental dressings of the Torah:

    the crowns (*keterim*) usually with bells

    a breastplate (*choshen*)

    a mantle, the outer cloth covering

    a Torah binder (*avnate*)

    a pointer (*yad*) that looks like a hand

- Be comfortable pointing out: how a Torah is rolled; how the Torah is undressed and dressed; the last word of the Torah; the last story in the Torah about the death of Moses; the first word in the Torah; the first story in the Torah, the creation of the world; the letters of the Hebrew *alef bet*. (If you cannot identify the Hebrew letters, find someone in the group who can help with this.)

Procedure

- The Facilitator tells the families that they are going to the sanctuary (or room where the Ark is) to view the Torah. (If this is done in the regular meeting room, take a pretend trip to a sanctuary where the Torah is kept in the Ark.)

- The Facilitator takes the Torah out of the Ark. Let the families know that it is customary to stand when the Torah is standing and to sit when the Torah is sitting or laying down. This is the same respect we show to a king or queen.

- March the Torah so that everyone can see it and touch it. Introduce the custom of kissing the Torah. As we kiss a person we love, so we kiss the Torah, too.

- Ask the families why we dress the Torah with such beautiful ornaments and clothing. Undress the Torah for the families. Say the name of the Torah ornaments as you take them off: crowns (*keterim*), pointer (*yad*), breastplate (*choshen*), mantle, and binder (*avnate*). Let a different family hold each of the Torah ornaments. Or, pass the ornaments around.

- Place the Torah on a table or lectern. The easier for the children to see and gather around, the better. Spread out the Torah so that you can see several columns.

- Explain that the Hebrew in the Torah is a very fancy lettering, calligraphy. Have the children and parents look for the letter that they used in making their flag, the *Lamed* or *Bet*. Help a few families at a time find those two letters in the Torah.

- If you can, show them the last word in the Torah — the word *Yisrael*.

- Optional: Ask each child his/her name. Look for a Hebrew letter that corresponds to one of the sounds in their English name. Beginning and ending sounds are easier to hear. For example, with Jennifer, you can look for the letter *Resh*. Show them the letter, and tell them the sound it makes (e.g., *Resh* makes an "r" sound).

- Dress the Torah again with the assistance of the families. Put the Torah back in the Ark.

Note: If desired, have music and movement now in the sanctuary. This allows families to practice some Hebrew songs and dances with the Torah. It will also help the children to feel more comfortable when there are hordes of participants present for the actual Simchat Torah celebration.

00:40 – 00:50
Snack: Honey for the Sweetness of the Torah and for Jewish Learning

Simchat Torah has become a time for welcoming children to the beginning of their Jewish studies. Children are given honey or candy, a sweet treat, upon beginning their Jewish studies. This was to associate sweetness with the joy of learning.

Materials

honey graham crackers
Bit O'Honey or any other candy made with honey
apple juice
cups
napkins
tray for serving

- Serve honey graham crackers, Bit O'Honey candy, or any other honey product you can find that the children will enjoy. Serve with apple juice.

- Remember to recite the appropriate blessing (see Blessing #8, page 488).

00:50 – 01:10
Activity: The Jewish People are the Heart of the Torah

During this activity, families make a mobile of the Five Books of the Torah and a heart. The heart is symbolic of our love for Torah throughout the ages. This project introduces the families to the Hebrew and English names of the Five Books of the Torah. It reinforces the Mind Warmer presentation of the first and last words in the Torah, *Beresheet* (meaning beginning) and *Yisrael* (Israel).

Materials

1 set per child of The Simchat Torah Mobile Pattern I-V photocopied on the five colors of card stock in sequence with the colors of the rainbow (see Directions and Patterns):
blue – Genesis/*Beresheet*
green – Exodus/*Shemot*
yellow – Leviticus/*Vayikra*
orange – Numbers/*Bamidbar*
red – Deuteronomy/*Devarim*
1 The Torah is the Heart of the Jewish People copied on pink card stock (see Directions and Patterns)
1 18" strand of yarn in each of the following colors: blue, green, yellow, orange, red, and pink per child
1 6" cardboard cake round (if desired, substitute 6" round cut out of poster board with six holes pre-punched)
scissors
single hole punches
1 copy Simchat Torah Mobile Directions sheet per family (see Directions and Patterns)

Advance Preparation by the Facilitator

- Make a sample mobile.

- On the supply table, place these items, each in a separate container: scissors and single hole punches.

- On the supply table, place these supplies: five colored set of the books of the Torah, six colors of yarn or string, 6" cardboard cake rounds, The Torah Is the Heart of the Jewish People sheets, and Simchat Torah Mobile Directions sheets.

Procedure

- Each Family makes a mobile. They fold each of the 5 sheets of the 5 different books of the Torah in half to look like a book.

- They punch holes in the upper right-hand corner of each of these five folded books of the Torah. (They should use the upper right-hand corner to emphasize the way a Hebrew book opens.)

- They cut out the heart shaped sign: The Torah is the Heart of the Jewish People.

- They punch a hole in the heart in the upper middle part.

- They punch holes in the 6" cardboard cake round at 2, 4, 6, 8, 10, and 12 o'clock.

- They knot together the 6 pieces of the 6 different colors of yarn.

- They thread one strand of yarn down, around, and down again into each hole of the 6" pie circles.

- They tie the remaining end of each strand of thread to the corresponding color of either a book of the Torah or the heart sign (i.e., blue thread to blue book).

01:10 – 01:30
Closure: Simchat Torah Music and Dance

End the program with singing, dancing, sharing, and holiday greetings.

- Use Simchat Torah music and movement related to: the Torah, the Five Books of the Torah, creation, Moses, beginnings, endings, the parts of the Torah, the joy of the Torah, Hebrew letters, honey, *Yisrael*.

Recommended Songs:

"Hands Hold the Torah" (*To See the World Through Jewish Eyes*, Volume I, Union of American Hebrew Congregations)

"Toralee," (*Especially Wonderful Days* by Steve Reuben, A.R.E. Publishing, Inc.)

"The Torah" (*Especially Jewish Symbols* by Jeff Klepper, A.R.E. Publishing, Inc.

- Be certain to do some *Hakafot* — marching the Torah around the room. Or, do some Israeli dancing.

- Have participants share their reactions to the program. Ask families to complete one of these phrases:

Simchat Torah is . . .

Our family enjoyed . . .

Our family learned . . .

For Simchat Torah, we . . .

- Send everyone off with a Simchat Torah greeting: "*Chag Sameach!*" (Happy Holiday!)

Simchat Torah Letter Flag Pattern I — Lamed

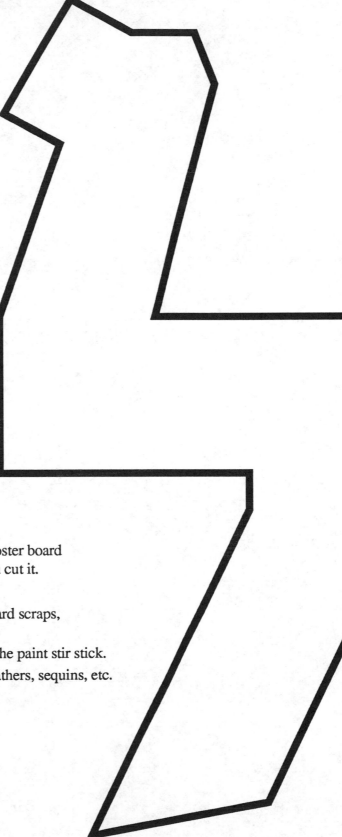

1. Staple this sheet onto a piece of poster board so the *Lamed* won't slip when you cut it.
2. Cut out the *Lamed*.
3. Discard this pattern, the poster board scraps, and any extra staples.
4. Staple the poster board *Lamed* to the paint stir stick.
5. Decorate the *Lamed* with eyes, feathers, sequins, etc.
6. Enjoy!

Simchat Torah Letter Flag Pattern II — Bet

1. Staple this sheet onto a piece of poster board so the *Bet* won't slip when you cut it.
2. Cut out the *Bet*.
3. Discard this pattern, the poster board scraps, and any extra staples.
4. Staple the poster board *Bet* to the paint stir stick.
5. Decorate the *Bet* with eyes, feathers, sequins, etc.
6. Enjoy!

1

בראשית

Genesis
I

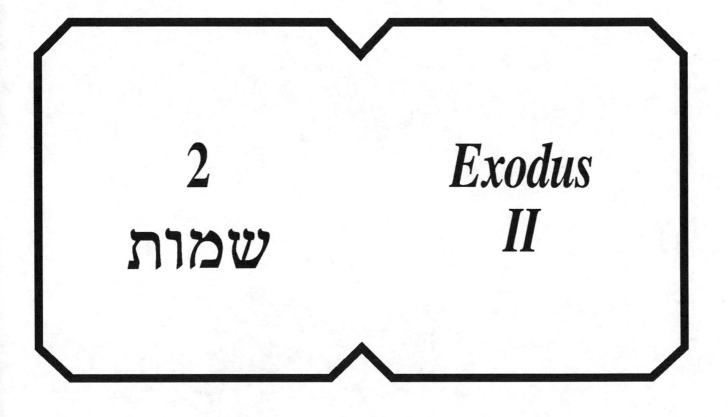

2

שמות

Exodus
II

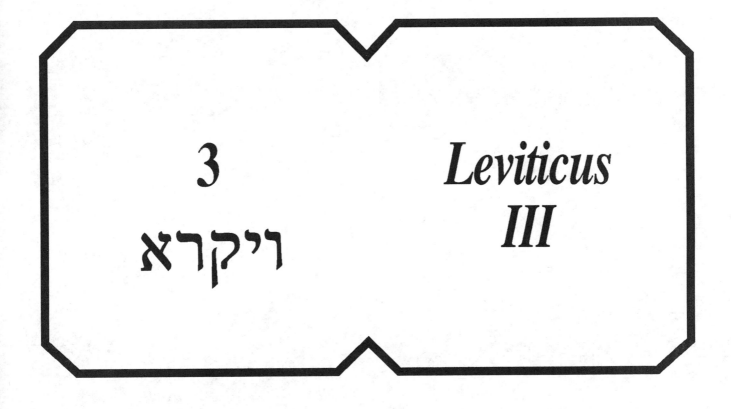

3

ויקרא

Leviticus
III

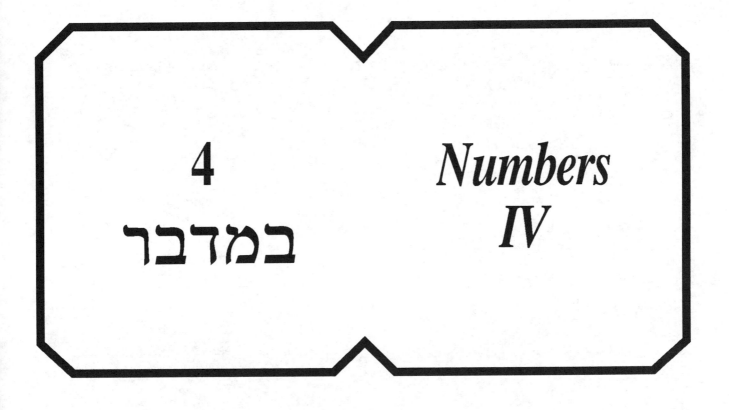

4

במדבר

Numbers
IV

5

דברים

Deuteronomy
V

The Torah is the ♥
of the Jewish people.

The Jewish people are
the ♥ of the Torah.

ישראלבראשית

Simchat Torah Mobile
(Directions)

Collect these materials:

    1 set of Simchat Torah Mobile Patterns (pages 1-6)

    1 6" cake circle

    6 18" lengths of rug yarn in 1 strand each of the following colors:
        blue, green, yellow, orange, red, and pink.

To assemble the mobile:

1. Cut out each book of the Torah (pages 1-5).
Fold each book in half and punch a hole near the fold.

2. Cut out the heart (page 6).
Punch a hole near the top.

3. Punch holes in the cake circle at 2, 4, 6, 8, 10, and 12 o'clock.

4. Knot the rug yarn about 2 inches from one end.

5. Thread the mobile. With the brown side of the cake circle facing up,
take the blue strand of yarn and thread it through the 12 o'clock hole.

Bring it around and down through the hole again.

Repeat this process with each strand
of yarn and each empty hole.

6. Tie the long free end of the yarn to the color of the
book of the Torah or heart it matches. For example,
tie the blue yarn to the blue book, Genesis.

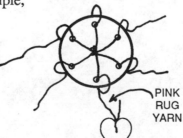

PINK
RUG
YARN

7. Take home and hang in a special place.

A Sensational Shabbat
Shabbat, Year 2

Postcard and/or Flier

To include:
Program Title
Sponsored by
Audience (age group, members only or general public, etc.)
Date
Time
Location
Cost (if applicable)
RSVP or For Further Information

Physical Set Up

work area: tables and chairs
tables for supplies
table for name tags and sign-in sheet
large trash cans
trash bags

Holiday Symbols, Customs, Terms, and Concepts

Shabbat as a five sense experience
foods of Shabbat
symbols of Shabbat
songs of Shabbat
warmth of Shabbat
light
the Shabbat table
Shabbat at home
Shabbat as sweet
Shabbat as family time
Shabbat as a taste of the world to come
Shabbat symbols in the synagogue
Shabbat blessings

00:00 – 00:15
Mind Warmer: A Sensational
Shabbat Sampler

Shabbat involves all five senses. There are Shabbat sights, sounds, smells, textures, and tastes. Families assemble a sampler — a page or montage of Shabbat sensations — that focuses on the senses of sight, touch, and smell.

Materials

name tags
markers
sign-in sheet
1 Sense-ational Shabbat Sampler per child enlarged and copied on white paper 11" x 17" (see Directions and Patterns)
Havdalah candles
matches
tissue paper or live flowers
aluminum foil
sesame or poppy seeds
scrap cloth preferably including velvet or upholstery cloth
paper napkins
cinnamon sticks
whole cloves
gluesticks
scissors
crayons

Advance Preparation by the Facilitator

- On the supply table, place these supplies: Sense-ational Shabbat Samplers (one per child), Havdalah candles, matches, tissue paper or live flowers, aluminum foil, sesame or poppy seeds, scrap cloth, paper napkins, cinnamon stick flakes, and whole cloves.

- On the supply table, place these items, each in a separate container: gluesticks, scissors, and crayons.

Procedure

- The Facilitator greets families as they arrive. Have them fill out a name tag for each family member and sign in.

- Direct families to the supply table to pick up the materials for the project.

- Families go to the work tables where they will be making a Sense-ational Shabbat Sampler. Some examples: cut and glue scrap cloth for the feel of a Shabbat *challah* cover, glue cinnamon stick pieces or whole cloves for the touch and fragrance of Havdalah (the service separating the end of Shabbat from the rest of the week), drip wax from Havdalah candles for the feel of Shabbat candles.

- The families will need to fill in the child's name on the top, indicating ownership: _____'s Sense-ational Shabbat Sampler.

- Ask families to bring their Sense-ational Shabbat Samplers to the Introductions and Announcements area.

- Families clean up, recycling scraps and returning supplies to their proper place.

00:15 – 00:25
Introductions and Announcements

Materials

1 copy of each of Shabbat Sense Pattern I to V on card stock of any color (see Directions and Patterns)

5 paint stir sticks or paper towel rolls
gluestick
scissors
stapler

Advance Preparation by the Facilitator

- Cut out each of the five sense patterns.

- Staple each five sense prop to a paint stir stick or paper towel roll.

Procedure

- The Facilitator welcomes everyone on behalf of the sponsoring agency/institution.

- The Facilitator introduces himself/herself and any other official representatives of the program or the agency/institution.

- Have a member of each family introduce himself/herself and other family members.

- Announce any upcoming events for the sponsoring agency/institution that are pertinent for this group.

- Instruct people as to how they can get on the mailing list if they are not already on it.

Setting the Stage

- Say: Shabbat is "sense-ational." Shabbat is a five sense experience. (Hold up each of the five sense props. Ask various children to hold each of the five sense props.) The five senses are (engage participants in pointing to eyes, ears, fingers, etc., for each of the senses): hearing, tasting, smelling, seeing, and touching.

  You just made a Sense-ational Shabbat Sampler of different tastes, smells, sights, and textures of Shabbat. Let's go through the five senses and figure out which Shabbat item goes with each of the five senses. Find something on your Sense-ational Shabbat Sampler that you see (get responses), taste (get responses), smell (get responses), hear (get responses), and touch (get responses). Encourage audience participation as you go through the five senses and connect them to Shabbat sensations. For example, touching — we touch the Shabbat candles which feel smooth and cool; seeing — we see the light of Shabbat candles. We can see ourselves in the nicely polished silver Shabbat candle-sticks.

We will spend the remainder of this Shabbat program focusing on the sensations of Shabbat.

00:25 – 00:45
A Sense-ational Shabbat Scavenger Hunt

Participants first make popsicle stick puppets of Shabbat objects. Then the preschoolers and parents together go on a scavenger hunt looking for these objects. If this program is in a synagogue, they search for the objects in their usual place. In other locations, or with limited space, you can "hide" the objects, and have the families look for them.

Materials

6 popsicle sticks per child
1 set per child of Shabbat Scavenger Hunt Symbols: candlesticks, *Kiddush* cup, prayerbook, Torah, *kipah*, and *challah* copied on card stock (see Directions and Patterns)
1 set of Shabbat candlesticks
1 *Kiddush* cup
1 Shabbat prayerbook
1 Torah or miniature Torah (the type given out at Consecration, available from KTAV Publishing House)

1 *kipah*
1 *challah*
staplers
staples
crayons
scissors
pencils

Advance Preparation by the Facilitator

- Make and staple on popsicle sticks a sample of Shabbat Scavenger Hunt Symbols

- Arrange for the following six objects to be found in the building or room you are using: prayerbook, Torah (use a miniature Consecration Torah or a book if absolutely necessary), *kipah*, *Kiddush* cup, *challah*, and candlesticks.

- On the supply table, place these materials: sets of the six Shabbat symbols photocopied on colored card stock.

- On the supply table, place the following items, each in a separate container: popsicle sticks, scissors, crayons, staplers, staples, and pencils.

Procedure

- The Facilitator explains that families will be going on a Sense-ational Shabbat Scavenger Hunt. They will look for six symbols associated with Shabbat celebration in the synagogue. Hold up the sample stick puppets. First, they will make popsicle stick puppets of these symbols.

- Ask one or two representatives from each table to get the materials for this project from the supply table.

- Instruct families to color, cut out, and staple onto a popsicle stick the six shapes of the Shabbat symbols: Prayerbook, Torah, *kipah*, cup, candlesticks, and *challah*.

- Families clean up, returning supplies to their proper place.

- All begin the Sense-ational Shabbat Scavenger Hunt, looking for the six symbols. The families can each do this on their own. An adult from each family will need a pencil.

- Families will need to bring along their six puppets. As this is a Sense-ational hunt, allow time for everyone to touch, see, and observe each object. Have families comment on texture, sounds, colors, etc., of each object.

- Emphasize that these six symbols are part of Shabbat celebration in synagogues in your community and throughout the world.

- Whenever an object is found, a parent writes on the popsicle stick symbol where it was found.

00:45 – 01:10
Snack and Activity:
A Sense-ational Shabbat Snack

This combined extended snack and activity simulates a home Shabbat celebration. The first part of the activity involves the families setting a Shabbat table.

Materials

1 paper white tablecloth per table
1 cup per person
1 plate per person
1 fork per person
1 knife per person
1 napkin per person
1 *challah* per table
grape juice
2 or 3 frozen Empire kosher chicken nuggets per person

trays for cooking or plates for microwaving the chicken nuggets
serving forks
1 frozen or canned or fresh mini-carrot per person
pot for cooking the mini-carrots
bowls for serving the mini-carrots
serving spoons
1 *challah* cover per table
1 set of candlesticks per table
1 set of Shabbat candles per table
1 book of matches per table
1 *Kiddush* cup per table
1 vase and flower(s) per table (use fresh, dried, or paper flowers)
access to a stove (a microwave can substitute)
access to an oven (a microwave can substitute)
1 copy of the Shabbat blessings per family (see Blessings #1, 2, 3, and 4, page 487).

Advance Preparation by the Facilitator

- Prepare copies of the four Shabbat blessings for distribution to the families.

- In advance, cook the chicken nuggets. If possible, serve them warm.

- If using fresh carrots, wash and peel them. Serve them raw or cooked. If using frozen mini-carrots, either cook them in advance and warm them up or arrange for a volunteer to prepare them.

- On the supply table, place all the items needed for setting each table and the Shabbat meal: paper tablecloths, cups, napkins, forks, knives, plates, *challah*, grape juice, chicken nuggets, carrots, *Kiddush* cup, candlesticks, candles, matches, *challah* cover, flower(s), vase, and copies of the blessings.

Procedure

- The Facilitator explains that participants will now simulate a sense-ational home Shabbat celebration. Encourage comments at each point on what they see, hear, smell, taste, and touch throughout the celebration.

- Much of Shabbat celebration involves preparation. On Thursday night or Friday, participants make and bake *challah* for Shabbat. The group will pretend to "make *challah*," with parents using the children's bodies to simulate the *challah* making.

- Orally, the Facilitator goes through the steps of making *challah*, guiding the parents and children. Say: Mix together all the ingredients. Stir the yeast in the water. Add honey. Watch it bubble. Stir in eggs, raisins, and melted butter. Add lots of flour until the dough is no longer sticky. Knead the bread with the heel of your hands. Get out all those air bubbles. Form the dough into a ball. Let it rise and expand. Now punch it down with your knuckles getting out all the air. Knead it again with the heel of your hands.

  Now divide it into three balls. Roll each ball into a long strand. Braid the *challah*. Brush egg on the top. Add poppy or sesame seeds. Bake. Watch it rise. Smell the *challah* as it bakes. Tap the *challah* with your fingers to make certain the crust is hard and the *challah* is done. Take it out of the oven. Enjoy the smell! Bring your *challah* to the sense-ational Shabbat dinner table.

- Ask families to take a seat. Since each table will become a family, make certain everyone knows one another.

- Instruct each family table to set the table for Shabbat (including the food).

- Give families time to experience all the sensations of the objects, symbols, and foods. Touch! See! Taste! Smell! Hear! (Ask that they leave some food for the blessings.)

- Recite the blessings over the candles, *Kiddush*, children, and *HaMotzi*.

- For this program, you may elect to have music and movement around the Shabbat table. This models another option for a family home Shabbat celebration.

01:10 – 01:30
Closure: Sense-ational Shabbat Music and Movement

End the program with singing, sharing, and Shabbat greetings.

- Sing and move to music related to: the five senses, Shabbat symbols, the Shabbat blessings, Shabbat at home, Shabbat in the synagogue, Shabbat foods, candles, wine, family, celebration.

  Recommended Songs:

  "*L'Cha Dodi*" (*Especially Wonderful Days* by Steve Reuben, Denver: A.R.E. Publishing, Inc.),

  "*Shabbat Shalom*" (*To See the World Through Jewish Eyes,* Volume I, Union of American Hebrew Congregations)

- Have participants share their reactions to the program. Ask families to complete one of these phrases:

  Shabbat is . . .

  We want Shabbat to be . . .

  Next Shabbat . . .

  Our family enjoyed . . .

  Our family learned . . .

- Send everyone off with a Shabbat greeting: "*Shabbat Shalom!*" (literally, a Shabbat of peace and wholeness).

Sense-ational Shabbat Sampler

Use the materials on the table to fill in the spaces on your sampler.
There are two blanks for you to add your own ideas.

_____'s SENSE-ational Shabbat Sampler

On Shabbat I can feel:

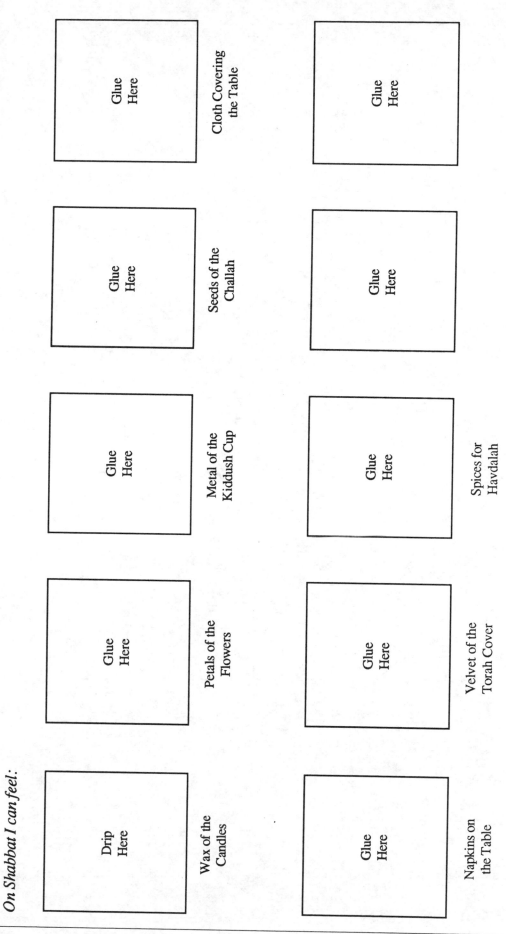

Drip Here	Glue Here	Glue Here	Glue Here	Glue Here
Wax of the Candles	Petals of the Flowers	Metal of the Kiddush Cup	Seeds of the Challah	Cloth Covering the Table
Glue Here	Glue Here	Glue Here	Glue Here	
Napkins on the Table	Velvet of the Torah Cover	Spices for Havdalah		

Shabbat Sense Pattern I — See

Cut out and mount on a paint stir stick or paper towel roll.

Shabbat Sense Pattern II — Hear
Cut out and mount on a paint stir stick or paper towel roll.

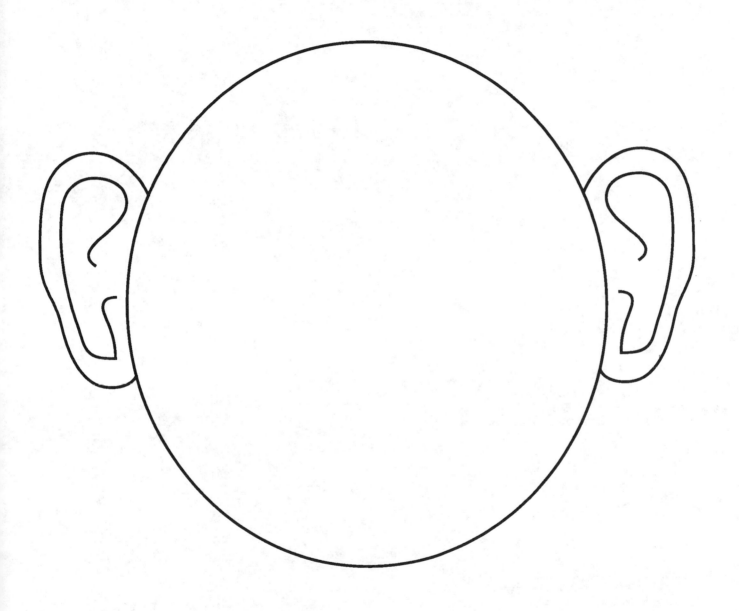

Shabbat Sense Pattern III — Taste

Cut out and mount on a paint stir stick or paper towel roll.

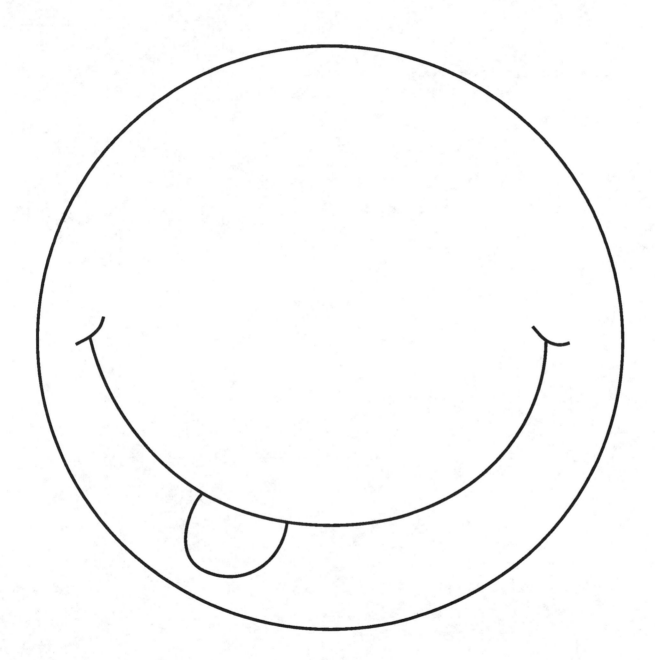

Shabbat Sense Pattern IV — Touch

Cut out and mount on a paint stir stick or paper towel roll.

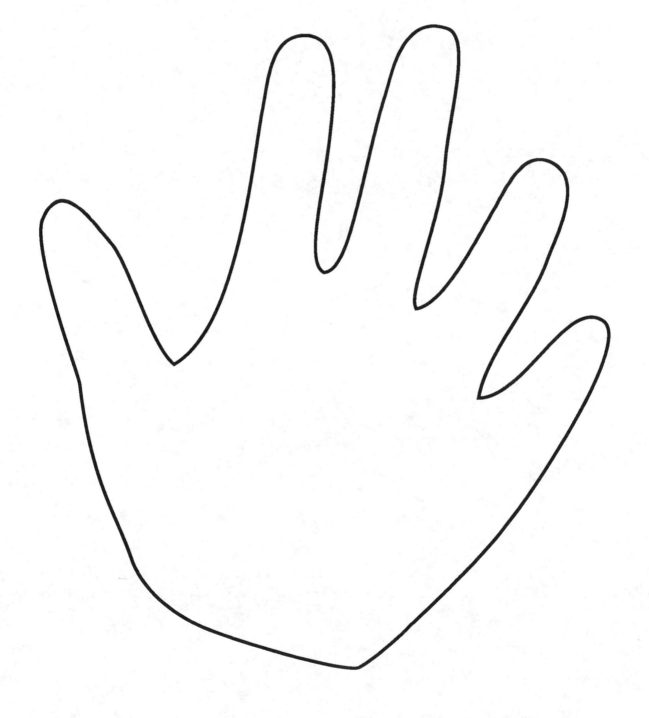

Shabbat Sense Pattern V — Smell
Cut out and mount on a paint stir stick or paper towel roll..

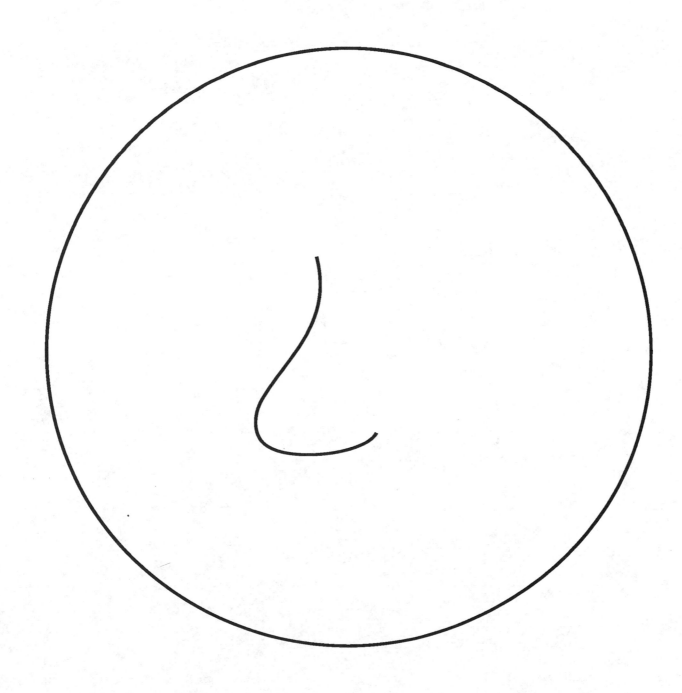

Scavenger Hunt Symbols

1. Color these symbols and then cut them out.
2. Mount on popsicle sticks to make puppets.
3. "Tour" the synagogue and see if you can find the actual objects (You could also try this at home).
4. Write where you found your object on the line on your clue shape.

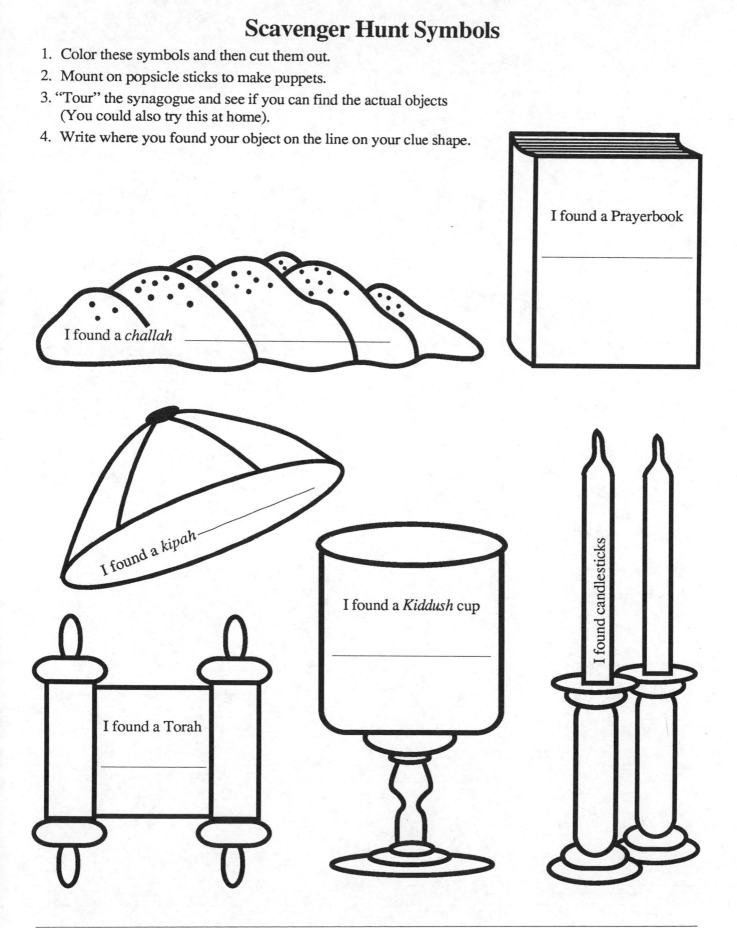

I found a Prayerbook

I found a *challah*

I found a *kipah*

I found a Torah

I found a *Kiddush* cup

I found candlesticks

Nes Gadol Hayah Sham
Chanukah, Year 2

Postcard and/or Flier

To include:
Program Title
Sponsored by
Audience (age group, members only
    or general public, etc.)
Date
Time
Location
Cost (if applicable)
RSVP or For Further Information
Bring a 3" x 5" or 4" x 6" family picture for
    a Chanukah project.

Physical Set Up

work area: tables and chairs
tables for supplies
table for name tags and sign-in sheet
large trash cans
trash bags
place for baking the frozen *latkes* or a place
    to reheat them

Holiday Symbols, Customs, Terms,
and Concepts

chanukiah
Nes Gadol Hayah Sham — a great miracle
    happened there
dreidel
miracles
overcoming obstacles and hardships
standing up for being a Jew
the Maccabees
Mattathias
Judah Maccabee
the story of Chanukah from the Book of
    Maccabees and the Talmud

cruse of oil
the Temple in Jerusalem
worshiping one God, not idols
latkes made in oil
Chanukah as the festival of light

00:00 – 00:15
Mind Warmer: Nes Gadol Hayah Sham —
The Dreidel Centerpiece

The letters on a *dreidel* — *Nun, Gimel, Hay,*
and *Shin* — stand for the Hebrew words *Nes
Gadol Hayah Sham* (a great miracle happened
there). The *dreidel* celebrates the miracles of
Chanukah: the small band of Maccabees and
friends defeating the Syrians; the oil needed
for rededicating the Temple, lasting not one,
but eight days; and the enthusiasm with which
Jews celebrate Chanukah today. This activity
involves making *dreidel* centerpieces to
decorate the home.

Materials

name tags
markers
sign-in sheet
1 Chanukah Dreidel Centerpiece Pattern
    per 3-4 families copied onto white paper
    (see Directions and Patterns)
colored poster board, one 12" x 9" piece
    per child
colorful stickers of dots, squares, and/or
    other shapes
wiggly eyes
sequins
glitter (optional)
gluesticks

scissors
crayons
pencils

Advance Preparation by the Facilitator

- On the supply table, place these supplies: poster board, wiggly eyes, sequins, stickers in shapes or designs, Chanukah Dreidel Centerpiece Pattern sheets, and glitter in cups (optional).

- On the supply table, place these items, each in a separate container: gluesticks, scissors, crayons, pencils.

- Prepare a sample of how the two *dreidel* pieces fit together and stand up freely. This will cut down on the verbal directions you will need to give.

Procedure

- The Facilitator greets families as they arrive. Have them fill out a name tag for each family member and sign in.

- Tell the families to go to the supply tables where they will find all the materials for making a *dreidel* centerpiece.

- Instruct the families to trace two *dreidel* shapes onto poster board using the paper *dreidel* shapes.

- Families cut out the two *dreidel* shapes from the poster board.

- They decorate the *dreidel* shapes on both sides using stickers, sequins, wiggly eyes, crayons, etc.

- With five minutes to go, the Facilitator explains how to assemble the *dreidel* centerpiece.

- Parents make two slits, one per *dreidel* piece. On one piece, they cut down a few

inches from the top. On the other piece, they cut up a few inches from the bottom. The two *dreidels* will fit perpendicular to one another, allowing the *dreidel* centerpiece to stand up on its own. They slide the piece with the slit on the bottom over the piece with the slit on the top.

- Have the families write their family name in pencil in a corner of their *dreidel* so that each family can take their own *dreidel* home.

- Families clean up, returning materials to the supply table.

00:15 – 00:25
Introductions and Announcements

Materials

1 *dreidel*

Procedure

- The Facilitator welcomes everyone on behalf of the sponsoring agency/institution.

- The Facilitator introduces himself/herself and any other official representatives of the program or the agency/institution.

- Have a member of each family introduce himself/herself and other family members.

- Announce any upcoming events for the sponsoring agency/institution that are pertinent for this group.

- Instruct people as to how they can get on the mailing list if they are not already on it.

Setting the Stage

- The Facilitator holds up a *dreidel*.

- The Facilitator says: On the *dreidel* are the four letters — *Nun, Gimel, Hey,* and *Shin.*

These Hebrew letters stand for the phrase *"Nes Gadol Hayah Sham"* (a great miracle happened there). Where is there? In Israel.

The *dreidel* reminds us of a great miracle associated with Chanukah. What is that miracle? (Have the families answer. Hopefully, they will volunteer the miracle of the oil lasting for eight days.) There are other great miracles of Chanukah: a small band of Jews, the Maccabees, stood up for religious freedom and won. Even our celebration of Chanukah so many years after the Maccabees is a miracle.

Now we will hear the Chanukah story, "A Great Miracle Happened There."

00:25 – 00:45
The Chanukah Story: A Great Miracle Happened There

Relate the Chanukah story. It begins with the Maccabees' determination to practice their Judaism through the rededication of the Temple in Jerusalem. The families will hold up pre-made stick puppets and props of the key symbols (see immediately below for instructions).

Materials

1 copy of the Chanukah Story Props I-V on white card stock (see Directions and Patterns)

8 copies of the Chanukah Story Props VI on white card stock (see Directions and Patterns)

5 copies of the Chanukah Story Props VII on white card stock (see Directions and Patterns)

scissors

markers

stapler and staples

gluestick

paint stir sticks or paper towel rolls

Advance Preparation by the Facilitator

- Photocopy the Chanukah Story Props I-VII on white card stock.

- Color and cut out the story props.

- Glue and then staple these story props to a paint stir stick or paper towel roll.

Procedure

- The Facilitator passes out the story props to volunteers. Ask them to hold up the symbols, characters, etc., whenever these are mentioned in the story.

- The Facilitator tells the story:

A Great Miracle Happened There

A long time ago, the Syrians, who adopted Greek ways and Greek gods, ruled Israel. The Syrians, under the mean rule of Antiochus, made many mean rules against the Jews. The Syrians ordered the Jews to bow down to idols instead of to God. The Syrians took control of the Temple in Jerusalem. In the Temple, they placed idols. They made a mess of God's house, the place where the Jews came to worship God.

In a little town in Israel called Modi'in, Mattathias Maccabee hid his family from the mean Syrians. Mattathias and his sons went to fight the Syrians. Judah Maccabee, called "The Hammer," and his brothers were strong and brave. The Maccabees wanted to worship only the one God, *Adonai*. The Maccabees did not want to bow to the false gods, the idols of the Syrians. The Maccabees did not like the Syrians.

The Maccabees led the Jewish people in battle against the big Syrian army. The Maccabees fought until the Syrians lost and gave up.

After their victory over the Syrians, the Maccabees went to Jerusalem. In Jerusalem, they cleaned up the Temple. They threw out all the Greek idols, all the statues of false gods. They put everything back in its place.

The Rabbis of the Talmud tell us that when the Temple was all clean, it was time to light the Eternal Light that burned there. A cruse of oil was needed — pure olive oil that was made especially for use in the Temple. The Jews looked and looked and looked, until finally, one cruse, one small container of oil was found. They lit the cruse of oil which was enough for a day. But the oil burned, one, two, three, four, five, six, seven, and eight days. It is said that a great miracle happened there — *Nes Gadol Hayah Sham* — a one day supply of oil lasted eight days.

Today, we remember all the miracles of Chanukah when we light our own *chanukiah*. We remember the miracle of the Maccabee's victory and the miracle of the oil lasting eight days. It is a miracle that the Jews have continued to light Chanukah candles for hundreds of years!

00:45 – 00:55
The Miracle Oil Snack: Latkes

Latkes are a Chanukah favorite. Generally they are sizzled in that Chanukah miracle substance, oil. Homemade *latkes* are always a treat. For your convenience, frozen mini-*latkes* (or regular size *latkes*) are now available. These can be baked rather than fried, which takes less time.

Materials

latkes
baking sheets
spatula
juice
apple sauce
sour cream (optional)
plates
forks
cups
napkins
serving spoons
bowls for apple sauce and sour cream

Advance Preparation by the Facilitator

- Make arrangements in advance of the program to have the *latkes* baked or zapped in a microwave. (A volunteer can do this.)

- Dish out the apple sauce and sour cream into bowls.

Procedure

- Serve the *latkes* with apple sauce, sour cream, and juice. Be certain to point out the connection of *latkes* to the Chanukah story.

- Remember to recite a blessing (see Blessing #9, page 488). It will be a miracle if no one gets a stomach ache!

00:55 – 01:10
Activity: Our Family Coat of Arms

The Maccabees were proud to be Jews. Their shields identified them as Jews. Each family now makes its own coat of arms, displaying their Jewish pride.

Materials

1 Our Family Coat of Arms sheet per child enlarged and photocopied on 11" x 17" paper (see Directions and Patterns)
pencils
crayons
gluesticks

Advance Preparation by Facilitator

- Photocopy Our Family Coat of Arms onto 11" x 17" white paper.

- On the supply table, place Our Family Coat of Arms sheets.

- On the supply table, place these items, each in a separate container: pencils, gluesticks, and crayons.

Procedure

- The Facilitator describes the making of family coats of arms.

- Have a representative or two pick up the materials from the supply table.

- Each family decorates an Our Family Coat of Arms sheet as follows:

  - They glue on the family photograph.

  - They draw in a picture of their favorite Jewish light.

  - They draw a picture of a Jewish object in their home.

  - They make up a rebus (picture symbols) of their last name.

  - Families clean up, returning the materials to the supply table.

01:10 – 01:30
Closure: Miraculously Performed Chanukah Songs and Movement

End the program with singing, blessings, sharing, and holiday greetings.

Materials

1 copy per family of the Chanukah story,

"A Great Miracle Happened There" (see Directions and Patterns)

Advance Preparation by Facilitator

- Prepare and make copies of the Chanukah story.

Procedure

- Sing and move to Chanukah music related to: miracles, the miracle of the oil, the Maccabees, Maccabees standing up for what they believed, Jewish pride, *dreidel, Nes Gadol Hayah Sham*, worshiping one God, and *latkes* made in oil.

Recommended Songs:

"Where's the Dreidle?"(*Apples on Holidays and Other Days* by Leah Abrams, Tara Publications)

"A Latke Recipe," (*Apples on Holidays and Other Days* by Leah Abrams, Tara Publications)

"Chanukah" (*Seasoned With Song* by Julie Auerbach, Tara Publications)

- Review and recite the Chanukah blessings.

- Have participants share their reactions to the program. Ask families to complete one of these phrases:

  It is a miracle . . .

  Chanukah is about . . .

  Our family enjoyed . . .

  Our family learned . . .

- Send everyone off with copies of the Chanukah story and practicing *Nes Gadol Hayah Sham* and *"Chag Sameach"* (Happy Chanukah).

Chanukah Dreidel Centerpiece Pattern

Cut two of these *dreidel* patterns out of poster board.

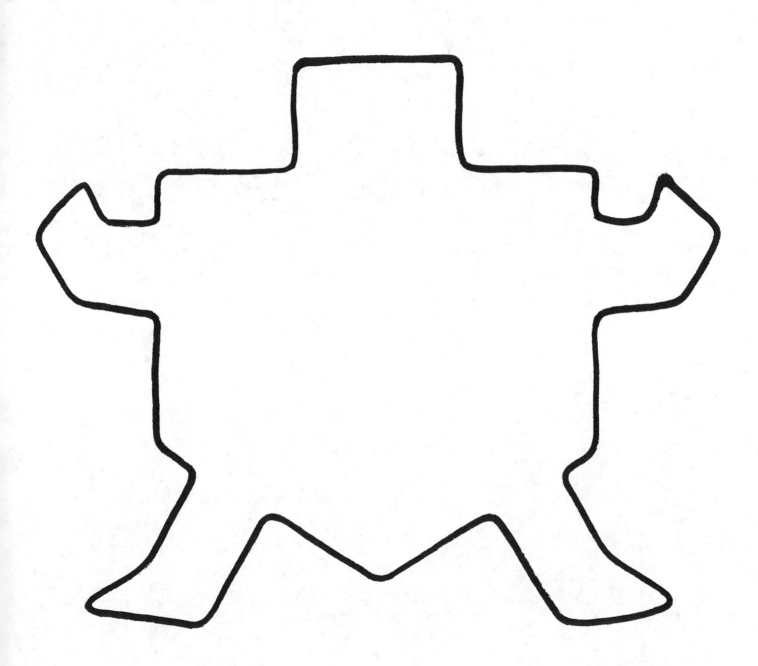

Chanukah Story Props I — Chanukiah

Cut out and mount on a paint stir stick or paper towel roll.

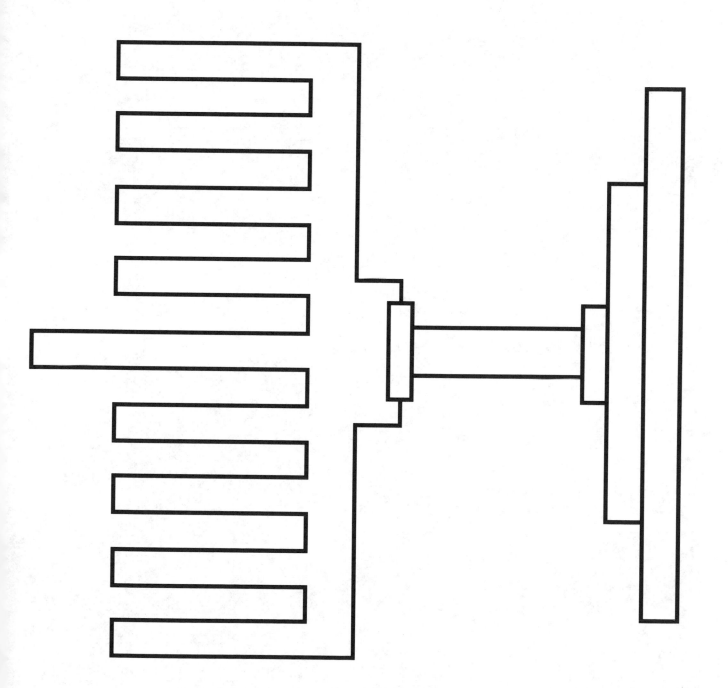

Chanukah Story Props II — Jerusalem

Cut out and mount on a paint stir stick or paper towel roll.

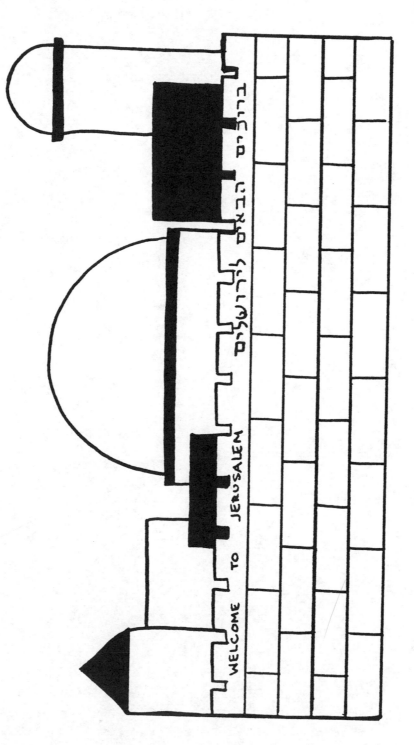

Chanukah Story Props III — The Temple

Cut out and mount on a paint stir stick or paper towel roll.

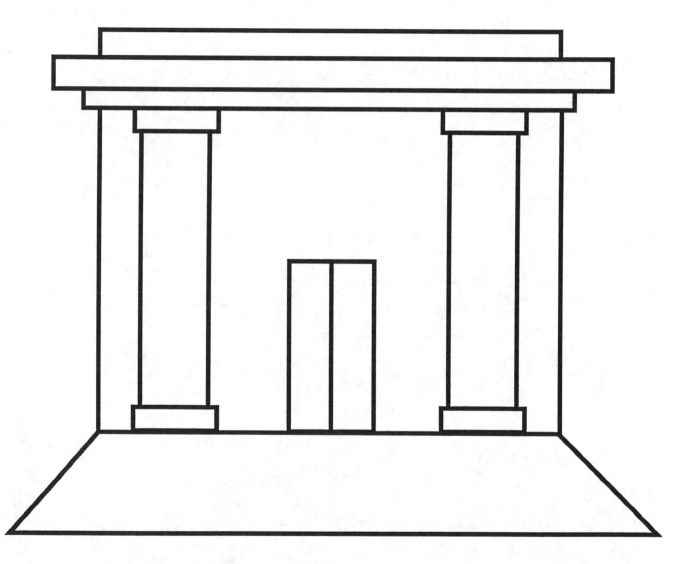

Chanukah Story Props IV — Antiochus

Cut out and mount on a paint stir stick or paper towel roll.

Chanukah Story Props V — Cruse of Oil
Cut out and mount on a paint stir stick or paper towel roll.

Chanukah Story Props VI — Syrian Soldier

Make 8 copies of this page. Cut out and mount each on a paint stir stick or paper towel roll.

Chanukah Story Props VII — Maccabee

Make 5 copies of this page. Cut out and mount each on a paint stir stick or paper towel roll.

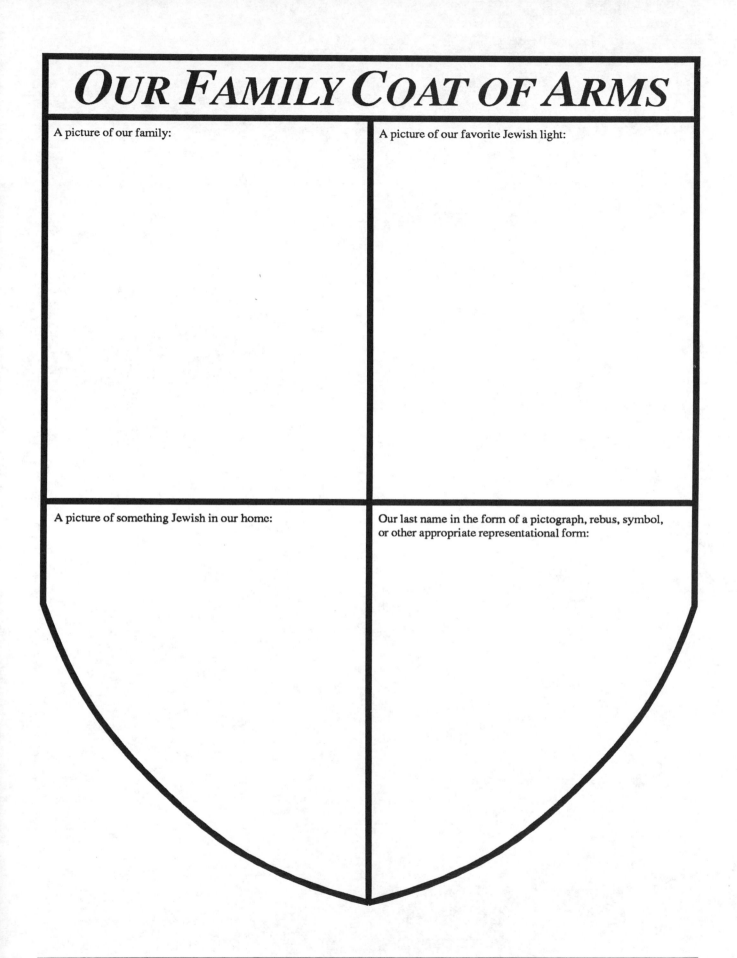

OUR FAMILY COAT OF ARMS

A picture of our family:

A picture of our favorite Jewish light:

A picture of something Jewish in our home:

Our last name in the form of a pictograph, rebus, symbol, or other appropriate representational form:

Mark Your Calendar, It's the New Year of the Trees
Tu B'Shevat, Year 2

Postcard and/or Flier
- Program Title
- Sponsored by
- Audience (age group, members only or general public, etc.)
- Date
- Time
- Location
- Cost (if applicable)
- RSVP or For Further Information
- Bring hand shovels for planting.
- Wear jeans and clothes appropriate for planting.

Physical Set Up
- work area: tables and chairs
- tables for supplies
- table for name tags and sign-in sheet
- trash cans
- trash bags
- table for the Fruit Salad Bar

Holiday Symbols, Customs, Terms, and Concepts
- Tu B'Shevat, the 15th of the month of Shevat
- the New Year of the Trees
- the Jewish calendar
- lunar calendar versus solar calendar cycles
- the life cycle of a plant
- the value of trees to nature, humans
- products of trees
- planting for the future
- taking care of the earth

00:00 – 00:15
Mind Warmer: Mark Your Calendar, It's the New Year of the Trees

The families will assemble a Jewish calendar. As Tu B'Shevat is the New Year of the Trees, they will decorate trees representing the four seasons of the calendar year.

Materials
- name tags
- markers
- sign-in sheet
- 1 sheet per child of construction paper 12" x 18"
- 6 sheets of the Blank Calendar Page copied on white paper (see Directions and Patterns)
- 1 calendar January through June (Shevat through Sivan) per child (see Preparation below)
- 1 copy of Trees Have New Years, Too per child copied on letter size white paper (see Directions and Patterns)
- cotton balls
- tissue paper in yellow, orange, red, pink, and white
- green crayons
- punched hole reinforcers
- ribbon or thick yarn
- pencils
- gluesticks
- staplers
- staples
- single hole punches
- scissors

1 copy per family A New Year Calendar for Tu B'Shevat Directions on white paper (see Directions and Patterns)

Advance Preparation by the Facilitator

* Make 6 copies of the blank calendar page.

* Fill in the January through June or Shevat through Sivan calendar, the days of the week and dates. (If Tu B'Shevat falls in February, you may elect to skip January.) Allow one page per month. Fill in the Hebrew and English dates. Also fill in the dates of the Jewish holidays, any institutional events pertinent for this group, and the dates of the upcoming preschool holiday programs (see sample calendar page filled out with dates in Directions and Patterns).

* Once the calendar is filled in, photocopy each of the month pages to make a complete set for each child.

* Prepare a sample to show how the major pieces of the calendar fit together. Staple together the pages of the calendar. Then staple these pages to the bottom half of the construction paper. Glue on the top half a copy of Trees Have New Years, Too, which outlines four seasons in the life of trees.

* On the supply table, place these supplies: 12" x 18" construction paper; sheets of the calendar of dates; copies of the directions and diagram sheets; copies of Trees Have New Years, Too; cotton balls; tissue paper in red, yellow, orange, pink, and white; green crayons; hole reinforcers; and ribbon or thick yarn.

* On the supply table, place these items, each in a separate container: pencils, gluesticks, staplers, staples, single hole punches, and scissors.

Procedure

* The Facilitator greets families as they arrive. Have them fill out a name tag for each family member and sign in.

* The Facilitator tells families that in honor of Tu B'Shevat, the New Year of the Trees, they will assemble and decorate a Jewish calendar.

* Send the families to the supply table to gather the needed materials. (They should also get a copy of the sheet that lists the materials needed and a copy of the step-by-step directions.)

* Families staple the calendar sheets in order.

* They staple the calendar of dates to the bottom half of the 12" x 18" construction paper.

* Using scissors, they trim the edges of the Trees Have New Years, Too sheet.

* They glue the Trees Have New Years, Too to the top half of the 12" x 18" construction paper.

* They decorate the four seasonal trees of the Trees Have New Years, Too sheet. Use red, yellow, and orange tissue paper for fall leaves, white cotton balls for snow, pink and white for spring blossoms, and green crayons for summer leaves. (Adapt these to your climate and surroundings.)

* They punch two holes in the top of the calendar about 5" apart, putting hole reinforcers on both sides (front and back of the paper). Cut a piece of ribbon or thick yarn. Thread the ribbon or thick yarn through the holes. Tie and knot the ends of the ribbon or thick yarn. Now the calendar is ready for hanging on a hook or nail.

* They circle Tu B'Shevat on their calendar.

- The Facilitator encourages families to add birthdays and any other important dates to the calendar as time permits or at home.

- Families clean up, returning materials to the supply table.

00:15 – 00:25
Introductions and Announcements

- The Facilitator welcomes everyone on behalf of the sponsoring agency/institution.

- The Facilitator introduces himself/herself and any other official representatives of the program or the agency/institution.

- Have a member of each family introduce himself/herself and other family members.

- Announce any upcoming events for the sponsoring agency/institution that are pertinent for this group.

- Instruct people as to how they can get on the mailing list if they are not already on it.

Setting the Stage

- Say: You just made a Hebrew calendar in honor of the New Year of the Trees, Tu B'Shevat. The "Tu" in Tu B'Shevat stands for the number fifteen. The new year of the trees falls on the 15th day of the month of Shevat.

  Trees go through a cycle. Most trees look different at diffent times of the year. Sometimes their leaves are green, sometimes they have no leaves at all. Sometimes they have beautiful pink, yellow, or white blossoms. Some trees even have fruit that we eat.

  Let's play a game — *Trees Grow*. It is about the foods from trees. Trees are important to us because they give us food.

I will say the name of a food. If the food comes from a tree, stand up. If the food is not from a tree, sit down. (The families may suggest some foods, too. Play for one or two minutes.)

Later, we will eat a variety of foods from trees as part of celebration of the New Year of the Trees, Tu B'Shevat. Now we will hear a story about trees.

00:25 – 00:45
A Tree-mendous Story:
Honi and the Carob Tree

"Honi and the Carob Tree" is a story from the Talmud. It is a Jewish Rip Van Winkle story. Have fun telling the story. Use props, costumes, puppets, tree branches, carob chips, and other enrichments as you tell it.

Procedure

- Tell the following story.

Honi and the Carob Tree

Once upon a time, there was a young man named Honi. Honi was about the age of most high school students. That is the age when you are sure that you know everything. Honi lived in Israel. Honi loved to walk. Honi walked to school, to the store, to his friends, to the edge of town, and to the center of town.

One day, when Honi was on one of his walks to the edge of town, Honi saw an old man with a long, long, long white beard. Honi was used to seeing old men. His father was old; his grandfather even older. So what made Honi stop and stare? Honi could not believe that this old man was planting a little seedling of a tree.

Honi began to laugh. First he laughed quietly. Then Honi laughed loudly. The old man heard Honi. "Young man, why are you laughing?" Honi was laughing so hard he could hardly talk.

"Old man," Honi said, "I do not mean to hurt your feelings. But why are you planting that tree? You will never see that little seedling of a tree grow into a tall tree with many branches. In your lifetime, that little tree will never be big enough to give you shade, or fruit, or even wood."

Now it was the old man's turn to laugh. "Ah, foolish young man. I am planting this little seedling for the future. You will see." With that, the man went into his house.

Honi continued on his way to the edge of the town. When he reached the edge of town, he stretched his legs and arms. He yawned. He sat down under a tree with lots of shade, and closed his eyes for a short nap.

Honi slept and slept and snored and snored and slept and snored and slept a very long time. When he awoke, he had a long, long, white beard. When he got up, he almost tripped over the long, long white beard.

"Where did this beard come from?" he wondered. "I only slept an hour or two longer than I usually do for my afternoon nap. I'm hungry. I should be going home. I sure hope my Mom has a meal ready."

Honi started walking back to his home. He was a little stiff. His legs didn't go as fast as he remembered. When he came across a big branch, he was happy to use it as a walking stick, a cane.

On his way back, Honi passed by the old man's house. From afar, he saw an old woman in the yard. She was picking fruit from a tree. Honi stared and stared and stared at the old woman picking the carob

fruit, but this time he did not laugh.

"Old man," said the old woman to Honi, "why are you staring at me?" Honi knew he had been a little rude to the old man, so he did not want to tell this woman that he was a young man, not an old man.

"I am staring at the tree with its fruit. Why, just earlier today, I saw the old man planting a little seedling of a tree."

The old woman laughed and laughed. "Silly old man, this tree was not planted today. My grandfather planted this tree many, many, years ago when I was born. In our family, there is a story my grandfather told about this tree. On the day he planted it, a young man passed by. This young man laughed and laughed at my grandfather. This young man could not understand why an old man would plant a tree. My grandfather then laughed at the young man, saying, 'Ah, foolish young man, I am planting this seedling for the future. You will see.' I, too, have planted a little seedling for my grandchild. Look, it's over there."

Honi walked home — a little slower, a little older, and much, much wiser.

00:45 – 00:55
Snack: A Fruit Tree Salad Bar

The snack is a fruit salad bar. Use the available seasonal and/or regional fruits for your salad bar. Choose toppings that come from trees, too! Try to use some carob as a follow up to the story of "Honi and the Carob Tree."

Materials

a selection of seasonal or regional fruits from trees: apples, oranges, grapefruit, peaches, pears (use canned or fresh fruits) a selection of toppings that come from trees: almonds, coconut flakes, raisins, carob chips, maraschino cherries

knife to cut fresh fruit or can opener for canned fruit

bowls

serving spoons

spoons for eating

apple juice

napkins

cups

refrigerator for cool storage of fruits and toppings

Advance Preparation by the Facilitator

- Cut up the fruits (or open the cans of fruit) and cut the toppings into small pieces. Place each fruit or topping in a bowl with a spoon for easy service. Refrigerate as necessary.

- Place the bowls with fruit and topping on the table reserved for the Fruit Salad bar.

Procedure

- Point out that all the fruits and toppings are from trees .

- Teach and recite the blessing for products from trees (see Blessing #7, page 488).

- Have families make and eat their own Tu B'Shevat fruit salad.

- Enjoy your delicious and thematic snack!

00:55 – 01:10
Activity: Planting for Our Future

This activity involves planting plants. Depending on your geographical location, there is an outdoor planting option or an indoor planting option. The idea here is to plant something that many people, not just the families, will have the opportunity to enjoy and appreciate. With either activity,

you need to make arrangements with the building manager to plant or place the plants in a public place.

Materials

flats or plants for planting outdoors

extra hand shovels

watering can

   or

several large planters

variety of indoor plants

bag of dirt

watering can

markers

Advance Preparation by the Facilitator

- With the administrator of the building, arrange for a place for planting outdoors or a place for putting indoor plants.

Procedure

For Outdoor Planting:

Because planting seeds is too risky in terms of a success rate, plant flowers or bulbs instead.

- The Facilitator brings the flats of flowers or bulbs and extra hand shovels to the place where you will be planting.

- Instruct the families how deep to dig. Plant the flowers or bulbs. Fill in the dirt. Water the flowers.

- When finished planting, have everyone take the time to look at all the flowers or at the place where the bulbs were placed.

For Indoor Planting:

- Have available one large planter per 3-4 families and small household indoor plants. Also have markers and other appropriate supplies so that families can decorate the planters.

- The Facilitator places a planter, dirt, and a variety of plants on each work table.

- Explain that families will need to work as a group to put together this planter.

- Families decorate the planter as they see fit. Have markers available so that families can sign their names to the planter or in some way decorate it.

- Place dirt in the base of the planter. Add the household plants, using more dirt as necessary. Pat down the dirt. Water.

- Take the planters to the agreed upon site.

- Spend time admiring the new plants.

01:10 – 01:30
Closure: Tree Tops Whispering and People Singing

End the program with singing, moving, sharing, and holiday greetings.

Materials

1 copy per family of the story "Honi and the Carob Tree"

Procedure

- Sing and move to Tu B'Shevat music related to: trees, new year, products from

trees, uses of trees, planting, gardening, taking care of the earth, the calendar, the Jewish calendar, cycles, growing, planning and planting for the future.

Recommended Songs:

"Tu B'Shevat" (*Especially Wonderful Days* by Steve Reuben, A.R.E. Publishing, Inc.)

"*Ma Mezeg Ha'avir*" (*Seasoned With Song* by Julie Auerbach, Tara Publications)

"The Jewish Calendar Song" (*Seasoned With Song* by Julie Auerbach, Tara Publications)

- Have participants share their reactions to the program. Ask families to complete one of these phrases:

Tu B'Shevat is . . .

Trees are . . .

Our family enjoyed . . .

Our family learned . . .

We wish . . .

- Send everyone off with a "Happy Tu B'Shevat," "*Chag Ha'ilanot Sameach*," or "*Yom Huledet Sameach L'ilonot*" (Happy Holiday of the Trees).

- Pass out copies of the story "Honi and the Carob Tree" for families to take home.

Sample Calendar Page for Facilitators

(Use this calendar page as a basis for the calendar pages you provide the families.)

Month, Year
Hebrew Months/Hebrew Year

Hebrew Date

Portion of the Week

Torah & Haftorah Readings

Sunday	Monday	Tuesday	Wednesday	Thursday	Friday	Saturday
			1 25 Tevet	**2** 26 Tevet	**3** 27 Tevet	**4** 28 Tevet Va-Era Ex. 6:2-9:35 Ezek. 28: 25-29:21
5 29 Tevet Family Holiday Program for Tu B'Shevat	**6** 1 Shevat ROSH CHODESH	**7** 2 Shevat	**8** 3 Shevat	**9** 4 Shevat	**10** 5 Shevat	**11** 6 Shevat Bo Ex. 10:1-13:16 Jer. 46:13-28
12 7 Shevat	**13** 8 Shevat	**14** 9 Shevat	**15** 10 Shevat	**16** 11 Shevat	**17** 12 Shevat	**18** 13 Shevat SHABBAT SHIRAH BeShallach Ex. 13:17-17:16 Judges 4:4-5:31
19 14 Shevat	**20** 15 Shevat TU B'SHEVAT	**21** 16 Shevat	**22** 17 Shevat	**23** 18 Shevat	**24** 19 Shevat	**25** 20 Shevat Yitro Ex. 18:1-20:23 Isa. 6:1-7:6, 9:5
26 21 Shevat	**27** 22 Shevat	**28** 23Shevat	**29** 24 Shevat	**30** 25 Shevat	**31** 26 Shevat	

Special Events

Room for Families to Write

Jewish Holidays

Blank Calendar Page

Sunday	Monday	Tuesday	Wednesday	Thursday	Friday	Saturday

Use cotton, colored tissue paper, colored cellophane, etc., to dress each tree in its seasonal splendor.

A New Year Calendar for Tu B'Shevat

(Directions)

Collect:

    1 piece of 12" x 18" construction paper
    1 set of calendar sheets
    1 Trees Have New Years, Too! sheet
    1 piece of ribbon
    4 punched hole reinforcers

To assemble the calendar:

1. Staple the calendar sheets to the bottom half of the construction paper (see diagram).

2. Trim off the margins and glue the Trees Have New Years, Too! sheet to the top half of the construction paper.

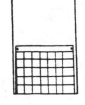

3. Use cotton, colored tissue paper, colored cellophane, etc., to dress each tree in its seasonal splendor.

4. Punch 2 holes at the top of the calendar. Reinforce the holes front and back

5. Thread the holes with ribbon.

6. Circle Tu B'Shevat on the calendar.

7. Add family birthdays and occasions to your calendar.

It Sounds Like Purim Is Here
Purim, Year 2

Postcard and/or Flier

To include:
Program Title
Sponsored by
Audience (age group, members only
    or general public, etc.)
Date
Time
Location
Cost (if applicable)
RSVP or For Further Information
Come dressed as a favorite Purim character —
    Queen Esther, Mordecai, King Ahasuerus,
    or Haman.

Physical Set Up

work area: tables and chairs
tables for supplies
table for name tags and sign-in sheet
trash cans
extra trash bags
tray for snack

Holiday Symbols, Customs, Terms, and Concepts

the sounds of Purim
gragger
blotting out Haman's name
the Purim story characters: Esther, Mordecai,
    King Ahasuerus, and Haman
hamantaschen, a pastry like Haman's hat
Mishloach Manot, sending gifts to friends
caring for others
sharing as a form of celebration
reaching out to other Jews
making people feel part of the community

00:00 – 00:15
Mind Warmer: The Sound of Purim

The families will be making *graggers* that
resemble tambourines.

Materials

name tags
markers
sign-in sheet
1 copy per family of Tambourine Gragger
    directions (see Directions and Patterns)
2 paper plates per child (the flatter the plate
    rim, the fewer staples needed to securely
    fasten the *gragger* shut)
dried beans and or small bells (if using beans,
    use large ones, such as brown beans or
    garbanzo beans, rather than lentil or pinto
    beans)
streamers or ribbons in a variety of colors
1 paint stir stick per child
staplers
staples
scissors

Advance Preparation by the Facilitator

- On the supply table, place these supplies:
  Tambourine Gragger directions, paper
  plates, beans or small bells, multi-colored
  streamers, and paint stir sticks.

- On the supply table, place these items, each
  in a separate container: staplers, staples, and
  scissors.

Procedure

- The Facilitator greets families as they arrive. Have them fill out a name tag for each family member and sign in.

- Let the families know that they will be making a *gragger* for the Mind Warmer.

- Send families to the supply table to gather all the supplies, as well as the Tambourine Gragger Directions.

- Families place one of the paper plates right side up on the table. They lay one end of the paint stir stick and the ends of the crepe paper on the rim of the plate.

- They staple the paint stick and streamers and ribbons to the rim of the plate in at least two places.

- They lay the other plate face down on top of the first plate.

- They match up the rims of the plates and staple every 1" to 2", leaving an opening at the top. They should staple a few extra times near the paint stir stick and streamers.

- They drop the beans or bells in the opening, then staple the opening shut.

- Have participants gather for the Introductions and Announcements and bring their *graggers*.

- Families clean up, returning materials to the supply table.

Note: This activity can be done without the paint stir sticks, resulting in a tambourine-like *gragger*.

00:15 – 00:20
Introductions and Announcements

- The Facilitator welcomes everyone on behalf of the sponsoring agency/institution.

- The Facilitator introduces himself/herself and any other official representatives of the program or the agency/institution.

- Have a member of each family introduce himself/herself and other family members.

- Announce any upcoming events for the sponsoring agency/institution that are pertinent for this group.

- Instruct people as to how they can get on the mailing list if they are not already on it.

Setting the Stage

- The Facilitator holds up someone's newly made *gragger*, and asks the families what they have made. Ask everyone to show off the sound of their *graggers*.

- Ask: Why do we use a *gragger* on Purim? (Get responses.) Say: We use a *gragger* to blot out the name of Haman, as if to blot out Haman himself, and all the wicked people like him. You will have the opportunity to use your *graggers* as we hear *Megillat Esther* (the Scroll of Esther). In the *Megillah*, Haman's name is mentioned many times, and each time we hear it, we make noises to blot it out.

00:20 – 00:40
The Purim Characters in Costume

Families will have the opportunity to use their newly made *graggers* during the telling of *Megillat Esther*. This particular rendition emphasizes the characters in the story. It is for this reading that the children and parents were asked to wear costumes.

Materials

1 copy of *Megillat Esther* (see Purim, Year 3 Directions and Patterns)

Procedure

- The Facilitator introduces the major characters of the Purim story: Queen Esther, Mordecai, King Ahasuerus, and Haman. As each character is introduced, ask the children dressed as that person to stand up and parade around.

- Ask those children who forgot to come in costume to stand up when you mention the Purim character they wish to be. Or, these children can be the Jewish People or Esther's servants in the Purim story.

- Instruct the families to stand up every time you read the name of the character they are dressed as. They should also use their *graggers* when Haman's name is said.

- Read or chant the blessing over the reading of *Megillat Esther* (see Blessing #12, page 489).

- Tell the Purim story. You can use the abbreviated version of *Megillat Esther*, the Scroll of Esther, found in Directions and Patterns for Purim, Year 3.

Have a noisy and colorful costume time!

00:40 – 00:50
Snack: The Search for the Hamantaschen Monster

The snack consists of *hamantaschen*, more *hamantaschen*, and more yummy *hamantaschen*, and juice. Rumor has it that a *hamantaschen* monster is on the loose. Perhaps the creature dresses as a parent or a preschooler. Families must protect their *hamantaschen*.

Materials

hamantaschen
juice
napkins
cups

Procedure

- Serve the *hamantaschen* and juice. Remember to recite a blessing (see Blessing #8, page 488).

00:50 – 01:10
A Tisket, A Tasket, A Purim Mishloach Manot Basket

After Haman is done in and the Jewish People saved, the Scroll of Esther mentions how the Jews celebrated. One of the things the Jews did, was to send gifts to one another. In Hebrew, this act is called *Mishloach Manot*.

Today, *Mishloach Manot* is still a Purim custom. We send gifts of at least two different types of foods, usually sweets or nuts or fruit, to a Jewish person we know. This is a way of sharing in the joy of Purim. This activity involves the making of such a basket.

Materials

1 copy per child of the Mishloach Manot Basket Directions
1 paper plate per child
1 strip per child of colored poster board pre-cut to 12" long and 1½" wide
1 paper napkin per child
ribbon
cookies or *hamantaschen*
candy
raisins
(Substitute other foods as desired.)
scissors
crayons
staplers
staples
single hole punches
pencils

Advance Preparation by the Facilitator

- Assemble a sample basket with just the handle. This will help families put the basket together.

- On the supply table, place these supplies: paper plates, Mishloach Manot Basket Directions sheets, pre-cut strips of colored poster board, paper napkins, ribbon, and the assorted foods and candies.

- On the supply table, place these items, each in a separate container: scissors, staplers, extra staples, single hole punches, crayons, and pencils.

Procedure

- The Facilitator explains to families that they will be making a *Mishloach Manot* basket. Familiarize the families with this custom (paraphrase the description of this activity on page 265).

- Instruct one or two representatives from each work table to gather the needed materials and copies of the directions.

- Families take a paper plate. They turn it upside down and decorate the border.

- They turn the plate right side up, then fold in thirds. They take the top of the plate and fold the top one third down toward the center. They then fold the bottom up one third.

- They turn the plate 90 degrees and fold in thirds again, bringing the top third down toward the center and the bottom third up.

- They open up the plate. It now has a tic-tac-toe pattern.

- They cut along the four fold lines indicated on the diagram.

- They fold the sides of the basket up at the fold lines to form a square basket, then staple it.

- They staple a 1½" x 12" poster board handle on the inside of the basket.

- They cut out the card that reads "Mishloach Manot, Gifts of Food for You at Purim" found on the Mishloach Manot Basket Directions.

- They fold the card in half so that the printed message is on the outside.

- The family signs the inside of the card.

- They punch a hole in the top left corner of the card, then attach it with ribbon to the handle of the basket.

- They fill the basket with two diffferent kinds of food and take it home to give to someone special.

- Families clean up, returning materials to the supply table.

- Have fun sharing your Purim joy with a special friend, relative, or neighbor!

01:10 – 01:30
Closure: More Sounds of Purim

End the program with more sounds of Purim — some favorite Purim tunes, and blessings.

- Sing and move to Purim music related to: the sounds of *graggers*, the Purim characters, *hamantaschen*, *Mishloach Manot,* sharing with others, and putting on costumes.

    Recommended Songs:

    "Purim's a Time" (*Seasoned With Song* by Julie Auerbach, Tara Publications)

    "*Al Hanisim*" (*Especially Wonderful Days* by Jeff Klepper, A.R.E. Publishing, Inc.)

- Recite some Purim blessings. Include *Shehecheyanu* (see Blessing #5, page 488) and the blessing recited upon hearing the *Megillah* read (see Blessing #12, page 489).

- Have participants share their reactions to the program. Ask families to complete one of these phrases:

  Purim is . . .

  My favorite Purim figure is . . .

  Our family enjoyed . . .

  Our family learned . . .

  For Purim, we . . .

- Send everyone off with a Purim greeting of "*Chag Sameach*!" (Happy Holiday!) or "Be happy it's Adar." Have fun making lots of Purim noise!

Tambourine Gragger
(Directions)

Collect the following materials:
  - 2 paper plates
  - 1 paint stir stick
  - a few crepe paper streamers
  - a few small jingle bells or a handful of beans

To assemble the tambourine *gragger*:

1. Lay one plate right side up. At the edge of the plate, lay one end of the paint stir stick and the ends of the crepe paper streamers.

2. Staple the paint stir stick and streamers to the paper plate.

3. Lay the other plate face down. Be sure to match the edges of the plates.

4. Starting at the paint stir stick, staple the plate edges together all the way around, leaving a small opening at the top.

OPENING

5. Put a few extra staples where the plates, streamers, and paint stir stick are joined.

6. Drop the bells or beans into the opening.

7. Staple the opening.

8. Use the *gragger* to make noise when Haman's name is mentioned.

Mishloach Manot Basket
(Directions)

1. Turn a paper plate upside down and decorate the border.

2. Turn the plate right side up. Fold into thirds — fold the top third down towards the center, then fold the bottom third up.

3. Turn the plate 90° and fold into thirds again. (When the plate is unfolded, it will have a tic-tac-toe pattern folded into it.)

4. Make 4 cuts along the dotted lines as shown in the diagram.

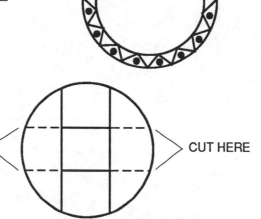

5. Fold the sides of the paper plate up at the fold lines to form a square basket and staple.

6. Staple a 1½" x 12" poster board handle on the inside of the basket.

7. Cut out this card:

> ## Mishloach Manot
> *Gifts of Food*
> *For You on*
> ### Purim

8. Fold the card in half so that the printed message is on the outside.

9. Sign the inside of the card.

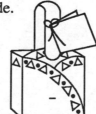

10. Punch a hole in the top left corner of the card and attach it with ribbon to the basket handle.

11. Fill the basket with two different kinds of food (e.g., fruit and candy).

12. Give the Mishloach Manot Basket to someone special.

Counting on Passover
Passover, Year 2

Postcard and/or Flier

To include:
Program Title
Sponsored by
Audience (age group, members only or
general public, etc.)
Date
Time
Location
Cost (if applicable)
RSVP or For Further Information
Bring your favorite Sesame Street resident.

Physical Set Up

work area: tables and chairs
tables for supplies
table for name tags and sign-in sheet
large trash cans
trash bags
floor space for the *Seder Scotch* (*Hopscotch*)
game board

**Holiday Symbols, Customs, Terms,
and Concepts**

the numbers of Passover
Echad Mi Yodeah? (Who Knows One?)
three *matzot* (plural of *matzah*)
four cups of wine
four questions
four children
seven weeks of the Omer
ten plagues
15 steps of the *Seder*
numbers as symbolic
an orientation to Jewish time

using the holidays as milestones in time
and in one's life

00:00 - 00:10
**Mind Warmer: A Three-Layered
Matzah Cover**

Passover means *matzah*! The *Seder* table is set
with three *matzot*. One half of the middle
matzah becomes the *Afikomen*. Families make
a three-layered *matzah* cover for use at their
Seder.

Materials

name tags
markers
sign-in sheet
2 pieces per child of 12" x 18" construction
paper in light colors
gluesticks
staplers
staples
gold and silver glitter
yarn, braid, rick-rack, etc.
crayons

Advance Preparation by the Facilitator

- Make a sample *matzah* cover (see
Procedure).

- On the supply table, place these materials:
the sheets of 12" x 18" construction paper,
gold and silver glitter, and yarn.

- On the supply table, place these items,
each in a separate container: staplers, extra
staples, crayons, and gluesticks.

Procedure

- The Facilitator greets families as they arrive. Have them fill out a name tag for each family member and sign in.

- Tell the families that they will be making a three-layered *matzah* cover at the work tables. Show them the sample.

- Instruct families to pick up the supplies from the supply table.

- Families place two pieces of 12" x 18" construction paper evenly, one on top of the other. They fold the papers in half so that they are now 12" x 9".

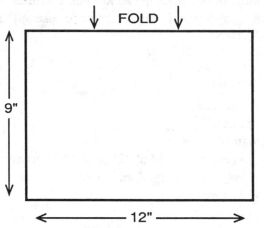

- They staple the two 9" sides every 3" to 4", but do not staple the front (the side opposite the fold). They now have a folder with three pockets — a three-layered *matzah* cover.

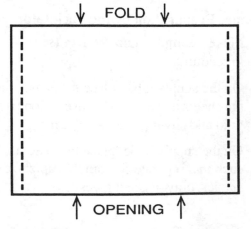

- Families decorate their cover as desired, using gold and/or silver glitter, crayons, yarn, braid, rick-rack, etc.

- The Facilitator asks families to clean up, returning materials to the supply table.

00:10 – 00:20
Introductions and Announcements

Materials

1 puppet or picture of the Count from Sesame Street

Procedure

- The Facilitator welcomes everyone on behalf of the sponsoring agency/institution.

- The Facilitator introduces himself/herself and any other official representatives of the program or the agency/institution.

- Have a member of each family introduce himself/herself and other family members.

- Announce any upcoming events for the sponsoring agency/institution that are pertinent for this group.

- Instruct people as to how they can get on the mailing list if they are not already on it.

Setting the Stage

- The Facilitator asks everyone to hold up three fingers.

- Say: Three is the number of *matzot* that we place in a *matzah* cover for Passover. As in the Passover song, "*Echad Mi Yodeah?*" (Who Knows One?), some numbers have special significance at the *Seder*.

  With the help of the Count (pull out puppet or picture of the Count from "Sesame Street"), we will count our way through these important numbers.

00:20 – 01:10
Extended Activity and Snack:
We're Counting on Passover

With the help of the Count from "Sesame Street," families participate in a variety of activities, associating the numbers 3, 4, 7, 9, 10, and 15 with Passover symbols and rituals. They count out each number as they learn about the Passover symbols and rituals associated with that number.

Materials

1 puppet or picture of the Count from "Sesame Street"

macaroons

grape juice for drinking and dripping

napkins

cups

1 dinner-size paper plate per child (the lightweight, plain white dinner-size paper plates are best for this activity)

1 pre-cut set of Frog Body Parts per child — eyes, tongue, and legs (see Directions and Patterns)

construction paper (green, red, white, black)

4 brads (small size) per child

1 Seder Scotch Game Board for the 15 steps of the *Seder* (see next page)

1 copy per child of the Omer Calendar on light colored paper (see Directions and Patterns)

1 puppet or picture of Cookie Monster (Matzah Monster for this occasion)

1 copy of *Only Nine Chairs* by Deborah Miller (Rockville, MD: Kar-Ben Copies, Inc., 1982)

masking tape

magnetic tape (2" strip per child)

gluesticks

scissors

crayons

Advance Preparation by the Facilitator

Seder Scotch Game

- Make a Seder Scotch Game Board (similar to *Hopscotch*) by enlarging the Seder Scotch Game Board on the next page on a piece of oilcloth 12" long and at least 3" wide. (Purchase the oilcloth at a fabric store.)

- Tape the *Seder Scotch* game board to the floor.

Paper Plate Frog

- The Facilitator pre-cuts all frog body parts so that families can assemble the frog quickly. Using the Frog Body Parts Pattern, prepare the parts as follows:

- Cut out the 5 Frog Body Parts outlines.

- Trace and cut as follows for each frog:

  2 black construction paper pupils

  2 whites of eyes on white contruction paper

  1 red construction paper tongue

  4 green construction paper legs

- Make a sample paper plate frog (see Procedure).

Seder Scotch Game Board

Draw this *Seder Scotch* game onto oilcloth. Write the instructions next to each box. If desired, copy an illustration from the Seder Order Cards on pages 465 and 467 into each box. Place the oilcloth on the floor for participants to play on.

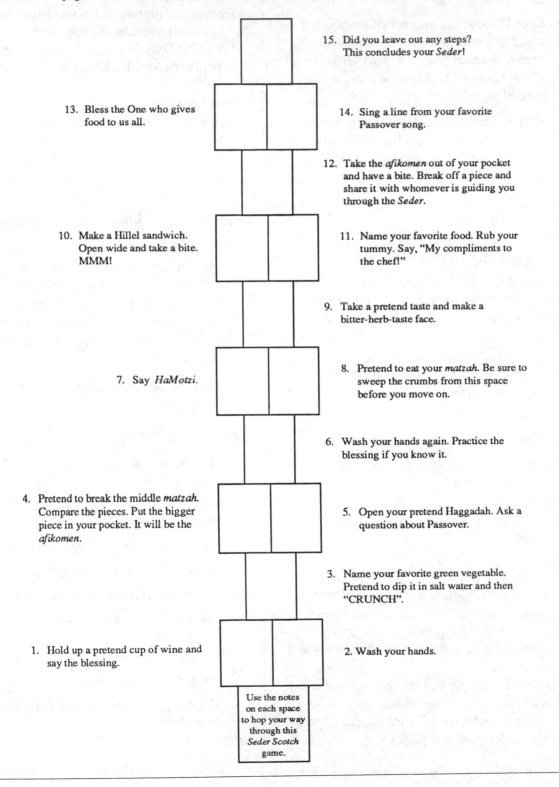

15. Did you leave out any steps? This concludes your *Seder*!

13. Bless the One who gives food to us all.

14. Sing a line from your favorite Passover song.

12. Take the *afikomen* out of your pocket and have a bite. Break off a piece and share it with whomever is guiding you through the *Seder*.

10. Make a Hillel sandwich. Open wide and take a bite. MMM!

11. Name your favorite food. Rub your tummy. Say, "My compliments to the chef!"

9. Take a pretend taste and make a bitter-herb-taste face.

7. Say *HaMotzi*.

8. Pretend to eat your *matzah*. Be sure to sweep the crumbs from this space before you move on.

6. Wash your hands again. Practice the blessing if you know it.

4. Pretend to break the middle *matzah*. Compare the pieces. Put the bigger piece in your pocket. It will be the *afikomen*.

5. Open your pretend Haggadah. Ask a question about Passover.

3. Name your favorite green vegetable. Pretend to dip it in salt water and then "CRUNCH".

1. Hold up a pretend cup of wine and say the blessing.

2. Wash your hands.

Use the notes on each space to hop your way through this *Seder Scotch* game.

Other Parts

- Have these supplies by your side for the Passover Count:

    puppet or picture of the Count
    from Sesame Street

    puppet or picture of Cookie Monster
    (Matzah Monster)

    4 cups per relay team

    the book *Only Nine Chairs*

- On the supply table, place the following materials: macaroons, napkins, cups (for drinking and game), grape juice, paper plates (for making the frog), brads, cut frog body parts, copies of the Omer Calendar, magnetic tape.

- On the supply table, place these items, each in its own container: gluesticks, scissors, crayons.

Procedure

- A recommended time allotment follows the title of each counting activity below. Remember, count aloud and together for each number!

- For each appropriate activity, send one or two representatives from each work table to collect the materials from the supply table.

- Families clean up after each of the following activities, returning the materials to the supply table.

#3: Three Matzot (3 minutes)

- The Facilitator says: Meet the Matzah Monster, alias Cookie Monster. (Hold up the Count and count to three. Hold up Matzah Monster). Matzah Monster explains, "You don't eat cookies on Passover. You eat *matzah*." Look at the *matzah* cover you made earlier during the Mind Warmer. Count the number of pockets in the *matzah* cover.

#4: Four Cups of Wine, Four Questions, Four Children (10 minutes)

- The Facilitator holds up the Count and counts to four.

- This is a relay race done at the work tables. Mention that there are a lot of Passover "fours": four cups of wine, four questions, and four children.

- The Facilitator explains the game. The object of the race is for each person on a team to unstack and restack the four cups. Ask each team to count as cups are stacked. Once a player on each team unstacks and restacks the four cups, pass them to the next player. All teams which unstack and restack all four cups win. (Teams at tables may need to be evened out so that all have the same number of players. Or, some players can go twice.)

#7: The Seven Weeks of the Omer — the Seven Weeks between Passover and Shavuot (7 minutes)

- The Facilitator holds up the Count and counts to 7.

- The Facilitator explains that Jews count the 50 days between Passover and Shavuot. It is a custom tied to the harvest. We begin counting on the second day of Passover. There are 7 weeks in total.

- Hold up the Jewish calendar (optional). Count the weeks.

- Families color the Omer Calendar and cut it out.

- They put one piece of magnetic tape on the

back of the Omer calendar near the center of the top edge.

- They color the Omer Calendar marker and cut it out.

- They put a piece of magnetic tape on the back of the Omer Calendar marker.

- Families take an Omer Calendar home and hang it on their refrigerator.

#9: *Only Nine Chairs* (15 minutes)

- The Facilitator holds up the Count and counts to nine.

- The Facilitator reads the story *Only Nine Chairs,* which is a review of the Passover *Seder.* The story's title fits in well with counting.

- Together recite the appropriate blessings (see Blessings #2, page 487 and #8, page 488).

- Everyone eats macaroons and drinks grape juice.

#10 — The Ten Plagues (15 minutes)

- The Facilitator holds up the Count and counts to 10.

- The Facilitator reads the ten plagues from the Haggadah:

  Dam, Blood

  Tzfardeyah, Frogs

  Kinim, Lice

  Arov, Wild Beasts

  Dever, Blight

  Sh'chin, Boils

  Barad, Hail

  Arbeh, Locusts

  Hoshech, Darkness

  Makat B'chorot, Slaying of the Firstborn

- The Facilitator drips a drop of grape juice for each plague, the second of which is frogs. Participants pretend to drip the drops. Before starting the frog activity, explain that another activity awaits them, the *Seder Scotch* game. They can play it before, during, or after completing the frog.

To assemble the frogs:

- Families fold the paper plate in half.

- They glue the tongue to the inside of the plate.

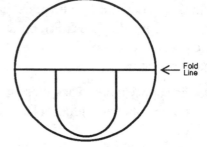

- With the 4 brass fasteners, they attach the legs to the underside of the folded plate.

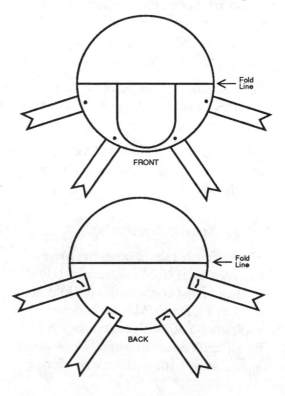

- They make frog eyes by gluing black pupils onto the whites of eyes and centering the eyeballs on the green eyelids. They do this twice.

- They glue the eyes onto the top flap of the folded plate.

- The Facilitator suggests that families take their frog to their family *Seder*.

#15: The Fifteen Parts of the *Seder*

- Each family plays the *Seder Scotch* game before, during, or after they finish making their frog. They jump and hop, or even just walk, doing the activities written on each square. Parents read the instructions to the child. More than one family can be on the board at a time.

01:10 – 01:30
Closure: Echad Mi Yodeah?
Who Knows One?
  End the program with singing, blessings, sharing, and holiday greetings.

- Be certain to sing at least the refrain from *"Echad Mi Yodeah?"* (Who Knows One?)

This Passover song associates numbers with significant Jewish people, books, concepts, and things. It is thematically connected to this program.

- Sing and move to other Passover music related to: three *matzot*, four cups of wine, four questions, four children, ten plagues, frogs, 15 parts of the *Seder*, numbers, *matzah*, the Jewish calendar, the counting of the Omer (the weeks between Passover and Shavuot).

  Recommended Songs:

    "Pesach Is _____." (*Apples on Holidays and Other Days* by Leah Abrams, Tara Publications)

    "The Ten Plagues" (*Bible People Songs* by Jeff Klepper, A.R.E. Publishing, Inc.)

    "Chad Gadya" (Haggadah)

- Recite a Passover blessing or two.

- Have participants share their reactions to the program. Ask families to complete one of these phrases:

    A Passover number is . . .

    Our family enjoyed . . .

    Our family learned . . .

    For Passover, we will count . . .

- Send everyone off with a Passover greeting: *"Chag Sameach*!" (Happy Holiday!)

Omer Calendar

1. Color the Omer Calendar below and cut it out.
2. Put one piece of magnetic tape on the back of the Omer calendar near the center of the top edge.
3. Color the Omer Calendar Marker on the right and cut it out.
4. Put a piece of magnetic tape on the back of the Omer Calendar Marker.
5. Take the Omer Calendar home and hang it on your refrigerator.
6. Each night, beginning with the second night of Passover, say the prayer at the top of the Omer Calendar and move the marker to count the Omer.

Omer Calendar Marker:

 **Omer Calendar**

בָּרוּךְ אַתָּה, יְיָ אֱלֹהֵינוּ, מֶלֶךְ הָעוֹלָם, אֲשֶׁר קִדְּשָׁנוּ בְּמִצְוֹתָיו וְצִוָּנוּ עַל סְפִירַת הָעֹמֶר.

BARUCH ATAH ADONAI ELOHEYNU MELECH HA-OLAM
ASHER KIDSHANU B'MITZVOTAV V'TZVEEVANU AL SEFIRAT HAOMER.

Blessed are You, Eternal our God, Ruler of the universe, Who makes us holy with Your *mitzvot*, and Who commanded us to count the Omer.

1	2	3	4	5	6	7	1 whole week!
8	9	10	11	12	13	14	2 whole weeks!
15	16	17	18	19	20	21	3 whole weeks!
22	23	24	25	26	27	28	4 whole weeks!
29	30	31	32	33	34	35	5 whole weeks!
36	37	38	39	40	41	42	6 whole weeks!
43	44	45	46	47	48	49	7 whole weeks!

…when you count… it will be seven complete weeks. By the day after the seventh day of the seventh week, you will have counted fifty days… Leviticus 23:15-16

Frog Body Parts

For each frog you will need:
   4 brads
   1 paper plate

You will also need:

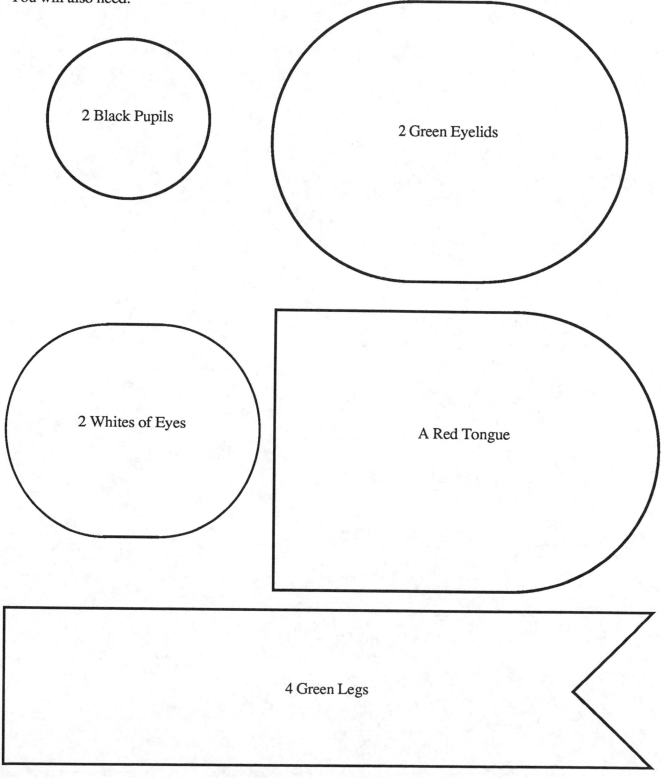

2 Black Pupils

2 Green Eyelids

2 Whites of Eyes

A Red Tongue

4 Green Legs

A Pilgrimage to Israel
Yom HaAtzma' ut, Year 2

Postcard and/or Flier

To include:
Program Title
Sponsored by
Audience (age group, members only or
general public, etc.)
Date
Time
Location
Cost (if applicable)
RSVP or For Further Information

Physical Set Up

work area: tables and chairs
tables for supplies
table for name tags and sign-in sheet
large trash cans
trash bags
corner or wall of a room for Western Wall
set up

**Holiday Symbols, Customs, Terms,
and Concepts**

the Land of Israel
Yom HaAtzma'ut (Israel Independence Day)
visiting Israel
the Land of Israel as every Jew's
heritage and homeland
Israel as the responsibility of all Jews
the sites in Israel
the Western Wall, the wall associated
with the Temple
Israel as the Holy Land
sacred space
hiney mah tov — how good it is for all of us
to dwell together
handicrafts of Israel

produce from Israel
music of Israel
the connection between Jews in Israel
and Jews around the world

**00:00 – 00:15
Mind Warmer: Passport to Israel**

The Land of Israel is the focus of this Mind
Warmer. Families fill out a passport for their
child, write a prayer to place in the Western
Wall, and make a paper airplane.

Materials

name tags
markers
sign-in sheet
1 Passport per child photocopied on white
paper (see Directions and Patterns)
1 piece of plain paper 8$^{1}/_{2}$" x 11" per child
1 piece of lined paper per child
pencils
8-15 empty brown boxes to make a
Western Wall
at least 1 poster or large picture of
Jerusalem and Israel
crayons

Advance Preparation by the Facilitator

- Build the Western Wall out of cardboard
boxes in a corner or along a wall of the
room you will be using for the program.
Build it taller than the tallest child in the
group.

- On the supply table, place these materials:
Passports, plain white paper, and lined
paper.

- On the supply table, place these items, each in a separate container: crayons and pencils.

Procedure

- The Facilitator greets families as they arrive. Have them fill out a name tag for each family member and sign in.

- Inform the families that today's Mind Warmer on Israel involves filling out a passport for their child, writing a prayer to place in the Western Wall, and making a paper airplane to fly to Israel.

- Direct the families to the supply table to collect the materials.

- The families go to the work tables and begin filling out the passports. This process includes: drawing a picture of the child and coloring in eye color and hair color. They fold the passport in half and in half again.

- The Facilitator instructs each family to write a prayer together — a prayer to put in the Western Wall. (They will place the prayer in the Western Wall later.)

- Have the families make a paper airplane.

- Instruct each family to come to the Introductions and Announcements area with their family prayer, paper airplane, and passport.

00:15 – 00:25
Introductions and Announcements

Materials

1 stamp and ink pad (preferably, the stamp has something to do with Israel or Judaism. Or, use a date stamp that most bookkeepers or librarians have.)

Procedure

- The Facilitator welcomes everyone on behalf of the sponsoring agency/institution.

- The Facilitator introduces himself/herself and any other official representatives of the program or the agency/institution.

- Have a member of each family introduce himself/herself and other family members.

- Announce any upcoming events for the sponsoring agency/institution that are pertinent for this group.

- Instruct people as to how they can get on the mailing list if they are not already on it.

Setting the Stage

- The Facilitator says: Yom HaAtzma'ut is Israel's Independence Day. It is on the 5th of Iyar, which this year is _____. In the United States, Independence Day is celebrated on the fourth of July and in Canada on July 1st. Israel is the Homeland of the Jews. Israel is the birthplace of the Jewish People.

  For this year's celebration of Yom HaAtz–ma'ut, we will "visit" Israel. Now that you have your passports filled out, get your paper airplanes ready. It is time to fly to Israel. (Families fly the paper airplanes toward the set up of the Western Wall. Or, the Facilitator secures the poster or picture of Israel or Jerusalem to the wall, and families aim the airplanes as they would a dart at a bulls eye.) Now that you are in Israel, come and get your passport stamped. (The Facilitator stamps each passport.)

00:25 – 00:40
Story: Brothers

Brothers is a legend of two brothers who care for one another. Their caring, as legend goes, merits the building of the Temple on the site of their fields.

Materials

at least one poster or large picture of Jerusalem and Israel

1 copy of *Brothers* by Florence Freedman (New York: Harper and Row, 1985)

1 Aliyah Certificate per child photocopied on ivory or beige parchment-like paper (see Directions and Patterns)

markers

Advance Preparation by the Facilitator

- Make certain that the picture(s) of Jerusalem and Israel, as well as the Western Wall you built from boxes, are visible during story time.

- Sign the Aliyah Certificates.

- Have the Aliyah Certificates and markers ready for distribution.

Procedure

- The Facilitator says: Soon we will visit the Western Wall. The Western Wall was part of the wall around the Temple where Jews worshiped in Jerusalem. This is a picture of Jerusalem. First, we will hear a story about two brothers and how the place for the Temple was chosen.

- Tell the story. The story is about two brothers, one married and one unmarried, who display kindness toward one another. Because of this kindness, their fields were considered an appropriate, sanctified place for building the Temple in Jerusalem.

- The brothers displayed kindness toward one another. Sing the popular folk song, "*Hiney Mah Tov,*" which reflects their attitude.

The words are:

> *Hiney Mah Tov U'ma'Nayim Shevet Achim Gam Yachad.*
>
> How good it is for all of us to live together.

- Instruct families to go to the Western Wall and to place their family prayers in the Wall.

- After families put their prayers in the Western Wall, the Facilitator distributes Aliyah Certificates (acknowledging that they have visited Israel) and markers. Have the families fill in the child's name or family name.

00:40 — 00:50
Snack: The Foods of Israel

The snack introduces families to Israeli produce.

Materials

almonds
raisins
honey graham crackers
orange juice
napkins
cups

Procedure

- Serve the families a snack of produce from Israel, including almonds, raisins, honey graham crackers (honey for a land flowing with milk and honey), and *mitz tapuzim* (orange juice).

- Together recite a blessing (see Blessing #8, page 488).

- Enjoy the Israeli noshes.

00:50 – 01:10

Activity: Shalom! From the Holy Land

These three short activities reinforce Israel as a land to visit and a place where we can explore our roots. The activities can be done in any order. In one of the activities, families are photographed with a Polaroid camera. Keep a steady flow of families at the photography corner.

Materials

1 blank 5" x 8" card per child (either an index card or card stock)

1 6" x 9" manila envelope per child for mailing photographs

a small quantity of sand or corn meal

magazines, travel brochures, posters with pictures of Israel (obtain from a *Sheliach*, the Israeli consulate, El Al, or a travel agent)

Polaroid camera

enough film for one picture of each child

enough flashs bulbs for one picture of each child

tourist props — pick several of the following props or comparable ones (size of the item does not matter): sandals, T-shirts from Israel or with Hebrew writing, *kafia, kovah tembel (kibbutz* hat), beads, Israeli jewelry, embroidered dresses or shirts, etc.

gluesticks

scissors

pens

pencils

1 Israeli flag

Advance Preparation by the Facilitator

* Place the following tourist props near the Western Wall: embroidered dresses and shirts, T-shirts from Israel or that have Hebrew on them, sandals, *kibbutz* hats, *kafias*, etc. Place an Israeli flag by the Western Wall, too.

* On the supply table, place these materials: 6" x 9" manila envelopes, the blank index cards or card stock, small quantities of sand or cornmeal in cups, and the magazines or brochures.

* On the supply table, place these items, each in a separate container: pencils, gluesticks, scissors, and pens.

Procedures

Families may do the following activities in any order.

Making a Postcard

* Families cut out pictures of Israel from magazines and brochures.

* They glue the pictures to one side of the index card or postcard.

Shalom from Israel!

* Families decide to which relative they will send their postcard from Israel.

* They write a note to that relative on the back side of their postcard telling them what they are doing and why they are writing.

* The Facilitator suggests that families enclose a bit of sand in the envelope.

* They may also enclose the picture of their child taken at the Western Wall in tourist clothing. (Or, families may keep this picture.)

* Have families address an envelope. Suggest that they actually mail the card and enclosures. (Doing so is good P.R. for the program!)

The Child's Picture in Israel

- Allow the children time to get dressed in the tourist props. Parents can help.
- The Facilitator takes each child's picture in front of the Western Wall, waving an Israeli flag. (If the family has more than one child present, take one picture for each child.)
- Families can enclose the picture in the envelope to their relative. Or, they can take it home as a souvenir.

01:10 – 01:30
Closure: Kumsitz — Songs from Israel

End the program with singing, sharing, and greetings.

- Folk music is the heart and soul of Israel. In Israel, when people sit in front of a fire and sing songs, it is called a *kumsitz*.
- Sing and move to Yom HaAtzma'ut music related to: Israel, freedom, living in Israel, the sites in Israel, Jerusalem, foods from Israel, Israel as the homeland, Israel as the holy land.

Recommended Songs:

"*Haveynu Shalom Aleichem*" (traditional melody)

"Let's All Take a Trip" (*Seasoned With Song* by Julie Auerbach, Tara Publications)

- Include some Israeli dancing, a line or circle dance, or just move to an Israeli tune.
- Have participants share their reactions to the program. Ask families to complete one of the following phrases:

Israel is . . .

I want to go to Israel because . . .

Our family liked . . .

Our family learned . . .

- Send everyone off with "*Lihitraot*" (*l' hit-ra-ot*) which is Hebrew for "Good-bye." Literally, it means "See you again!"

PASSPORT

This is my picture:

My Name is: _____

(color in each box)

I have [ ] Eyes

and [ ] Hair

Today I am going to learn about

ISRAEL

Official Stamp

Attestation of Pilgrimage

*To Anyone Who Should Ever Ask, Shalom —
Be It Known That*

נְעִידֵנִי
רַגְלֵינוּ
הָיוּ עֹמְדוֹת
בִּשְׁעָרַיִךְ
יְרוּשָׁלָ͏ִם
תהלים קכב

*has been to a family holiday program about Israel
and in doing so, ascended to Jerusalem, the Holy City,
Capital of Israel, and shall henceforth be known as a
Jerusalem Pilgrim.*

Special Representative of The Mayor of Jerusalem

Special Seal

I Have Been to the Mountain Top
Shavuot, Year 2

Flier and/or Postcard:

To include:
Program Title
Sponsored by
Audience (age group, members only or
    general public, etc.)
Date
Time
Location
Cost (if applicable)
RSVP or For Further Information

Physical Set Up

work area: tables and chairs
supply table
snack table for distributing snack
table for name tags and sign in sheet
large trash cans
trash bags

Holiday Symbols, Customs, Terms and Concepts

Ten Commandments
pilgrimage
going to the Temple in Jerusalem
bikkurim – first fruits
Megillat Ruth (The Scroll of Ruth)
eating dairy products
blintzes
Confirmation
Ruth
Boaz
peah (leaving the corners of the field for the
    poor, widow, and orphan)
the tablets of the Ten Commandments
Mount Sinai
standing at Sinai
synagogue
affirming belief in one God
the gift of Torah by God at Mount Sinai

00:00 – 00:15
Mind Warmer: Shavuot Magnets

Families will make Shavuot magnets for this
Mind Warmer. They will do this by cutting
out symbols associated with Shavuot, coloring
in the symbols, and sticking them on magnetic
tape. These magnets look great on refrigerator
doors!

Materials

name tags
markers
sign-in sheet
1 set per child of Shavuot Magnets on white
    card stock (see Directions and Patterns)
9" to 12" strips of magnetic tape per child
scissors
1 sandwich size Ziplock bag per child

Advance Preparation by the Facilitator

• On the supply table, place these items:
  sheets entitled Shavuot Magnets, magnetic
  tape, and Ziplock sandwich bags.

• On the supply table, place these materials,
  each in a separate container: scissors and
  markers.

Procedure

• The Facilitator greets families as they

arrive. Have them fill out a name tag for each family member and sign in.

- The Facilitator explains that families will be making magnets of various Shavuot symbols for the refrigerator.

- Direct participants to the supply table where they can get the materials needed for the project.

- Families color in the Shavuot symbols and cut them out.

- They cut a piece of magnetic tape approximately 1½" in length for each magnet.

- They write their family name on a piece of scrap paper, then place the scrap paper and the magnets in a Ziplock sandwich bag.

- Ask families to clean up, returning the materials to the supply table.

00:15 – 00:25
Introductions and Announcements

- The Facilitator welcomes everyone on behalf of the sponsoring agency/institution.

- The Facilitator introduces himself/herself and any other official representatives of the program or the agency/institution.

- Have a member of each family introduce himself/herself and other family members.

- Announce any upcoming events for the sponsoring agency/institution that are pertinent for this group.

- Instruct people as to how they can get on the mailing list if they are not already on it.

Setting the Stage

- The Facilitator says: Shavuot, the Festival of Weeks, is a harvest festival. Traditionally

Jews brought *bikkurim*, meaning "first fruits," the newest and best, as an offering to God to the Temple in Jerusalem. God gave the Ten Commandments on Mount Sinai to the Jewish people on the 6th of Sivan, the first day of Shavuot.

In many congregations, ninth or tenth grade students confirm or reaffirm their readiness to accept the values of Judaism. They stand before God as if they were at Mount Sinai.

On Shavuot, we read *Megillat Ruth*, the Scroll of Ruth. This is the story of one person's commitment to God, the Jewish people, the Ten Commandments, and the Torah. Soon you will complete your own Shavuot activity book.

Now we will hear a Shavuot story.

00:25 – 00:40
Story: Megillat Ruth in Play Form

Megillat Ruth, literally the Scroll of Ruth, is read on Shavuot. The most famous line in the book occurs when Ruth promises to follow Naomi, her mother-in-law, and to accept her people and her God. The connections between *Megillat Ruth* and Shavuot have to do with Ruth's harvesting the crops and her acceptance of God and all God's commandments.

This story will be done as a play with puppets. Parents will read the script while their child holds up the appropriate puppet.

Materials

8 lunch-size paper bags, any color
1 each Paper Bag Puppet Pattern I-VIII
   copied on white card stock (see Directions
   and Patterns)
markers
scissors

gluesticks
nine copies of the *Megillat Ruth* play

Advance Preparation by the Facilitator

- Make nine copies of the *Megillat Ruth* play for the readers.

- Make a sample paper bag puppet of Naomi, Elimelech, the two sons, Ruth, Orpah, Boaz, and King David.

- To make the puppets:

  - Using markers, color in the features of the face of each figure.

  - Cut out the faces and nametags from the card stock.

  - Glue each face and the character's name to the bottom on an unopened lunch-size paper bag.

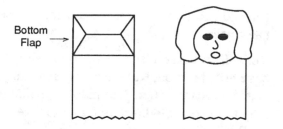

- Cut out the nametags. Glue each onto the "body" of the puppet.

- The Facilitator asks families to volunteer to read the script and hold the puppets. The parent reads. The child holds the puppet.

- Line up all the readers together so that the entire group can see them.

- Ask for nine volunteers. The nine parts are as follows: Narrator (this does not require a puppet, but the child can stand in front with the parent who reads), Elimelech, Naomi, two sons, Ruth, Orpah, Boaz, King David.

- Read the play using the puppets to emphasize who is speaking.

Play: Megillat Ruth

Narrator: A long time ago, in ancient Israel, Elimelech and Naomi lived in Bethlehem. They had two sons. They were a happy family. They celebrated the Jewish holidays and prayed to God.

One year, the land of Israel was dry. It did not rain enough. There was not enough food to eat in the land.

Elimelech: Naomi, there is no more food to harvest. The wheat is all dried up. No one in Bethlehem has any more food.

The two sons: Father we are hungry. Let us go to a land where there is food.

Elimelech: Yes, we shall soon set out to Moab. In Moab, they still have food.

Naomi: Elimelech, my husband, I am concerned about going to live in Moab. I do not want my children praying to another god. I want them to pray to the one God, *Adonai*. Who will our sons marry? I want our grandchildren to pray to *Adonai*.

Elimelech: It is better to eat in Moab than to starve in Bethlehem. Our God is everywhere. Even in Moab, we can pray to God.

Narrator: So Elimelech and Naomi took their sons to Moab. There they found food. They lived in Moab until the boys were adults and ready to marry. The sons each married Moabites.

The two sons: We are happily married to our wives, Ruth and Orpah.

Narrator: Then something bad happened. Many people in Moab got sick. First Elimelech died. Then the two sons died. That left Naomi and her two daughters-in-law all alone with no family to support them.

Naomi: My kind daughters-in-law, the time has come for me to return to Bethlehem. I have no family here to take care of me other than you two. I do not want to trouble you. I am getting older. I want to live out the rest of my life with my family.

Orpah: We will go with you, Naomi.

Naomi: You must not come with me. You should find husbands among your people, the Moabites. Someday, you too will grow old, and you will want to be near your families.

Orpah: You are right. I shall stay in Moab. Good-bye, Naomi. Be well.

Narrator: Orpah stayed in Moab. But Ruth loved her mother-in-law very much. She spoke some words that are now very famous. Listen to what she said.

Ruth: I am going with you to Bethlehem, Naomi.

Naomi: Why? I cannot support you. You are still young. Your home is here.

Ruth: Naomi, listen to me. I am going with you. Where you go, I will follow. Your family is my family. Your people will be my people. Your God will be my God.

Narrator: Naomi was touched by the promises that Ruth made. This was a special moment. It is not often that a Moabite agrees to pray to the one God, *Adonai*. Naomi kissed Ruth. Together they walked to Bethlehem. When they arrived in Bethlehem, they found

Naomi's house. They moved in. They slept well the first night.

Ruth: I slept well, but now I am hungry. How shall we get food to eat?

Naomi: Let me tell you how we will eat. There is a custom among Jews. At every harvest, when the crops are ready to pick, the farmers leave the corners of their fields for the poor, the orphan, and widows like us. Today, we can go to the fields, and get some food. Then I will cook us a meal.

Ruth: That is a wonderful custom, Naomi. I will go to the field now while it is still early.

Narrator: So Ruth set out to the fields. She began to gather the harvest foods. It was hot out. Soon she tired.

Boaz: Would you like some water? You look very warm.

Narrator: Ruth was surprised to hear the man talk to her.

Boaz: I am Boaz, Naomi's relative. Already I have heard of you, Ruth. Naomi says that you take good care of her. Naomi told me that you pray to the one God, *Adonai*. Please take as much food as you want.

Ruth: Thank you, sir. You are so kind. It is nice to see family members taking care of one another.

Boaz: I hope to see you again. You are welcome any time.

Narrator: Ruth returned to bring Naomi all the food and tell her about Boaz and his kindness, and their good luck. For many days, Ruth went to Boaz's field to gather wheat and to prepare the wheat. Every day, Boaz came over to see Ruth.

Boaz: For many days I have watched you. You are a special person. You take such good care of Naomi. You work hard. You pray often to *Adonai*, our God. I would like to marry you.

Ruth: Boaz, you, too, are kind and caring. I will marry you.

Narrator: So Ruth and Boaz were married. Naomi lived a long time. She lived well and happily thanks to Boaz. Ruth and Boaz had a son, Obed, who had a son named Jesse. Jesse also had a son; his name was David.

King David: My name is David, King David. I ruled over Israel for many years. You know who my great grandmother was? Ruth was my great grandmother. Ruth, who decided to become a Jew, had a good life. I like hearing the story of my great grandmother Ruth, don't you?

00:40 – 00:50
Snack: Let's Get Blintzed

Shavuot foods are customarily dairy foods. Enjoy a snack of blintzes, sour cream, apple sauce (the children will eat the apple sauce if they do not like the blintzes), and milk.

Materials

frozen blintzes
sour cream
apple sauce
milk
tray for heating up blintzes
cups
forks
knives
plates
serving spoons
serving bowls
serving platter
oven or microwave

refrigerator
spatula

Advance Preparation by the Facilitator

- Make arrangements for a volunteer to heat the blintzes while you are telling the story.

- The volunteer may also dish out apple sauce and sour cream into serving bowls and set the snack out on a table.

Procedure

- The Facilitator explains that it is a Shavuot custom to eat dairy products. The snack for today follows this tradition.

- Have each participant take a blintz, sour cream, apple sauce, and milk.

- Together recite a blessing (see Blessing #9, page 488.

- Enjoy getting blintzed!

00:50 – 01:10
Activity: "On Shavuot" Activity Book

At this point, families begin completing their own *On Shavuot* activity book. This activity book presents holiday customs, origins, and terms in a way that preschoolers can understand. It outlines the major characters and story line from the Book of Ruth.

Materials

1 *On Shavuot* activity book per child (see Directions and Patterns)
1 binder with a clear cover per child for the *On Shavuot* activity book (see Directions and Patterns)
1 plastic fork per child
1 plastic napkin per child

small quantities of grains: rice, cereal, or
   beans
magazines with pictures of food
gluesticks
pencils
scissors
crayons

Advance Preparation by the Facilitator

- On the supply table, place these materials:
  copies of the *On Shavuot* activity book,
  binders, plastic forks, paper napkins, grain
  in cups, and magazines with pictures of
  food.

- On the supply table, place these items, each
  in its own container: gluesticks, pencils,
  scissors, and crayons.

Procedure

- The Facilitator tells families that they will
  be creating their own activity book called
  On Shavuot.

- Emphasize that they should take their time
  in working on the book. Directions are
  found on each page of the activity book. If
  they don't finish, they may complete the
  book at home.

- Ask one or two people from each work
  table to get the materials from the supply
  table.

- At the end of the time period, ask families
  to clean up, returning the materials to the
  supply table.

01:10 – 01:30
Closure: We'll be Coming Round Mount Sinai When We Come

End the program with singing, sharing, and
holiday greetings.

Materials

1 copy of the *Megillat Ruth* play per family.

Procedure

- Sing and move to Shavuot music related to:
  Shavuot, the Torah, the Ten Commandments, Mount Sinai, Ruth, dairy products,
  two tablets, honoring parents, Confirmation, one God, first fruits, pilgrimage,
  standing, climbing, receiving.

  Recommended Songs:

  "Torah" (*Apples on Holidays and
  Other Days* by Leah Abrams, Tara
  Productions)

  "Shavuot" (*Especially Wonderful Days*,
  by Steve Reuben A.R.E. Publishing,
  Inc.)

  "The Synagogue" (*Especially Jewish
  Symbols* by Jeff Klepper and Susan
  Nanus, A.R.E. Publishing, Inc.)

  "*Al Shalosh Regalim*" (*Seasoned with
  Song* by Julie Auerbach, Tara
  Publications)

- Shavuot is one of three pilgrimage festivals
  on which Jews made a trip to Jerusalem to
  the Temple. March around to one of the
  holiday songs.

- Have people share their reactions to the
  program. Ask families to complete one of
  these phrases:

  Shavuot is . . .

  Our family enjoyed . . .

  Our family learned . . .

  For this Shavuot, we . . .

- Send everyone off with a Shavuot greeting,
  "*Chag Sameach!*" (Happy Holiday!)

- Distribute copies of the *Megillat Ruth* play
  to the families to read at bedtime.

ON SHAVUOT

An Activity Book
Written By

_____

This is my picture. I know lots about Shavuot.

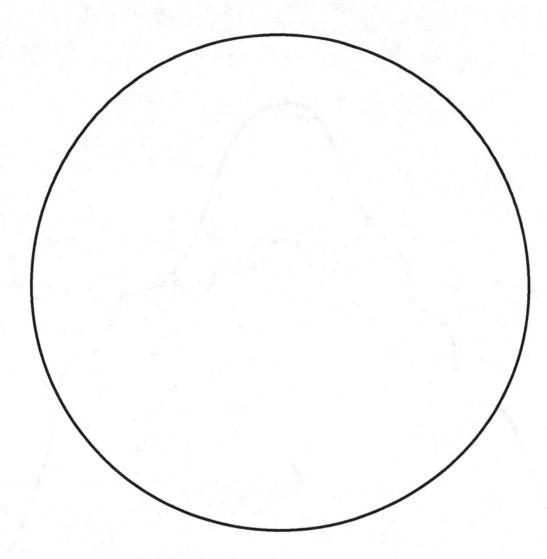

This is what I know . . .

Page 1

The Torah was given at Mount Sinai on Shavuot.

Draw your family at the base of the mountain.

On Shavuot we read the Ten Commandments from the Torah.

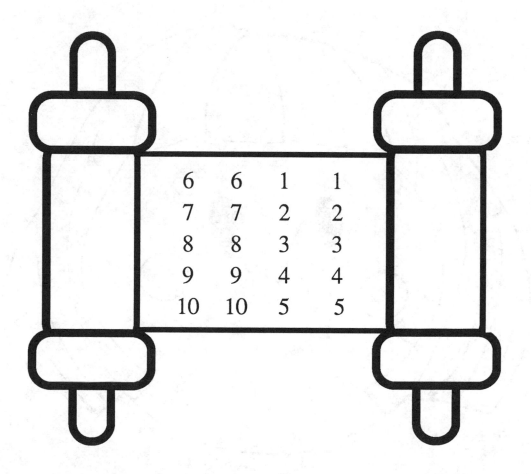

Connect the numbers to make ten lines on this Torah.

Page 3

On Shavuot we stand when the Ten Commandments are read.

Draw ears so that the child can hear the Ten Commandments.

On Shavuot our ancestors went on a pilgrimage to Jerusalem.
They walked to the Temple.

Color in your ancestors and give them some shoes.

Page 5

On Shavuot our ancestors brought BIKKURIM,
the best first fruits, vegetables, and animals to the Temple in Jerusalem.

Find a picture of a fruit or vegetable in a magazine.
Cut it out and glue it in these hands.

On Shavuot we read the story of Ruth.

Decorate this book jacket.

Page 7

We read the story of Ruth on Shavuot because Ruth gathered grain.
Boaz left grain in the corners of his field for Ruth and for others
who needed food.

Glue a grain of food (such as rice, cereal, oats, or corn)
in the four corners of this field.

On Shavuot many synagogues have CONFIRMATION.
Confirmation takes place in ninth/tenth/eleventh grade (circle one)
at our synagogue.

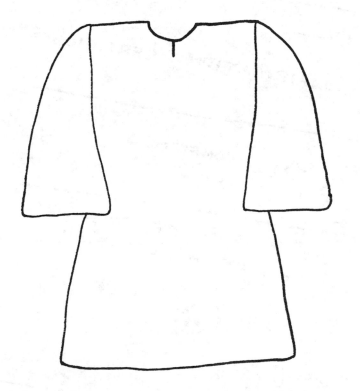

This is me in my Confirmation robe.

Page 9

On Shavuot, Confirmands affirm their faith in one God.

Fill in this Confirmation certificate.

On Shavuot people eat blintzes and other dairy products.

Recipe for

_____

_____

_____

_____

_____

_____

_____

_____

_____

from the kitchen of _____

This is my family's favorite dairy recipe.

Page 11

We eat blintzes on Shavuot because they resemble
the tablets of the Ten Commandments.

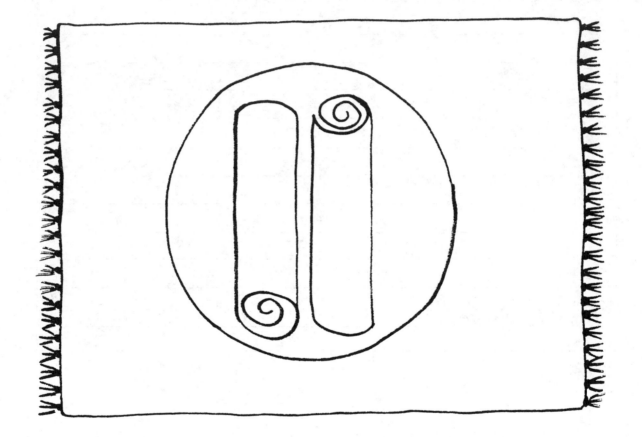

Glue a napkin and a plastic fork on the placemat
so that you can eat these blintzes.

Shavuot Magnets

1. Color these Shavuot symbols and cut them out.
2. Put a piece of magnetic tape on the back of each symbol.
3. Take the magnets home and use them on your refrigerator.

Torah
The Torah contains the Ten Commandments
and details of the first Shavuot.

Ruth and Naomi
We read the story of Ruth
on Shavuot.

Rose
Shavuot is known as the
Feast of Roses
in some Sephardic communities.

Road Sign
Shavuot is one of the three
pilgrimage festivals.

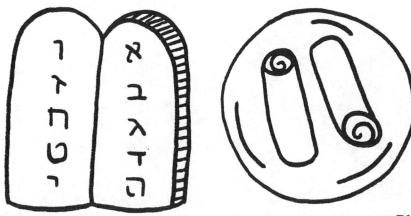

Ten Commandments
On Shavuot we celebrate the giving
of the Ten Commandments.

Blintzes
On Shavuot we eat dairy products.
This dairy product looks like the
two tablets of the Ten Commandments.

Paper Bag Puppet Pattern I

ELIMELECH

NAOMI

NAOMI

MAHLON
(Son)

CHILION
(Son)

RUTH

ORPAH

BOAZ

KING DAVID

Year 3

The Sweetness of the New Year
Rosh Hashanah, Year 3

Postcard and/or Flier:

To include:
Program Title
Sponsored by
Audience (age group, members only or
general public, etc.)
Date
Time
Location
Cost (if applicable)
RSVP or For Further Information

Physical Set Up

work area: tables and chairs
tables for supplies
table for name tags and sign-in sheet
large trash cans
trash bags

**Holiday Symbols, Customs, Terms,
and Concepts**

the Jewish year 57_ _
starting the new Jewish year
the color white as symbolic of purity on the
High Holy Days
dressing up for something special
dressing up the Torah for something special
the shofar
the "voices" of the shofar
circles/cycles
the sound of the shofar as a call to act
reflection: looking inside oneself

00:00 - 00:15
Mind Warmer: Greetings for the New Year

Families make New Year greeting cards.

Materials

name tags
markers
sign-in sheet
multiple colors of ¾" round dot labels
(stickers), available at office supply stores
copies of all three Shanah Tovah Greeting
Cards: Shofar, Apple, Torah — one of each
shape per child with the inside of the card
copied onto the back(see Directions and
Patterns)

Advance Preparation by the Facilitator

- Fill in the actual year of the Jewish New
Year before copying all three of the Shanah
Tovah Greeting Cards.

- The Shanah Tovah Greeting Cards have an
outside and an inside. Copy the cards on
white paper with the outside and inside
patterns back to back. Make certain that
when the card is folded, all pictures and
words are right side up.

- On the supply table, place the copies of the
Shanah Tovah Greeting Cards and colored
dot labels.

Procedure

- The Facilitator greets families as they
arrive. Have them fill out a name tag for
each family member and sign in.

- Inform the families that they will be making
Rosh Hashanah cards during the Mind
Warmer. Point them to the supply table
where they will find all the materials and
supplies.

- They fill in the shofar, apple, and Torah shapes with dot-shaped stickers.

- They finish decorating as desired.

Note: Families can mail the cards from home.

00:15 - 00:25
Introductions and Announcements

- The Facilitator welcomes everyone on behalf of the sponsoring agency/institution.

- The Facilitator introduces himself/herself and any other official representatives of the program or the agency/institution.

- Have a member of each family introduce himself/herself and other family members.

- Announce any upcoming events for the sponsoring agency/institution that are pertinent for this group.

- Instruct people as to how they can get on the mailing list if they are not already on it.

Setting the Stage

- The Facilitator says: Rosh Hashanah means "head of the year." It falls on the first day of the month of Tishri and is the first day of the year according to the Jewish calendar. Give families the first three digits of the current Jewish year. Have them guess the correct year. (Hopefully, someone will know the answer.)

Rosh Hashanah begins the cycle of all the Jewish holidays. As the Jewish New Year comes around again, we welcome it and use a round *challah.* During this program, we will learn about some of the other symbols and customs related to Rosh Hashanah. We say *L' Shanah Tovah u' Metukah,* which means "a good and sweet new year." (Have the participants repeat this greeting.)

00:25 - 00:45
Story: Announcing the Birthday of the World

This segment is a story and activity combined. In the story, a boy recognizes that Rosh Hashanah is the birthday of the world. He sets out to make a birthday party for the world. In keeping with the story, the families will play a game that teaches the shofar sounds.

Materials

1 copy of *The World's Birthday* by Barbara Diamond Goldin (New York: Harcourt, Brace and Janovich, 1990)
1 shofar
space to play the game

Procedure for Story

- The Facilitator reads *The World's Birthday.*

Procedure for Game

- Play the game *Tekiah, Shevarim, Teruah,* which is aimed at teaching the families the different shofar blasts.

- The Facilitator tells families that, through a game, they will learn the different blasts of the shofar. Each sound of the shofar will be associated with steps.

- Have the families stand in a row with everyone on the starting line. Now teach the sounds of the shofar and the accompanying steps:

Tekiah (families repeat the name) — everyone takes one long step

Shevarim (families repeat the name) — everyone takes three regular walking steps

Teruah (families repeat the name) — everyone takes nine short steps

- The Facilitator sounds the shofar. If unable

to do so, invite someone who can. Or, use a kazoo. Or, sing the blasts.

- Have the group practice taking the steps one more time.

- Now play the game. Players walk from the starting line to the finish line, using the appropriate size and number of steps dictated by the sounds of the shofar.

- Teach *Tekiah Gedolah*, one long blast, as a single giant step.

00:45 - 00:55
Snack: The New Year Comes Around Again

For this snack, serve apples, honey, pomegranate, apple juice, foods symbolic of a happy and sweet new year. *Rimonim* means pomegranate, and also means Torah crowns. According to legend, a pomegranate has 613 seeds, one for each commandment in the Torah.

Materials

lemon juice (optional)
apples
honey
pomegranate
apple juice
napkins
plates
cups
knife
serving spoon

Advance Preparation by the Facilitator

- Slice apples before the program. (Sprinkle apples with a little lemon juice to delay the browning.)

- Slice a pomegranate or two for families to sample.

Procedure

- The Facilitator explains the symbolism associated with this snack. Let the families know that after the snack, they will be looking at *rimonim* and other parts of the Torah dressings.

- With the group, recite the appropriate blessing (see Blessing #7, page 488).

- Teach the *Shehecheyanu* blessing, which is recited on the new year (see Blessing #5, page 488).

- Enjoy eating this High Holy Day treat.

00:55 - 01:15
Activity: The Torah Gets Special Clothes for the High Holy Days, Too

The Torah covers in the Ark are changed from their usual bright colored mantles to mantles of all white. This activity highlights that custom.

Materials

1 copy per family of the Dress Your Torah for the High Holy Days! Directions on white paper (see Directions and Patterns)
1 copy per child of the Torah and Binder on white card stock (see Directions and Patterns)
1 sheet per child of Torah Ornaments (breast plate, *yad, keter,* and *rimonim)* on gold card stock (see Directions and Patterns)
1 sheet per child of the Mantle for the Rest of the Year on colored card stock per child (see Directions and Patterns). If desired, choose the color of the Torah covers at your synagogue or institution.
1 sheet per child of the White Mantle for the High Holy Days on white card stock (see Directions and Patterns)
1 sandwich-size Ziplock bag per child

gold or silver glitter, gold braid, buttons, "jewels" (these items are optional)

gluesticks (optional)

scissors

1 additional set for the Facilitator of Torah and Binder, Torah Ornaments, and both Mantles enlarged onto 11" x 17" white paper (see Directions and Patterns)

poster board: one white sheet; one gold or yellow sheet; one red, green, or blue sheet

Advance Preparation by the Facilitator

- Enlarge the Torah and Binder, Torah Ornaments, and Mantles onto the 11" x 17" white paper. You need two Torah mantles, one in white and one in a bright color, such as red, green, or blue. Trace the Torah and two Mantle patterns onto sturdy white poster board. Cut these out.

- Trace the Torah Ornaments onto the gold or yellow poster board. Cut out the ornaments. Trace the Mantle and Torah Binder onto the green, red, or blue poster board. Cut these out.

- Dress the enlarged "Torah" with the colored mantle and all the ornaments.

- On the supply table, place the following materials: copies of the Torah and Binder, Torah Ornaments, Mantles, the Ziplock bags, the Dress Your Torah for High Holy Days Directions, and, if desired, decorations — glitter, braid, buttons, and jewels.

- On the supply table, place these items, each in a separate container: scissors and gluesticks.

Procedure

- The Facilitator holds up the poster board Torah. Ask: Why do people wear special clothes to synagogue on Rosh Hashanah

and when they celebrate the holiday at someone's home? (Let families respond.) Explain that the Torah gets special clothes for the High Holy Days, too. These special clothes are white.

- Discuss why the Torah has special clothes for Rosh Hashanah and why the Torah covering is white on Rosh Hashanah. (White is a symbol of purity, simplicity, mourning. We change the Torah covers to let people know this is a holy, very special day that is unlike other days.)

- Go over the names of the different Torah ornaments. Remove the ornaments.

- Change the mantle of the Torah from the regular bright blue, red, or green to white, as is done for Rosh Hashanah.

- Explain that families will now make their own Torah "paperdolls" with mantles and ornaments.

- Ask one or two representatives from each work table to get the materials from the supply table.

- Families cut out the Torah and Binder, Torah Ornaments, and both Mantles.

- (optional) Families decorate the Torah Mantles by gluing on glitter, braid, buttons, and jewels.

- Families practice dressing and undressing the paperdoll Torah, and practice the names of all the dressings.

- They place their Torah and Torah dressings in a Ziplock plastic bag.

01:15 - 01:30
Closure: Our Voices Welcome the New Year

End the program with singing, movement, sharing, and holiday greetings.

Materials

1 copy per family of Kolot (Voices) pattern on white paper (see Directions and Patterns)

Procedure

• Sing and move to Rosh Hashanah music related to: the new year, growth, colors, cycles, the Torah, the parts of the Torah, the shofar, the blasts of the shofar, warning sounds, reflecting, changing our ways, *L'Shanah Tovah.*

Recommended Songs:

"Sing Along Song: Rosh HaShanah" (*Especially Wonderful Days* by Steve Reuben, A.R.E. Publishing, Inc.)

"Happy Rosh Hashanah to You" (*Seasoned With Song* by Julie Auerbach, Tara Publications)

• Have participants people share their reactions to the program. Ask families to complete one of these phrases:

The High Holy Days are . . .

Our family learned . . .

Our family enjoyed . . .

For this Rosh Hashanah, we . . .

• Send everyone off with High Holy Day greetings, *"L'Shanah Tovah u'Metukah"* (A Good and Sweet New Year).

• Send famlies home with the Kolot (Voices) pattern. They can play the game at home.

Shanah Tovah Card — Shofar

Shanah Tovah
Happy New Year
This Year Is

Shanah Tovah Card — Apple

Shanah Tovah
Happy New Year
This Year Is

Shanah Tovah Card — Torah

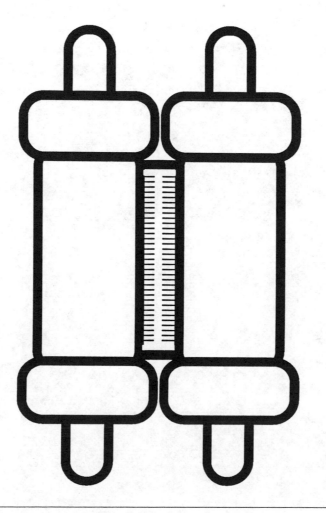

Shanah Tovah
Happy New Year
This Year Is _____

Dress Your Torah for the
High Holy Days!

(Directions)

1. Cut out your Torah, as well as all of its ornaments, and both mantles.

2. If desired, decorate the mantles.

3. Have fun dressing your Torah and learning the names of each ornament.

4. When the High Holy Days come, dress your Torah in its white mantle (the same color the High Priest wore during Yom Kippur services in Temple times), and put on its finest ornaments.

Torah and Binder

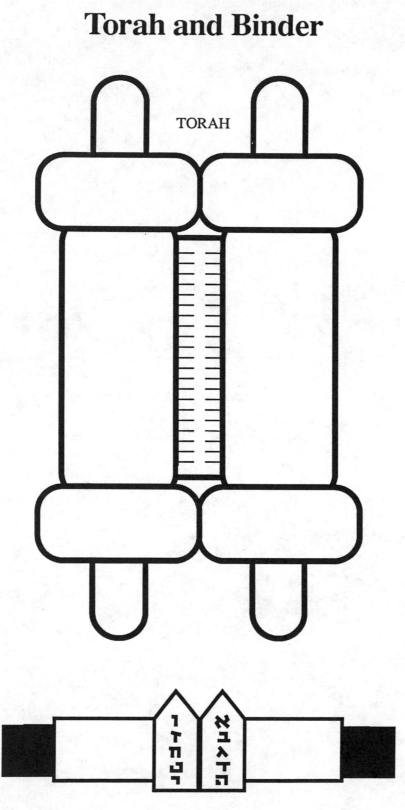

TORAH

BINDER

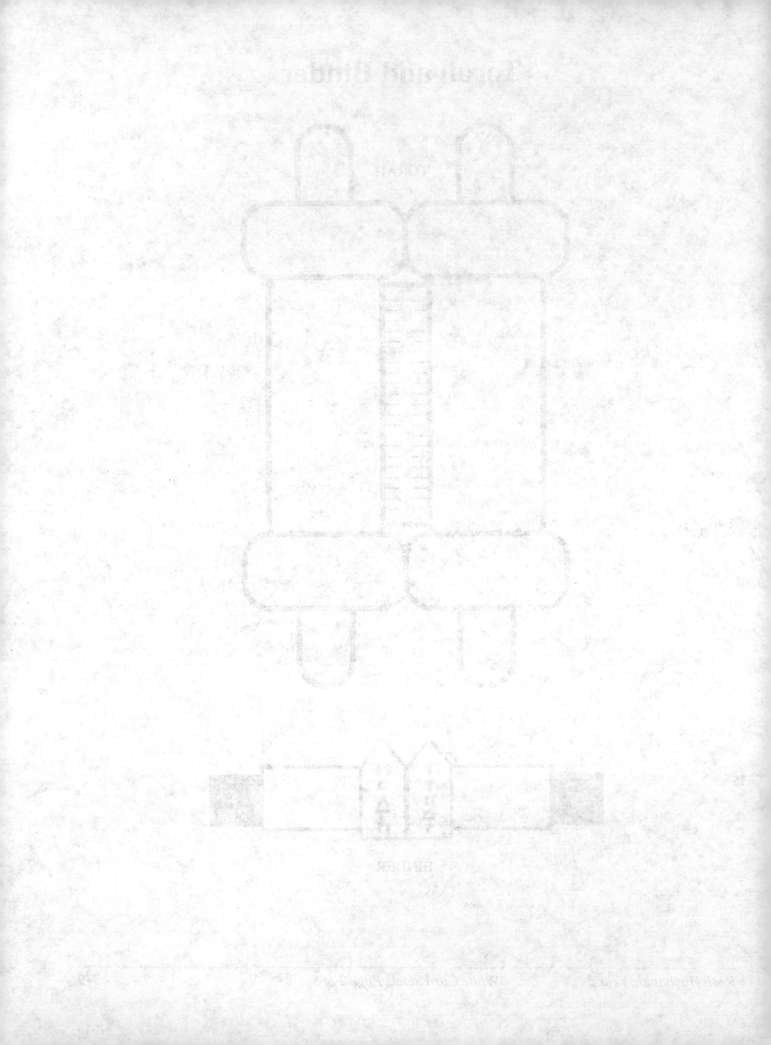

Torah Ornaments

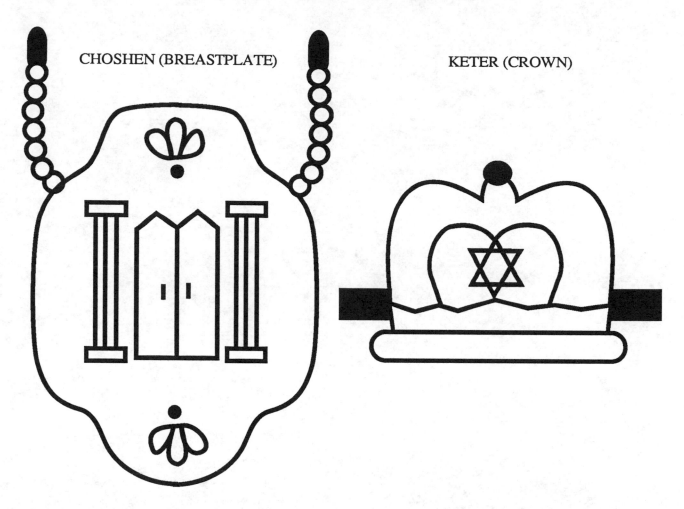

CHOSHEN (BREASTPLATE)

KETER (CROWN)

YAD
(from the Hebrew word for hand)

RIMONIM
(from the Hebrew word for pomegranate)

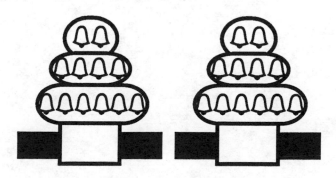

Mantle for the Rest of the Year

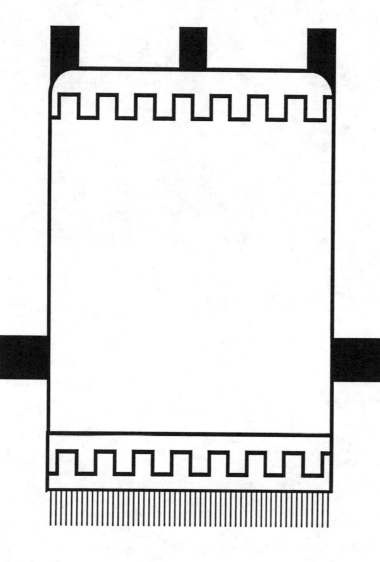

Feel free to add a decorative
design to this colored mantle.

White Mantle for the High Holy Days

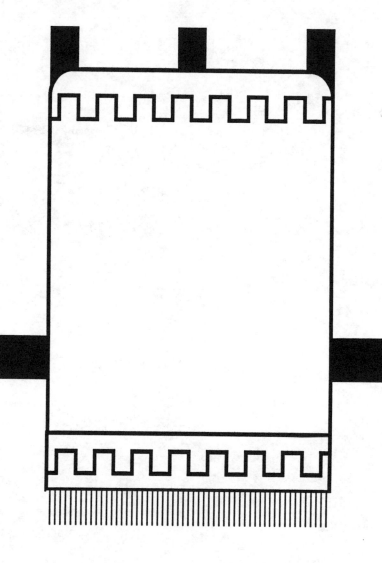

Feel free to add a decorative
design to this white mantle.

Kolot (Voices)

The shofar sounds out four blasts during the High Holy Days.

Tekiah

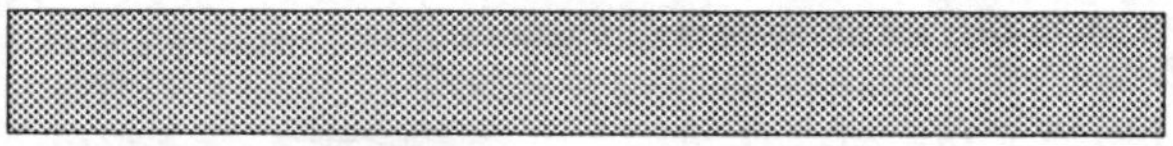

(1 long sound)

Shevarim

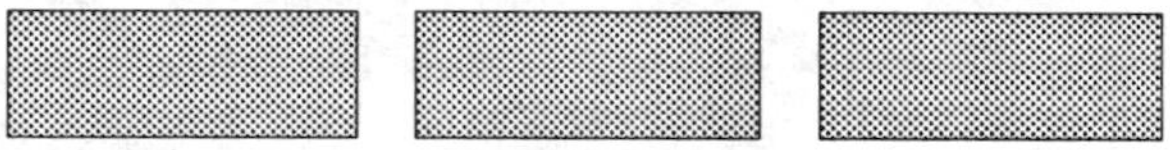

(3 short sounds)

Teruah

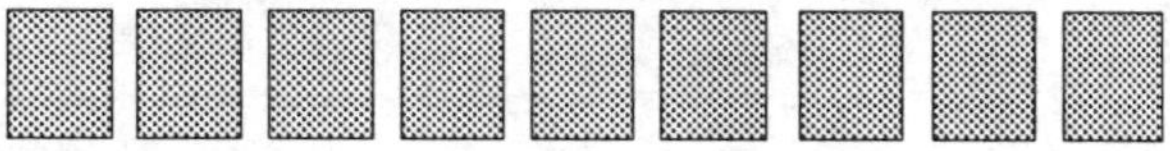

(9 quick sounds)

Tekiah Gedolah

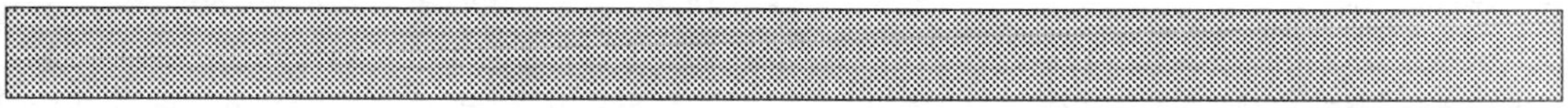

(a very long, loud sound)

Sukkot Under the Stars
Sukkot, Year 3

Postcard and/or Flier

To include:
Program Title
Sponsored by
Audience (age group, members only or
    general public, etc.)
Date
Time
Location
Cost (if applicable)
RSVP or For Further Information
Bring an empty tennis ball or Pringles can
    and top, or other can with a plastic or
    reusable lid.
Wear outdoor clothes suitable for working.

Physical Set Up

work area: tables and chairs
tables for supplies
table for name tags and sign-in sheet
table on which to display sample
    tzedakah boxes
large trash cans
trash bags
a *sukkah* for hanging food and projects
    (optional)

Holiday Symbols, Customs, Terms, and Concepts

the *mitzvah* of building a *sukkah*
decorating a *sukkah*
the *mitzvah* of eating in a *sukkah*
the *sukkah* as a temporary dwelling
the *sukkah* as shelter
elements of a *sukkah*: three free standing
    walls, a ceiling through which stars may be
    seen, a temporary structure
harvest festival
local or regional harvest foods
lulav and *etrog*: four species
tzedakah box
Mazon, the organization that fights against
    hunger
tzedakah as a modern day offering

00:00 – 00:15
Mind Warmer: A Modern Day Offering: The Family Tzedakah Box

Families make their own *tzedakah* box,
decorating it with pictures of food. Through
this activity, they associate the ancient tradition of bringing a harvest offering with the
symbolic act of giving *tzedakah*.

Materials

name tags
markers
sign-in sheet
enough Contact paper for each family to cover
    their *tzedakah* box
pictures of food for each child (labels from
    boxes or cans of food, food coupons, food
    stickers, or magazines with lots of food
    pictures)
extra tennis ball or Pringles cans
samples of *tzedakah* boxes (from organiza-
    tions such as the Jewish National Fund,
    UNICEF, Leukemia, Diabetes, etc.)
scissors
transparent tape
gluesticks

Advance Preparation by the Facilitator

- On the supply table, place these materials: name tags; magazines and coupons, etc., with food pictures; Contact paper; extra Pringle or tennis ball cans.

- On the supply table, place these items, each in a separate container: gluesticks, scissors, markers, and transparent tape.

- Set up a table with the sample *tzedakah* boxes for families to view as they enter the room.

- Prepare a sample of the *tzedakah* box that families will make.

Procedure

- The Facilitator greets families as they arrive. Have them fill out a name tag for each family member and sign in.

- The Facilitator shows families the sample *tzedakah* boxes.

- Direct families to the supply table where they will gather materials to make their own *tzedakah* box.

- At the work tables, families write their family name(s) on a name tag and decorate it.

- They glue and/or tape onto a tennis ball or Pringles can the pictures of food, covering the entire can.

- They stick on the extra name tag.

- They cut Contact paper large enough to cover the can and cover it.

- Using the scissors, adults cut a slit for coins in the plastic lid.

00:15 – 00:25
Introductions and Announcements

Materials

1 Mazon brochure per family

Procedure

- The Facilitator welcomes everyone on behalf of the sponsoring agency/institution.

- The Facilitator introduces himself/herself and any other official representatives of the program or the agency/institution.

- Have a member of each family introduce himself/herself and other family members. Have each family share a favorite food.

- Announce any upcoming events for the sponsoring agency/institution that are pertinent for this group.

- Instruct people as to how they can get on the mailing list if they are not already on it.

Setting the Stage

- The Facilitator introduces the word *mazon*, meaning food or sustenance. Explain that Sukkot began as a harvest festival.

  Say: On Sukkot, Jews brought the foods they grew (such as wheat for making bread, and grapes, etc.) to the Temple. Sukkot is a time for thanking God for our food.
  One way of showing our thanks to God is by sharing our food with others. Some people do not have enough food. On Sukkot, we give cans of food for the needy. Or, we give money to help feed the hungry.

  Mazon is a special Jewish group which is helping to do away with hunger. (Pass out the Mazon brochures.) Mazon reminds us that each time we celebrate with food, we need to think of others who are hungry.

Mazon is a good organization for the money you will collect in your new family *tzedakah* box. You can do this during Sukkot, or at any time during the year.

Contributing to a *tzedakah* box is a Jewish tradition. Some families put all their change, or just their pennies and nickels, in the *tzedakah* box every day. Some families contribute to the family *tzedakah* box before Shabbat begins. Some families put a few coins in the family *tzedakah* box every time something nice or good happens. As a family, you may decide on your own family custom.

We will spend the rest of the program preparing for Sukkot and learning about Sukkot customs and symbols.

00:25 – 00:50
Activity: Sukkot Hangings

Choosing from four possible projects, families make *sukkah* hangings and decorations.

Materials

wallpaper books or sheets of extra wallpaper
rug yarn or other thick yarn
onion sacks
curly ribbon
1 piece of fruit, vegetable, corn, or gourd for every 2-3 children
1 6" cardboard cake rounds per child
1 set per child of Sukkot Mobile I, II, III, and IV on the following colors of card stock:
backbone and eyes on white card stock
lips and heart on pink card stock
myrtle, palm, and willow branches on green card stock
etrog on bright yellow card stock
metallic or foil paper

scissors
gluesticks
single hole punches
staplers
staples
pencils
1 Shimmery Star Pattern for every 2-3 families (see Directions and Patterns)
1 Fruit Sack Pattern for hanging fruit for every 2-3 families on 11" x 17" white paper (see Patterns and Directions)
1 Sukkot Paper Chain Pattern for every 2-3 families (see Directions and Patterns)

Advance Preparation by the Facilitator

* Pre-cut four 18" strands of rug yarn per child.

* One the supply table, place the following materials: 6" cardboard cake rounds, 18" strands of rug yarn, Sukkot Mobile I, II, III, and IV copied onto card stock, metallic or foil paper, wallpaper books or sheets of wallpaper scraps, fruit or vegetables or gourds, onion sack meshing, ribbon, Shimmery Star Pattern sheets, Fruit Sack Pattern for hanging fruit sheets, and Sukkot Paper Chain Pattern sheets.

* Make samples of all the projects (see Procedures).

* On the supply table, place these items, each in a separate container: scissors, gluesticks, single hole punches, staplers, staples, and pencils.

Procedure

* The Facilitator explains that families will have their choice of four possible projects. The hangings and decorations they make may be hung in their home, in their home *sukkah*, or in the community's *sukkah*.

(Encourage families to make one project to take home and one for the community *sukkah*.)

- One project revolves around a *midrash* about the *lulav* and *etrog*. The *midrash* relates how a *lulav* and *etrog* are like a person. The *midrash* pairs palm and spine, myrtle leaves and eyes, willow leaves and mouth, *etrog* and the heart. Families will have an opportunity to make a mobile based on this *midrash*.

- The Facilitator holds up the samples of all the projects. Tell families to get the materials for their first project from the supply table. They can get additional materials for other projects when they are ready.

To Make Sukkot Mobiles:

- Families punch holes in the 6" cardboard cake round at 12, 3, 6, and 9 o'clock.

- Families knot together four pieces of 18" rug yarn at one end.

- They thread one strand of rug yarn down, around, and down again into each hole of the 6" pie circles.

- They cut out mobile parts from the card stock.

- They pair the mobile parts as follows:
  heart – *etrog*
  lips – willow
  eye – myrtle
  spine – palm

- They glue the body part and matching specie back to back.

- They punch a hole in the top of each of the glued back-to-back body part/matching specie.

- They attach pairs to string by tying knots through the holes.

To String Fruit:

- Families cut four 4' strands of curly ribbon.

- They cut out the circle from the Fruit Sack Pattern. They use the circle as a pattern to cut out a piece of onion sack.

- They tie the four ribbons together 6" from one end. At the knot, they divide the ribbon into two groups of two and thread the ribbons in and out of the net starting from the double holes (see circle pattern) and working in opposite directions (see arrows on circle pattern) to meet at the other set of double holes. (Be sure the knot is on the outside.)

- They place fruit, vegetable, or gourd in the center of the bag. Then gather it by pulling ribbons and tying together tightly.

- They tie a knot 6" from the top of loose ends.

- They curl the ribbon strands using the blade of a scissors.

To Make Glittery Stars:

- Families trace and cut out four stars so that they are all the same size. They make six-pointed Jewish stars.

- They fold the stars in half.

- They glue the folded star halves one on top of the other. (If the material has a dull side, it is the dull sides that are glued.)

- They open "loose" top half star and "loose" bottom half star, pulling them so that they are now back-to-back. They glue them together to create a multi-dimensional star.

- They punch a hole at the top.

- They attach a longish strand of ribbon.

To Make Paper Chains:

- Families cut out the paper chain from the Sukkot Paper Chain Pattern.

- They trace the shape on the wallpaper scraps and cut them out.

- They weave one strip through the other, making links.

- The Facilitator or a parent staples together the chains made by the various families.

Conclusion of Activity

- When everyone has had a chance to complete one or two projects, the Facilitator asks families to clean up, returning materials to the supply table.

- The Facilitator takes the group out to the *sukkah* and hangs the *sukkah* decorations. (If there is no community *sukkah* at your location, the group makes a human *sukkah*. Parents form the four walls, raising their hands above their heads and linking with other parents. The children decorate the *sukkah*, raising their hands with the projects in them. *Voila*, a decorated *sukkah*!)

00:50 – 01:00
Snack: Our Harvest Foods

This snack provides an opportunity to fulfill the *mitzvah* of eating in a *sukkah* (real or pretend). Participants will learn what foods are harvested nearby. Serve some of these foods. Be resourceful.

Materials

harvest foods and harvest drinks from your locale, region, or country

napkins
cups
other serving materials as needed

Procedure

This segment of the program should be done in the *sukkah* if possible.

- The Facilitator explains what a harvest is and describes the products that in biblical times were harvested in Israel at Sukkot — grains, grapes, dates, and figs.

- Ask the participants to come up with foods that are harvested in your area. Inform the families of the harvest foods selected for their snack.

- Teach the blessing for sitting in the *sukkah* (see Blessing #10, page 488).

- Recite the appropriate blessing from the Blessings section on pages 487-489. Eat the selected "harvest crop." Enjoy!

01:00 – 01:10
Story in the Sukkah

The story for today is about one family's urban *sukkah*, a *sukkah* on the roof. Weather permitting, join together in the *sukkah* for the reading.

Materials

1 copy of *The Sukkah on the Roof: A Sukkot Story* by David Adler (New York: Bonim Books, 1976)

Procedure

- The Facilitator reads the story *The Sukkah on the Roof: A Sukkot Story*.

01:10 – 01:30
Closure: Raising the Roof with Sukkot Music and Movement

End the program with singing, shaking, sharing, and holiday greetings. If available, and weather permitting, do this activity in the *sukkah* using a real *lulav*.

• Sing and move to Sukkot songs related to: the *sukkah*, *lulav*, and *etrog*, body parts, stars in the sky, harvesting, harvest foods, helping others, *tzedakah, tzedakah* box.

Recommended Songs:

"The Lulav" (*Seasoned With Song* by Julie Auerbach, Tara Publications)

"Sukkot Song" (*Especially Wonderful Days* by Steve Reuben, A.R.E. Publishing, Inc.)

"Build a Sukkah" (*Rabbi Joe Black Sings*, Temple Israel, 2324 Emerson Avenue S., Minneapolis, MN 55404)

• Practice shaking bodies like a *lulav* — right, left, forward, back, up, and down. (Optional: Wave a real *lulav*.)

• Have participants share their reactions to the program. Ask families to complete one of these phrases:

Our family likes Sukkot because . . .

Our family learned . . .

Our family enjoyed . . .

For Sukkot, we . . .

• Send everyone off with a Sukkot greeting, *"Chag Sameach!"* (Happy Holiday!)

Sukkot Mobile I

How is a *lulav* like my body?

EYES — myrtle leaves are round like my eyes.

SPINE — the *lulav* is shaped like my spine.

Sukkot Mobile II

How is a *lulav* like my body?

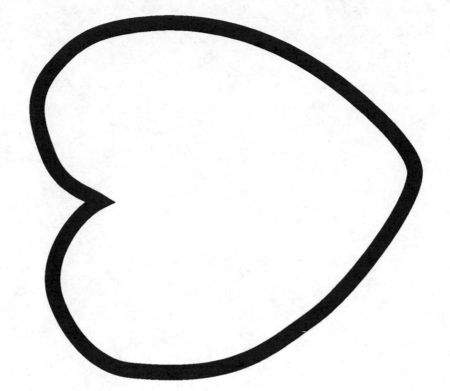

HEART — the *etrog* is shaped like my heart.

MOUTH — willow leaves are shaped like my mouth.

Sukkot Mobile III

How is a *lulav* like my body?

Myrtle leaves are round like my eyes.

Willow leaves are shaped like my mouth.

The *lulav* is shaped like my spine.

Sukkot Mobile IV

How is a *lulav* like my body?

The *etrog* is shaped like my heart.

Shimmery Star Pattern

1. Use this pattern to cut four stars from foil paper.

2. Fold each star in half (shiny sides together) along the imaginary fold line marked on the pattern.

3. Make a stack of folded stars by gluing the folded stars dull sides together.

4. Glue the top dull star half to the very bottom dull star half. This will open your star into a shimmery *sukkah* decoration.

5. Punch a hole in the top point. Thread with ribbon and hang in the *sukkah*.

Fruit Sack Pattern

1. Cut four strands of ribbon 4' long.

2. Use this circle as a pattern to cut a circle from an onion, potato, or citrus sack.

3. Tie the four ribbons together 6" from one end. At the knot, divide the ribbon into two groups of two and thread the ribbons in and out of the net circle starting from double holes and working in opposite directions (see arrows) to meet at the other set of double holes. Note: be sure the knot is on the outside (see example).

4. Place fruit in the center of the bag. Gather by pulling ribbons and tying together tightly.

5. Tie a knot 6" from the top of loose ends.

6. Curl all strands.

TWO RIBBONS   TWO RIBBONS

Knot

Sukkot Paper Chain Pattern

Place over wallpaper scraps. Fold and cut out shaded areas.

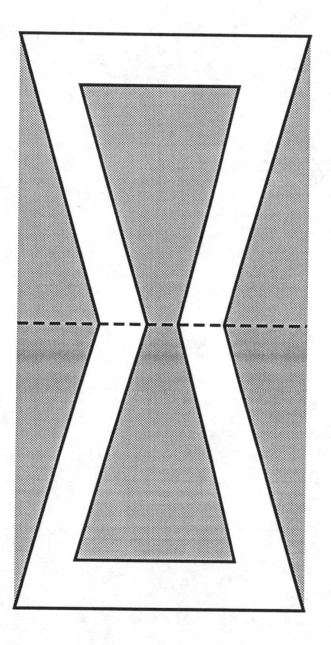

A Three Star Celebration: Star Light, Star Bright, It's Havdalah We Do Tonight
Shabbat, Year 3

Postcard and/or Flier:

To include:
Program Title
Sponsored by
Audience (age group, members only or
  general public, etc.)
Date
Time
Location
Cost (if applicable)
RSVP or For Further Information
Bring an empty 35mm film canister (extras
  are appreciated).

Physical Set Up

work area: tables and chairs
tables for supplies
table for name tags and sign-in sheet
large trash cans
trash bags

**Holiday Symbols, Customs, Terms,
and Concepts**

six days of creation and one day of rest
rest and work
God and human beings
day and night
holy and profane (ordinary)
experiencing a taste of *olam haba* (the world
  to come)
Havdalah
besamim (spice box)
braided Havdalah candle
sweetness of Shabbat
spices

Kiddush cup
stars — marking time
Shavuah Tov, a good week
ending Shabbat, beginning a new week
the Havdalah blessings
the five senses used in enjoying Shabbat

**00:00 – 00:10
Mind Warmer: Creating out of Clay**

Introduce Shabbat as a day of rest and
reflection.

Materials

name tags
markers
sign-in sheet
Play Dough or pliable clay, enough for each
  child to have a chunk

Procedure

- The Facilitator greets families as they
  arrive. Have them fill out a name tag for
  each family member and sign in.

- The Facilitator gives each family a lump of
  Play Dough or clay. (Or, this material may
  be placed on the supply table.) Instruct
  families to play with the clay, creating
  shapes, objects, aliens from outer space,
  whatever.

- When three minutes remain, the Facilitator
  asks families to bring a creation with them to
  the Introductions and Announcements area.

00:10 – 00:20

Introductions and Announcements

- The Facilitator welcomes everyone on behalf of the sponsoring agency/institution.

- The Facilitator introduces himself/herself and any other official representatives of the program or the agency/institution.

- Have a member of each family introduce himself/herself and other family members. Families show off and share their clay creations.

- Announce any upcoming events for the sponsoring agency/institution that are pertinent for this group.

- Instruct people as to how they can get on the mailing list if they are not already on it.

Setting the Stage

- The Facilitator says: Today's program is about Shabbat. Shabbat is a day of rest, the day on which God rested after six days of creating. We, like God, create and work and go to school for six days. But, on the seventh day — Shabbat — we rest. We stop creating and reflect and admire and think about all that happened during the week. Take a moment to look at and think about your Play Dough/clay creation(s). (Collect the clay.)

During today's program, we will pay special attention to Havdalah. Havdalah is the ceremony which ends Shabbat and begins a new week. We say blessings over wine, candle, spices, and the end of Shabbat. We sing a song about the prophet Elijah, and a song that wishes everyone a good week, "*Shavua Tov.*"

We perform Havdalah on Saturday evening after there are three stars in the sky. At that time, there is darkness except for our braided Havdalah candle.

Now we are going to hear a story about darkness. Then we will participate in a Havdalah service. You will see the Havdalah symbols, learn the Havdalah blessings, and sing some Havdalah songs.

00:20 – 00:40

Story: The Very First Darkness and Havdalah Service

This story, "Adam and Eve and the Very First Darkness," deals with light and darkness. In the Havdalah service, we recognize the separation between light and darkness, between Shabbat and the rest of the week, and between the holy and the ordinary. This story conveys the mystery of these contrasting images in a way understandable to pre-schoolers. After the story, families will participate in a Havdalah service.

Materials

1 copy of "Adam and Eve and the Very First Darkness" found in *Exploring Our Living Past,* edited by Jules Harlow (New York: Behrman House, 1979)

1 sample Havdalah Kit (see Activity), which is a Havdalah set consisting of a candle holder, braided Havdalah candle, *Kiddush* cup, wine, spice box with fragrant spices (if the synagogue or institution or agency has a Havdalah set, have it *and* the sample Kit available)

matches

Procedure

- The Facilitator reads the story "Adam and Eve and the Very First Darkness."

- The Facilitator introduces the Havdalah

service. Say: Havdalah is a service which marks the end of Shabbat, and the beginning of the new week. Traditionally, Havdalah takes place when there are three stars in the sky. Havdalah is a service, often held at home, sometimes held at a synagogue.

Havdalah involves all five senses: We *see* the light of the candle. (Hold up the braided candle.) We *smell* the spices that remind us of the sweetness of Shabbat. (Show the spice box.) We *taste* the wine symbolic of the joy of Shabbat. (Hold up the *Kiddush* cup.) We *hear* beautiful prayers and songs. We *touch* the symbols, and *feel* the closeness of others.

- The Facilitator leads a Havdalah service using the Owner's Manual from the Havdalah Kit made during the Activity. First darken the room. Practice each blessing as it is recited by having the participants repeat the Hebrew. (Aim for familiarity, not memorization.)

- Sing *"Eliyahu HaNavi"* and *"Shavua Tov."* The words are found in the Owner's Manual for the Havdalah Kit.

00:40 – 00:50
Snack: Star Grazing

Snack consists of star-shaped cookies called Zimsterne and grape juice. It is a European tradition to eat spicy star-shaped cookies for Havdalah, because of the three stars that must appear before Havdalah. The grape juice is symbolic of the wine drunk during the Havdalah service.

Materials

Zimsterne (star-shaped cookies)
grape juice

cups
napkins

Advance Preparation by the Facilitator

- Make these cookies using the Zimsterne recipe (see page 385). Add sprinkles to make the stars sparkle. (Or, find a bakery that will make star-shaped cookies.)

- Recite a blessing before eating (see Blessing #8, page 488).

00:50 – 01:10
Activity: Assembling a Havdalah Kit

Now that the families have participated in a Havdalah ceremony, they assemble a Havdalah Kit for use in their own homes. The Havdalah Kit includes all the symbols and comes with instructions.

Materials

1 copy per child of the Havdalah Kit Owner's Manual cover on any color card stock (see pages 387 and 388 in Directions and Patterns)
1 copy per child of the Havdalah Kit Owner's Manual sheets on white paper (see pages 383-386 in Directions and Patterns)
1 Our Havdalah Kit Label per child on bright colored paper (see Directions and Patterns)
1 Shavua Tov luggage tag per child on any color card stock (see Directions and Patterns)
3 thin candles per child in a variety of colors, or just blue and white
1 clear plastic wine cup per child
extra empty film canisters
whole cloves
cinnamon sticks
other desired whole spices
1 colorful gift bag with handles per child

ribbon or yarn
scissors
single hole punches
gluesticks
one bowl of warm water per work table

Advance Preparation by the Facilitator

- White out the information at the bottom of pages 383, 385, and 387. Make copies of the Havdalah Kit Owner's Manual cover and the inside pages. To make a sample Manual, fold in half so that the cover is on the outside and the inside pages are in order. Staple twice on fold.

- On the supply table, place the following materials: thin candles, clear plastic wine glasses, film canisters, Shavua Tov Luggage Tags, Our Havdalah Kit Labels, colorful gift bags, ribbon or yarn, spices in paper cups, and Havdalah Kit Owner's Manual.

- On the supply table, place these items, each in a separate container: crayons, single hole punches, scissors, and gluesticks.

Procedure

- The Facilitator explains that each family will make their own Havdalah Kit. This includes: a Havdalah Kit Owner's Manual, Havdalah candle, *Kiddush* cup, and spice box.

- Ask one or two representatives from each work table to collect the items they need for making their Havdalah Kit.

- Each family makes a Havdalah Kit. They dip the candles in warm water to soften the wax. They twist the candles. (Twisting works better than braiding.)

- They fill the film canister with spices.

- They punch a hole in their Shavua Tov Luggage Tag, then attach the tag to the gift bag with string or yarn.

- They fill out their name tag and glue it onto the gift bag.

- They decorate the cover of the Havdalah Kit Owner's Manual.

- They place all the items in the gift bag.

- The Facilitator asks families to clean up, returning materials to the supply table.

01:10 – 01:30
Closure: Twinkle, Twinkle Havdalah Star

End the program with singing, sharing, and a Shabbat greeting.

- Sing and move to Shabbat music related to: Shabbat, clay, creation, darkness, light, stars, Havdalah, Adam and Eve, spices.

    Recommended Songs:

    "Havdalah" (*Especially Jewish Symbols* by Jeff Klepper, A.R.E. Publishing, Inc.)

    "Menorah" (*Especially Jewish Symbols* by Jeff Klepper, A.R.E. Publishing, Inc.)

- Review the songs "*Eliyahu HaNavi*" and "*Shavua Tov.*"

- Have participants share their reactions to the program. Ask families to complete one of these phrases:

    Havdalah is . . .

    Our family enjoyed . . .

    Our family learned . . .

    Next Shabbat . . .

- Send everyone off with an end of Shabbat greeting, "*Shavua Tov!*" (Have a good week!)

Songs

Eliyahu HaNavi
(Elijah the Prophet)
Eliyahu Ha-navi.
Eliyahu Ha-tishbi.
Eliyahu, Eliyahu,
Eliyahu Ha-giladee.

Bimheyrah Ve' yameynu.
Yavo Aleynu.
Im Mashiach Ben David,
Im Mashiach Ben
David.

Eliyahu Ha-navi.
Eliyahu Ha-tishbi.
Eliyahu, Eliyahu,
Eliyahu Ha-giladee.

Elijah the Prophet.
Elijah the Tishbite.
Elijah, Elijah, Elijah,
the Giladee.

Come speedily in our time.
Come to us with the Messiah.
Son of David.

Shavua Tov
Shavua Tov (eight times).
Sing twice:
A good week.
A week of peace.
May gladness reign
and joy increase.
Shavua Tov! A Good Week!

אֵלִיָּהוּ הַנָּבִיא, אֵלִיָּהוּ
הַתִּשְׁבִּי; אֵלִיָּהוּ, אֵלִיָּהוּ,
אֵלִיָּהוּ הַגִּלְעָדִי.
בִּמְהֵרָה בְיָמֵינוּ, יָבוֹא
אֵלֵינוּ; עִם מָשִׁיחַ בֶּן
דָּוִד, עִם מָשִׁיחַ בֶּן
דָּוִד. אֵלִיָּהוּ . . .

שָׁבוּעַ טוֹב . . .

The final prayer signifies the separation between the days of the week and Shabbat, between the six days of creation and God's resting, between light and darkness, and between the sacred and the profane.

בָּרוּךְ אַתָּה יְיָ, אֱלֹהֵינוּ מֶלֶךְ הָעוֹלָם, הַמַּבְדִּיל בֵּין קֹדֶשׁ לְחוֹל, בֵּין אוֹר לְחֹשֶׁךְ, בֵּין יִשְׂרָאֵל לָעַמִּים, בֵּין יוֹם הַשְּׁבִיעִי לְשֵׁשֶׁת יְמֵי הַמַּעֲשֶׂה. בָּרוּךְ אַתָּה יְיָ, הַמַּבְדִּיל בֵּין קֹדֶשׁ לְחוֹל.

Baruch Atah Adonai Eloheynu Melech Ha-olam Ha-mavdil Beyn Chodesh L'chol, Beyn Or L'choshech, Beyn Yisrael La'amim, Beyn Yom Ha'sh'vi-ee L'shayshet Y'mai Ha-ma'aseh. Baruch Atah Adonai Ha-mavdil Beyn Chodesh L'chol.

Blessed are You, Eternal our God, Ruler of the Universe, Who distinguishes between sacred and profane, light and darkness, Israel and the other nations, the seventh day and the six days of creation. Blessed are You, Eternal our God, Who distinguished between sacred and profane.

Sip the wine. Extinguish the candle in the cup of wine or pour the wine on the plate and extinguish the candle in it.

Zimsterne

How often do we wish that what we treasure in our lives could last forever: a loving glance, a passionate kiss, the melodic, high-pitched trill of our children's laughter, or a day when our joyful mood seems to be matched by all that surrounds us. Knowing that the next moment will come with a relentlessness we can't control, we clutch the present one to us, savoring its sweetness before it becomes one more treasured memory.

So it is with the Sabbath, an all-too-short twenty-four-hour day when all of these, life's most tender experiences, are possible. Contemplating Sabbath's end is a bittersweet burden. We beg for time, wishing that tomorrow could be held at arm's length, if only for a few more minutes, just as Jews did many centuries ago when they lovingly created the ceremony of Havdalah. With its blessings, wine, braided candles, and spice box forged into a short ceremony at Sabbath's end, Havdalah has the power to distract us with its beauty from the inevitable pain that comes with the loss of something much loved and cherished.

Inevitably, the end of Sabbath comes with the appearance of three bright stars in the heavens. An ordinary day will follow but first there will be a sip of wine, a look at the bright light from the braided candle of Havdalah, and a breath of aromatic spice that will come from a little cache of cloves, mace, or perhaps cinnamon, held in a delicately crafted holder, the *hadas*. Before the ceremony is over, every sense will have been satisfied in order to emphasize that, yes, Judaism is a religion of prayer but also of action, pleasure, and joy.

One small culinary treasure comes down to us as being part of the Havdalah ceremony of Middle European and Eastern European Jews several centuries ago. Its origin is impossible to date but its raison d'être is easily understood. Called simply *zimsterne* (say *zim–stern–eh*), "to the stars" in Yiddish, it is a sweet, spicy morsel, an attempt to momentarily confine Sabbath's spiritual

Now say the blessing over the spices:

בָּרוּךְ אַתָּה יְיָ, אֱלֹהֵינוּ מֶלֶךְ הָעוֹלָם, בּוֹרֵא מִינֵי בְשָׂמִים.

Baruch Atah Adonai Eloheynu Melech Ha-olam Borey Miney Besamim.

Blessed are You, Eternal our God, Ruler of the Universe, Who creates many varieties of spices.

Smell the spices. Pass the spices around for all to smell. It is customary to try to capture the light of the candle in one's finger tips.

Recite the blessing over the light:

בָּרוּךְ אַתָּה יְיָ, אֱלֹהֵינוּ מֶלֶךְ הָעוֹלָם, בּוֹרֵא מְאוֹרֵי הָאֵשׁ.

Baruch Atah Adonai Eloheynu melech ha-olam, borey me-oray ha-esh.

Blessed are You, Eternal our God, Creator of the lights of fire.

sweetness and piquancy to a tidbit which will evanesce on the tongue just as surely as day becomes night. It was also the custom to eat *zimsterne* to break the Yom Kippur fast.

Shaped like a star and tasting of honey and cinnamon, ginger and cloves, the *zimsterne's* pleasant taste and all that had gone before it, it was hoped, would provide the spiritual and physical sustenance needed to face the days ahead.

Zimsterne

4 tablespoons butter or margarine (½ stick)	1⅛ teaspoons ground cinnamon
1 cup sugar	½ teaspoons ground cloves
3 eggs	¼ teaspoons ground mace or ground nutmeg
½ cup honey	1 egg yolk plus food coloring
5 cups flour, sifted	
¾ teaspoon baking soda	

1. Using an electric mixer, cream butter and sugar. Add eggs and beat at medium speed until mixture is well blended. Add honey.

2. At low speed, add 4 cups flour, a cup at a time, beating until mixture is thick and flour has been completely absorbed. Add the last cup of flour and spices by hand. Refrigerate dough for 2 hours.

3. Preheat oven to 300 degrees. Roll out dough on floured board or cloth. Cut into star shapes. Make glaze with beaten egg yolk to which a few drops of food coloring have been added.

4. Line a greased baking sheets with wax paper. Place cookies on baking sheet; brush or smear a little of the glaze over the tops. Bake for 15 minutes. Remove cookies from wax paper while they are still warm.

(Reproduced from *A Lexicon of Jewish Cooking: A Collection of Folklore, Foodlore, History, Customs, and Recipes* by Patti Shostek © 1979, by arrangement with Contemporary Books, Inc.)

Havdalah

Traditionally, we begin Havdalah when three stars appear in the Saturday evening sky. This occurs approximately three quarters of an hour after sunset. Shabbat may be extended by holding Havdalah later in the evening.

For a Havdalah service you need:

a *Kiddush* cup

wine

a braided candle

a plate or aluminum foil to catch the dripping wax

matches

a spice box filled with spices (whole sweet spices are best)

Begin by lighting the braided Havdalah candle.

Now fill the *Kiddush* cup with wine.

Recite the blessing over the wine. (Do not drink the wine until after you have recited all four Havdalah blessings.)

בָּרוּךְ אַתָּה יְיָ, אֱלֹהֵינוּ מֶלֶךְ הָעוֹלָם, בּוֹרֵא פְּרִי הַגָּפֶן.

Baruch Atah Adonai Eloheynu Melech Ha-olam Boray P'ri Hagafen.

Blessed are You, Eternal our God, Creator of the fruit of the vine.

Introduction

Havdalah signifies the end of Shabbat and the beginning of a new week. Havdalah, meaning separation, is a brief ceremony generally done in the home, and sometimes in the synagogue.

Shabbat is the day when we desist from our labors, stop creating, and reflect upon all that we have done. Shabbat gives us a taste of *olam haba*, the world to come. At the end of Havdalah, we sing about Elijah the Prophet who, according to tradition, is to join us on earth when the Messiah comes.

Havdalah involves all five senses:

We *see* the light of the braided Havdalah candle. It has at least three wicks to distinguish it from the two wicks of the Shabbat candles.

We *smell* the spices that remind us of the sweetness of Shabbat.

We *taste* the wine symbolic of Shabbat joy.

We *hear* beautiful prayers and songs.

We *touch* the symbols, and *feel* the closeness of others.

OWNER'S MANUAL
HAVDALAH KIT

Our Havdalah Kit Label

Glue this label to one side of the gift bag that will hold your Havdalah Kit.

When completed, your Havdalah Kit should contain: a plastic
Kiddush cup, a 35mm film canister spicebox (with spices), a Havdalah
candle twisted from very thin party tapers, and an Owner's Manual.

Shavua Tov Luggage Tag

Attach this luggage tag with ribbon to the handles of
the gift bag that will hold your Havdalah Kit.

Chanukah: The Festival of Lights
Chanukah, Year 3

Flier and/or Postcard:

To include:
Program Title
Sponsored by
Audience (age group, members only or
    general public, etc.)
Date
Time
Location
Cost (if applicable)
RSVP or For Further Information
Bring a *chanukiah* (Chanukah *menorah*)
    from home.

Physical Set Up

work area: tables and chairs
tables for supplies
table for name tags and sign-in sheet
table for "Lights Museum"
large trash cans
trash bags

**Holiday Symbols, Customs, Terms,
and Concepts**

lights
Jewish lights versus "Plain Ole Lights"
light that is holy versus light that is ordinary
light of freedom
light of God's presence
light as celebration
knowledge as light
Ner Tamid (Eternal Light)
light as time: sun, moon, and stars
light as life
sources of light: oil, electricity, candles,
    batteries, fire
light for dedication or rededication

Chanukah means dedication
the light in the Temple in Jerusalem
the miracle of the light: the oil that burned
    for eight days

00:00 – 00:15
Mind Warmer: A Lights Museum

Families tour a "Lights Museum" for
Chanukah, the Festival of Lights. This
Museum contains examples of Jewish lights
for holy or special occasions, and everyday
lights for routine or ordinary occasions.

Materials

name tags
markers
sign-in sheet
1 sign that says "Lights Museum" or
    "Welcome to the Lights Museum"
1 copy per family of Lights Museum Brochure
    enlarged onto 11" x 17" white paper with
    the two categories "Jewish Lights" and
    "Plain Ole Lights" on the back (see
    Directions and Patterns)
1 copy per child of the Lights Museum
    Catalog copied on yellow paper (see
    Directions and Patterns)
scissors
gluesticks
chanukiah (Chanukah *menorah*)
2 Shabbat candlesticks
2 Shabbat candles
1 light bulb
1 oil lamp or hurricane lamp
2 or 3 birthday candles (put them in a
    sufganiah, a jelly doughnut, or doughnut
    hole served for snack)

1 night light
1 *yahrzeit* candle
1 working flashlight
1 braided Havdalah candle
1 set of Display Labels I, II, III, and IV copied on yellow paper (see Directions and Patterns)
10 5" x 8" index cards

Advance Preparation by the Facilitator

- On a table or tables, set out the following actual lights in the order that they appear in the brochure:
    chanukiah
    birthday candles
    Shabbat candles
    night light
    Ner Tamid (use the display label)
    Yahrzeit candle only
    light bulb
    flashlight
    oil lamp
    Havdalah candle

- Make a sign that reads: "Welcome to the Lights Museum." Place it on this same table(s).

- On the supply table, place these materials: copies of the Lights Museum Brochure and Lights Museum Catalog.

- Cut out the 10 patterns from the four Display Label sheets. Glue them on half an index card. Fold lengthwise. Place the signs on the table beside the corresponding actual light.

- On the supply table, place these items, each in a separate container: gluesticks and scissors.

Procedure

- The Facilitator greets families as they arrive. Have them fill out a name tag for each family member and sign in.

- Give each family a copy of the Lights Museum Brochure.

- Explain to the families that you want them to look around the Lights Museum, viewing and touching the lights. Parents discuss with their child how each works (e.g., fire lights candles, electricity turns on the bulb). Parents also identify each light by name and talk to their child about when each light is used.

- Families cut out the ten lights from the Lights Museum Catalog and sort the ten different lights into the two categories, Jewish Lights and Plain Ole Lights.

- They glue the lights under the appropriate heading in the Brochure, either Jewish Lights or Plain Ole Lights.

- Each family carries the *chanukiah* they brought from home to the Introductions and Announcements area.

- The Facilitator asks families to clean up, returning materials to the supply table.

00:15 – 00:25
Introductions and Announcements

- The Facilitator welcomes everyone on behalf of the sponsoring agency/institution.

- The Facilitator introduces himself/herself and any other official representatives of the program or the agency/institution.

- Have a member of each family introduce himself/herself and other family members.

- Announce any upcoming events for the sponsoring agency/institution that are pertinent for this group.

- Instruct people as to how they can get on the mailing list if they are not already on it.

Setting the Stage

- The Facilitator says: You just toured the Lights Museum and sorted lights into two categories, Jewish Lights and Plain Ole Lights. Jewish Lights are special. Jewish Lights are used for celebrations. We light candles for Shabbat, Chanukah, and most Jewish holy days. Jewish Lights are found in Jewish homes, in synagogues, and in museums.

  Plain Ole Lights we use all the time: lighting up rooms, streets, refrigerators, and closets. Everyone uses Plain Ole Lights.

  We say a blessing every time we light a Jewish Light, such as a Havdalah candle. We do not say a blessing every time we turn on a light switch. Jewish Lights remind us that we are Jewish.

  Chanukah is called the "Festival of Lights." On Chanukah, we light many lights every night. Many of you brought a *chanukiah* from home. Where did your *chanukiah* come from? Who gave it to you? Let's hear now about your *chanukiot*. (Families respond.)

  You saw examples of lights that run on electricity, of lights that are run by batteries, and of candles that burn. In the time of the Maccabees, the heroes of Chanukah, most lights used oil. The oil came from olives. Now we will hear a story which shows how the light of celebration of Chanukah burns bright.

00:25 – 00:45
Story: Rekindling the Light

This story begins with Judah Maccabee at a young age. His favorite word was "no!" Even as an adult, Judah said "no" — he said "no" to bowing down to idols. This Chanukah story has a surprise ending.

Materials

1 copy of *Judah Who Always Said "No!"* by Harriet K. Feder (Rockville, MD: Kar-Ben Copies, 1990)
chanukiah
candles
matches (optional)
aluminum foil or other wax drip catcher (optional)

Procedure

- The Facilitator reads the story *Judah Who Always Said "No!"*

- After the story, in celebration of standing up for what we believe in, recite together the three Chanukah blessings together (see Blessings #11 on page 489 and 5 on page 488). If lighting the candles, place aluminum foil or other wax drip catcher under the *chanukiah*.

00:45 – 00:55
Snack: Chanukah Delights

This snack introduces families to a Sephardic custom from the Middle East, the eating of *sufganiot*, jelly doughnuts, on Chanukah, rather than *latkes*.

Materials

sufganiot, jelly doughnuts (or doughnut holes, which most younger children prefer)
light colored juice
chocolate *gelt*
cups
napkins

Procedure

- Serve *sufganiot* — jelly doughnuts, chocolate *gelt*, and light colored juice.

- The Facilitator explains that eating *sufganiot* is a Sephardic tradition. Like *latkes*, doughnuts are cooked in oil.

- Together recite the appropriate blessing (see Blessing #8, page 488).

00:55 – 01:10
Activity: Catching the Light — A Chanukah Sun Catcher

In accordance with the theme of light, this activity involves making a Chanukah sun catcher in the shape of a *chanukiah* and a cruse of oil. It will look like stained glass. Families can hang this sun catcher by a window, reminiscent of the *mitzvah* of placing Chanukah lights on one's windowsill for all to see.

Materials

1 copy per family of the Sun Catcher Directions sheets copied on white paper (see Directions and Patterns)
1 copy per child of The Lights That We Light I and II, each copied on separate sheets of gold card stock (see Directions and Patterns)
ribbon
cellophane in different colors
gluesticks
scissors
single hole punches

Advance Preparation by the Facilitator

- On the supply table, place these materials: 1 copy per family of the Sun Catcher Directions sheet, one copy per child of The

Lights That We Light I and II on gold card stock, cellophane, and ribbon.

- On the supply table, place these items, each in a separate container: gluesticks, scissors, and single hole punches.

- Make a sample sun catcher to show families (see Procedure below).

Procedure

- The Facilitator introduces the project to the families. Share with them the *mitzvah* of displaying a *chanukiah* where it can be seen by all. Tell them that they will be making a Chanukah decoration, a sun catcher, to hang in their window.

- Show the families the sample sun catcher.

- Ask that one or two people from each work table gather the materials from the supply table. Alert them to the fact that there are two different gold sheets that they will need — one with the prayer in Hebrew and English and the other without.

- Families cut out the shaded areas on both sheets of gold card stock. They then turn one sheet over.

- They glue different colored pieces of cellophane over the opening.

- They make a "sandwich" of the sheet with the cellophane and the second sheet, making sure to match up the cut out areas on each sheet.

- They punch holes in the top and thread with ribbon through the holes.

- The Facilitator asks families to clean up, returning materials to the supply table.

1:10 – 1:30
Closure: A Little Light Music

End the program with singing, sharing, and holiday greetings.

Materials

1 copy per family of the Chanukah blessings (see Blessings #11, page 489 and #5, page 488).

Procedure

- Review the Chanukah blessings.

- Sing and move to Chanukah songs related to: candles, Chanukah, *chanukiot*, lights (moon, sun and stars), oil, clay, Maccabees, the Temple in Jerusalem, praying to God, not praying to idols, freedom, saying a blessing over lights.

  Recommended Songs:

  "Nu in the Middle" (*Apples on Holidays and Other Days* by Leah Abrams, Tara Publications).

  "*Soufganiot*" (*Rabbi Joe Black Sings*, Temple Israel, 2324 Emerson Avenue South, Minneapolis, MN 55404)

  "Chanukah" (*Seasoned With Song* by Julie Auerbach, Tara Publications)

- Have participants share their reactions to the program. Ask families to complete one of these phrases:

  Chanukah is . . .

  Light means . . .

  Our family enjoyed . . .

  Our family learned . . .

  For Chanukah, we . . .

- The Facilitator distributes to families a copy of the Chanukah blessings for use at home.

- Send everyone off with a Chanukah phrase from the letters on the dreidel, *"Nes Gadol Hayah Sham,"* meaning "a great miracle happened there," and with a Chanukah greeting, *"Chag Sameach!"* (Happy Holiday!)

Lights Museum Brochure

Welcome to the LIGHTS MUSEUM! Read this brochure to ensure maximum enjoyment from your visit.

Be sure to pick up a Lights Museum Catalog at the start of your tour if one has not been inserted in this brochure.

Tour the museum. See if you can match each display to its picture in your museum catalog.

After you have toured the museum, go to a work table. At the table, cut out each picture from the Lights Museum Catalog and glue it under the appropriate heading inside this brochure.

In some way, highlight the light(s) used for Chanukah.

Plain Ole Lights

Jewish Lights

Lights Museum Catalog

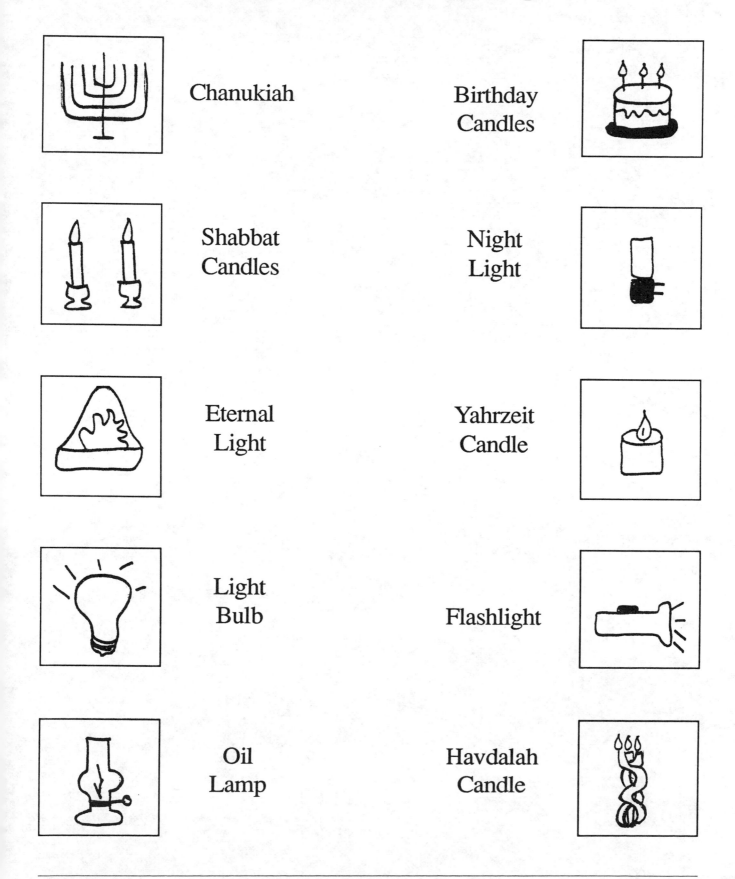

Chanukiah

Birthday
Candles

Shabbat
Candles

Night
Light

Eternal
Light

Yahrzeit
Candle

Light
Bulb

Flashlight

Oil
Lamp

Havdalah
Candle

Display Labels I

To make display signs for the Lights Museum, mount these labels on a
5" x 8" index card or on pieces of poster board folded lengthwise.

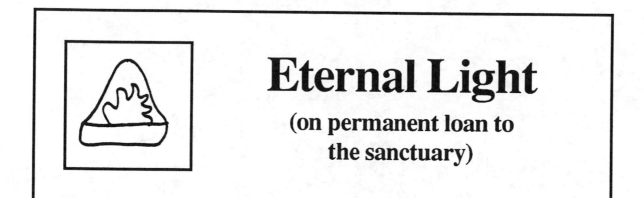

Eternal Light

(on permanent loan to
the sanctuary)

Light
Bulb

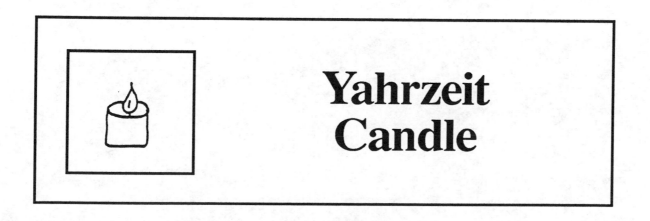

Yahrzeit
Candle

Display Labels II

To make display signs for the Lights Museum, mount these labels on a
5" x 8" index card or on pieces of poster board folded lengthwise.

Oil Lamp

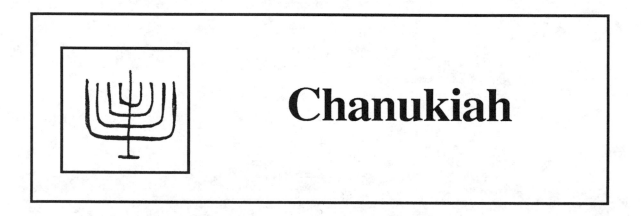

Chanukiah

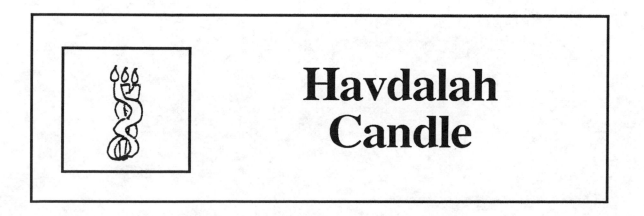

Havdalah Candle

Display Labels III

To make display signs for the Lights Museum, mount these labels on a
5" x 8" index card or on pieces of poster board folded lengthwise.

Night Light

Flashlight

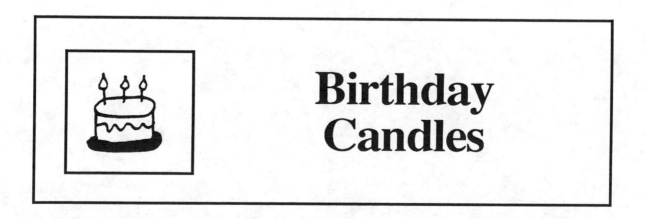

Birthday Candles

Display Labels IV

To make display signs for the Lights Museum, mount these labels on a
5" x 8" index card or on pieces of poster board folded lengthwise.

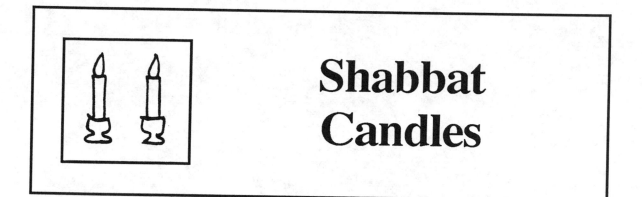

Shabbat Candles

Sun Catcher
(Directions)

To assemble your sun catcher:

1. Cut out the shaded areas on The Lights We Light I and II and throw away the shaded areas away.

2. Turn one sheet over.

3. Glue colored cellophane over the cut out area.

4. Make a "sandwich" of the sheet with the cellophane and the second sheet. Be sure to match up the cut out areas on each sheet (see sample).

5. Punch holes in the top. Thread with ribbon.

6. Hang in your window and enjoy.

The Lights That We Light I

הַנֵּרוֹת הַלָּלוּ

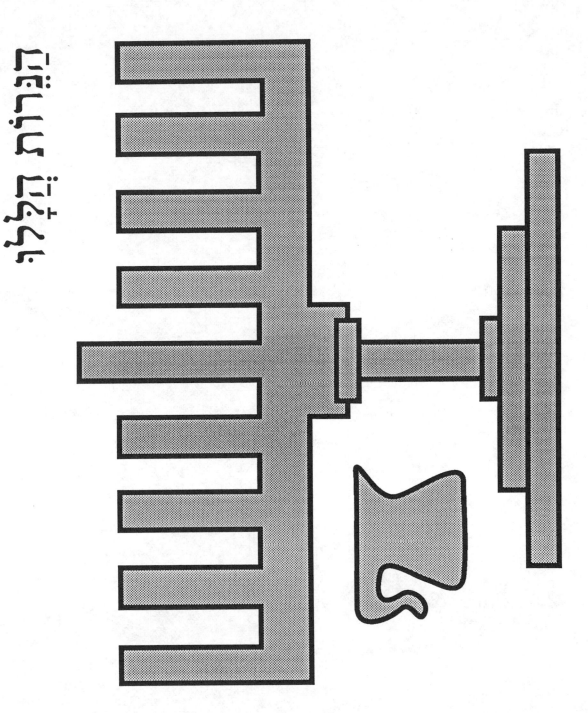

The Lights That We Light II

This is read after the candle blessings:

הַנֵּרוֹת הַלָּלוּ אָנוּ מַדְלִיקִין
עַל הַנִּסִּים וְעַל הַנִּפְלָאוֹת וְעַל
הַתְּשׁוּעוֹת, וְעַל הַמִּלְחָמוֹת
שֶׁעָשִׂיתָ לַאֲבוֹתֵינוּ בַּיָּמִים הָהֵם
בַּזְּמַן הַזֶּה עַל יְדֵי כֹּהֲנֶיךָ הַקְּדוֹשִׁים.
וְכָל שְׁמוֹנַת יְמֵי חֲנֻכָּה הַנֵּרוֹת
הַלָּלוּ קֹדֶשׁ הֵם, וְאֵין לָנוּ רְשׁוּת
לְהִשְׁתַּמֵּשׁ בָּהֶם אֶלָּא לִרְאוֹתָם
בִּלְבַד, כְּדֵי לְהוֹדוֹת וּלְהַלֵּל
לְשִׁמְךָ הַגָּדוֹל עַל נִסֶּיךָ וְעַל
נִפְלְאוֹתֶיךָ וְעַל יְשׁוּעָתֶךָ.

We light these candles because at this time of year You caused wondrous things to happen for our ancestors through actions of Your holy Kohanim. These candles are sacred during all eight days of Chanukah. We may not use the light of these candles in any way. We just look at these candles and think of Your Great Name, and Your wondrous miracles.

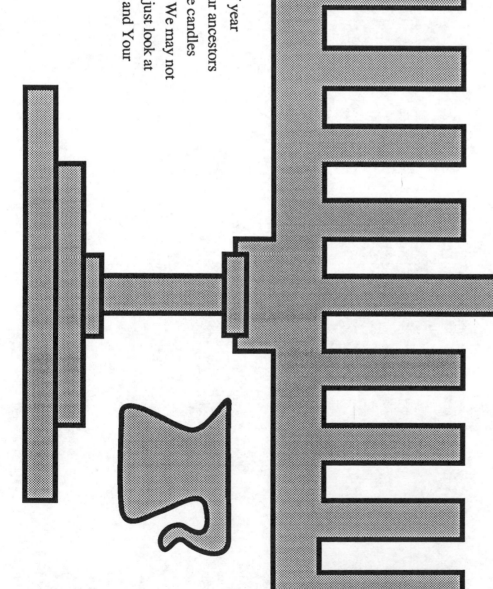

Growing To Like the 15th of Shevat
Tu B' Shevat, Year 3

Postcard and/or Flier:

To include:
Program Title
Sponsored by
Audience (age group, members only or general public, etc.)
Date
Time
Location
Cost (if applicable)
RSVP or For Further Information
Bring a measuring tape.

Physical Set Up

work area: tables and chairs
tables for supplies
table for name tags and sign-in sheet
table for snack
large trash cans
trash bags
room to roam and access to a sanctuary or room with an ark if possible

Holiday Symbols, Customs, Terms, and Concepts

New Year of the Trees
Birthday of the Trees
conservation
Israel
planting
planning for the future
Jewish National Fund
growth in general
individual growth
the Torah as an *eytz chaim* (tree of life)
family tree
use of trees
products of trees

00:00 – 00:15
Mind Warmer: My Growth Chart

Materials

name tags
markers
sign-in sheet
a few measuring tapes 6'-8' long
1 sheet per child of 6' x 8' butcher paper
1 copy per child of the Leaf Patterns and Directions for Assembly copied on bright green paper (see Directions and Patterns)
1 copy per child of A Chart of _____'s Growth copied on bright green paper (see Directions and Patterns)
1 copy per child of the verse from Psalm 92 copied on bright green paper (see Directions and Patterns)
brochures about trees in Israel
pencils
crayons
gluesticks
scissors

Advance Preparation by the Facilitator

- Obtain brochures about trees in Israel from a local *sheliach*, the Jewish National Fund, or an Israeli consulate.

- On the supply table, place these materials: butcher paper; copies of the sheet with the verse from Psalm 92; extra measuring tapes; brochures on trees in Israel; the Leaf Patterns and Directions for Assembly sheets; and A Chart of _____'s Growth sheets.

- On the supply table, place these items, each in a separate container: scissors, gluesticks, pencils, and crayons.

Procedure

- The Facilitator greets families as they arrive. Have them fill out a name tag for each family member and sign in.

- The Facilitator informs families that they will be making a life-size growth chart of their child.

- Direct families to the supply table where they will find the materials and directions.

- Suggest that families use the open area floor space rather than tables for making the growth charts.

- To make a growth chart, families use their creativity, doing any or all of the following:

- Each child lies down on the butcher paper. Parent(s) outline their child using a crayon.

- They glue the tape measure on the butcher paper (those who forgot measuring tapes, can simply measure the child's height).

- They fill in the blank with the child's name on A Chart of _____'s Growth.

- They cut out the big leaf. They glue it on the top of the butcher paper.

- They glue the verse from Psalm 92 to the bottom of the butcher paper.

- They write today's date on one of leaves on the Leaf Patterns and Directions for Assembly sheet. They cut out the leaf.

- Each child lies on the chart with his/her feet even with the bottom of the tape measure. Parents mark the height by gluing the leaf with the date at that point.

- As time permits, families decorate with more leaves or pictures of trees from the brochure of trees in Israel, etc.

- They take the growth chart home and hang it in a special place.

00:15 – 00:25
Introductions and Announcements

- The Facilitator welcomes everyone on behalf of the sponsoring agency/institution.

- The Facilitator introduces himself/herself and any other official representatives of the program or the agency/institution.

- Have a member of each family introduce himself/herself and other family members. Every child stands up and shares his/her height.

- Announce any upcoming events for the sponsoring agency/institution that are pertinent for this group.

- Instruct people as to how they can get on the mailing list if they are not already on it.

Setting the Stage

- The Facilitator introduces the holiday of Tu B'Shevat as the New Year or Birthday of the Trees, the time when crops are planted in Israel. Explain that the growth chart is a way of keeping track of growth.

- Ask families for comments on why one would like to "grow mighty like a cedar in Lebanon."

00:25 – 00:40
Story: Dates as Sweet as Honey

Materials

1 copy of *Dates as Sweet as Honey* by Betty Ann Ross (New York: Board of Jewish Education of Greater New York, 1982)

1 plate with samples of wheat, barley, grapes, pomegranate, figs, olives, and dates

Advance Preparation by the Facilitator

- Obtain a copy of the book *Dates as Sweet as Honey.*

- Prepare a plate with samples of the seven different foods mentioned in the book (wheat, barley, figs, pomegranate or pomegranate juice, olives, grapes, and dates). If necessary, use products that contain these foods like wheat crackers, cookies with fig filling, etc. (These food items may be used later for the snack.)

Procedure

- The Facilitator shows families the plate with samples of the seven species.

- Explain that you will read a Tu B'Shevat story about these special foods that are grown in Israel.

- The Facilitator reads the story *Dates as Sweet as Honey.*

- Point out the different foods as you say their name.

- Encourage families to chime in on the refrain: "Wheat and barley, grapes and pomegranates, figs and olives, and dates as sweet as honey."

- After the story, have participants identify each of the seven species on the plate of samples.

- Explain that today's snack will be a sampler of these seven special Tu B'Shevat foods.

00:40 – 00:50
Snack: A Sampler of the Seven Foods from Dates as Sweet as Honey

For the Birthday of the Trees, participants will eat products from trees and products that grow in the earth.

Materials

dates
wheat or wheat crackers
figs or cookies with fig filling
seedless grapes or raisins
barley
a pomegranate or pomegranate juice for tasting (found in health food stores)
olives (pitted)
juice for drinking
napkins
plates
serving plates or bowls
serving spoons
cups

Advance Preparation by the Facilitator

- Cut up the seven foods into sizes suitable for sampling. Place them on plates or in bowls. Lay them out on the supply table.

Procedure

- Have families get the snack and then eat it.

- Encourage parents to help their child identify the different foods on the plate.

- Teach and recite together the blessing for fruits that come from trees (see Blessing #7, page 488).

- Have fun sampling the foods.

00:50 – 01:10
Activity: The Tree Hunt

Families search throughout the building (including the sanctuary if you are in a synagogue) for products of trees and for examples of the many uses of trees. They then complete and decorate their own family tree.

Materials

1 magnifying glass per child (available at party stores or through carnival prize catalogues)

1 My Family Tree per child enlarged onto 11" x 17" white paper (see Directions and Patterns)

a Torah scroll or miniature Torah scroll, the type given to children at Consecration on Simchat Torah (available from KTAV)

pencils or pens

crayons

room to roam with access to a sanctuary or Ark if possible

Advance Preparation by the Facilitator

- On the supply table, place the My Family Tree sheets.

- On the supply table, place these items, each in a separate container: pencils, and crayons.

- For this activity you will need a Torah. If the program takes place in a building without a sanctuary, or if the sanctuary is not available, place an actual Torah scroll or a miniature Torah scroll where it can be discovered on the Tree Hunt.

Procedure

- The Facilitator tells the families that they will be going on a Tree Hunt to look for tree products, to discover the uses of trees.

- As families will be detectives, they must be equipped with a magnifying glass. Pass out the magnifying glasses.

- Together, tour the facility. Hunt for all the trees in the facility's art, architecture, and displays (including bulletin boards). Encourage families to announce aloud when they find a new and different type of tree product or tree. Allow all to come see the product or tree under their magnifying glasses.

- When they come across the Torah, the Facilitator reminds people of the prayer, "*Eytz Chaim Hee*" (It is a tree of life) which refers to the Torah. Say: The Torah's wooden post are each called an *eytz chaim* (a tree of life). The Torah itself is referred to as an *eytz chaim*. The Torah contains the oldest Jewish family tree, that of our ancestors, Abraham and Sarah, Isaac and Rebekah, Jacob and Leah and Rachel.

- As the guide, the Facilitator can also point out such things as: the *menorah* with branches like a tree; the *Ner Tamid*, which is like the Burning Bush and reminds us of God's presence; prayerbook pages that are sometimes called leaves and are made of paper.

- Back in the room where the Hunt began, the Facilitator instructs families to complete and decorate their family trees.

- Each family writes on the My Family Tree sheet all the names they can, then decorates the family tree with leaves, pictures of trees, etc.

01:10 – 01:30
Closure: A Tribute to Trees

End the program with singing, swaying, sharing, and holiday greetings.

- Sing and move to Tu B'Shevat music related to: growing, growing up, types of trees, fruits from trees, uses of trees, the Torah, *eytz chaim*, Israel, plants and trees in Israel, the months in the Jewish calendar.

  Recommended Songs:

  "Planting" (*Apples on Holidays and Other Days* by Leah Abrams, Tara Publications)

  "The Torah" (*Especially Jewish Symbols* by Jeff Klepper, A.R.E. Publishing, Inc.)

- Have participants share their reactions to the program. Ask families to complete one of these phrases:

  Trees are . . .

  Our family enjoyed . . .

  Our family learned . . .

  Tu B'Shevat is . . .

- Send everyone off singing "Happy Birthday to the Trees" and saying "Happy Tu B'Shevat!"

Leaf Patterns and Directions for Assembly

Collect the following materials:

    1 verse sheet
    1 label sheet
    1 length of butcher paper about 6'-8' long and not less than 15" wide

To assemble:

1. Lay the butcher paper on the floor.
2. Glue the tape measure onto the butcher paper.
3. Fill in the blank on the big leaf: A Chart of _____ 's Growth.
4. Glue the sheet with the verse from Psalm 92 on the bottom of the chart.
5. Write today's date inside on one of the leaves below. Then cut out the leaf.
6. Have the child whose height is going to be recorded lay on the chart with his/her feet even with the bottom of the tape measure. Mark the height.
7. Glue the leaf with today's date at the mark.
8. Take the chart home and hang it in a special place.
9. Use the remaining leaves to mark future dates and as a pattern for cutting more leaves.

A CHART OF GROWTH 's

צַדִּיק כַּתָּמָר יִפְרָח

כְּאֶרֶז בַּלְּבָנוֹן יִשְׂגֶּה

Like the palm their growth will be;

They will rise tall and upright

As a stately cedar tree.

Psalm 92

My Family Tree

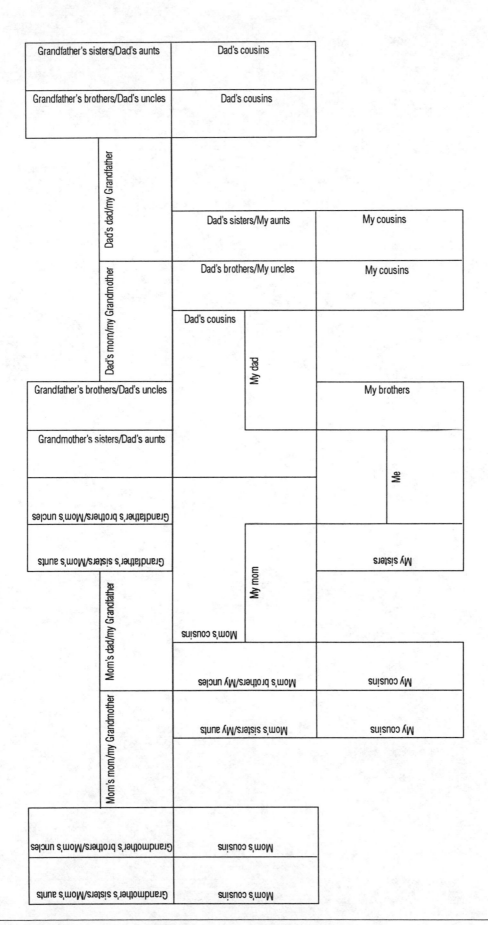

Grandfather's sisters/Dad's aunts	Dad's cousins
Grandfather's brothers/Dad's uncles	Dad's cousins

Dad's dad/my Grandfather

Dad's mom/my Grandmother

Dad's sisters/My aunts	My cousins
Dad's brothers/My uncles	My cousins

Dad's cousins

My dad

Grandfather's brothers/Dad's uncles

Grandmother's sisters/Dad's aunts

Grandfather's brothers/Mom's uncles

Grandfather's sisters/Mom's aunts

My brothers

Me

My sisters

My mom

Mom's dad/my Grandfather

Mom's mom/my Grandmother

Mom's cousins

Mom's brothers/My uncles

Mom's sisters/My aunts

My cousins

My cousins

Grandmother's brothers/Mom's uncles

Grandmother's sisters/Mom's aunts

Mom's cousins

Mom's cousins

Purim Is Rolling In
Purim, Year 3

Postcard and/or Flier:

To include:
Program Title
Sponsored by
Audience (age group, members only or
general public, etc.)
Date
Time
Location
Cost (if applicable)
RSVP or For Further Information
Bring an empty paper towel roll.

Physical Set Up

work area: tables and chairs
tables for supplies
table for name tags and sign-in sheet
large trash cans
trash bags

**Holiday Symbols, Customs, Terms,
and Concepts**

Megillah (scroll)
Megillat Esther (the Scroll of Esther)
the Purim Characters: Mordecai, Esther,
Haman, King Ahasuerus
reading and hearing the *Megillah*
blotting out Haman's name
gragger
the hats people wear
hamantaschen

00:00 – 00:15
Mind Warmer: Megillat Esther

Families assemble their own *Megillat Esther*
(Scroll of Esther).

Materials

name tags
markers
sign-in sheet
1 set of pages for a *Megillat Esther* per child
(see Directions and Patterns)
1 paint stir stick per child
extra empty paper towel rolls
1 piece of wood grained Contact paper per
child cut in approximately 5" x 12" sheets
(obtain at a hardware store)
variety of small stickers in the shape of stars
and shapes
other supplies for decorating the *Megillah* case
(optional)
scissors
gluesticks
staplers
staples
double sided tape

Advance Preparation by the Facilitator

- On the supply table, place these materials:
copies of the pages for a *Megillat Esther*,
paint stir sticks, wood grained Contact
paper, extra paper towel rolls, stickers, and
other items for decorating the *Megillah*
cases.

- On the supply table, place these items, each
in a separate container: double sided tape,
scissors, gluesticks, staplers, and staples.

- Assemble a sample *Megillat Esther* (see
Procedure).

Procedure

- The Facilitator greets families as they arrive. Have them fill out a name tag for each family member and sign in.

- Let families know that they will be assembling their own *Megillat Esther*, the Scroll of Esther, which is read on Purim.

- Show them a sample of how the pages and pieces fit together.

- Send families to the supply table to pick up all the materials.

- Families tape or glue the pages together side to side with overlap, making a scroll of paper as indicated on the *Megillat Esther* story sheets..

- They attach the scroll of paper to the paint stir stick with staples where indicated on the *Megillat Esther* story sheets.

- They remove the backing from the Contact paper and place it on the paper towel roll. They cut slits in the Contact paper that goes over the ends of the roll. These ends will fold in nicely inside the paper towel roll.

- They decorate the wood grained *Megillah* holder with stickers or other decorative items.

- To complete their *Megillat Esther,* each family rolls the paper around the paint stir stick. Insert inside the wood grained *Megillah* holder.

00:15 – 00:25
Introductions and Announcements

Materials

1 actual *Megillat Esther* (if available)

Procedure

- The Facilitator welcomes everyone on behalf of the sponsoring agency/institution.

- The Facilitator introduces himself/herself and any other official representatives of the program or the agency/institution.

- Have a member of each family introduce himself/herself and other family members.

- Announce any upcoming events for the sponsoring agency/institution that are pertinent for this group.

- Instruct people as to how they can get on the mailing list if they are not already on it.

Setting the Stage

- The Facilitator asks each family to hold up their *Megillat Esther*. The Facilitator then holds up the actual *Megillat Esther* and says: This is the *Megillah*, or scroll. (Have everyone repeat the word *Megillah*.) The *Megillah* read on Purim is called *Megillat Esther,* meaning the "Scroll of Esther." On this scroll is written the Book of Esther from the Bible.

  Ask: How is a *Megillah*, a scroll, different from a book? Show off the parts of the *Megillah*: the case, the Hebrew text, the parchment, the way the scroll rolls.

  It is a *mitzvah* to hear *Megillat Esther* read on Purim. Today, we will hear the story of Esther, Mordecai, King Ahasuerus, and Haman. We will make lots of noise for each of these people. We will make hats much like they wore, too. Of course, we will munch on *hamantaschen*, the three-cornered pastry some say looks like Haman's hat. And we will sing Purim songs.

00:25 – 00:45
Story: The Esther Symphony Accompanies the Reading of Megillat Esther

This *Megillah* reading adds some new noise making to the story — noise made by the "Esther Symphony." Players are equipped with rhythm instruments, each one associated with a Purim character. Of course, all the instruments play loudly to blot out Haman's name.

Materials

1 rhythm instrument per child (bells, cymbals, triangle, drums, etc.) If necessary, substitute homemade instruments: pots, pans, wood blocks, or store bought instruments, such as kazoos, or *graggers*.

Procedure

- The Facilitator passes out the instruments so that every child has one.

- Ask each child to sound his/her instrument. Be certain to go through all the instruments.

- Ask participants to associate each instrument with one of the Purim figures. Ask: Which sounds sweet like Esther? Which sounds rough like Haman? Which reminds you of a king? Which sounds strong and solid like Mordecai?

- Ask families what happens when Haman's name is read. Remind them of the custom of making so much noise that Haman's name cannot be heard. This is done to get rid of Haman forever and ever from the lives of the Jewish People.

- Using the *Megillat Esther* made by one of the families, tell the Purim story. A combination of telling and reading is recommended. If any of the children can read, they may follow along in their own *Megillah*.

- Ask families to play their instruments whenever they hear the name of the character their instrument is like.

- Encourage families to read their *Megillat Esther* as a bedtime story.

00:45 – 00:55
Snack: Noshing on Haman's Hat

Hamantaschen literally means "Haman's pocket." There is a controversy over the meaning of the word *hamantaschen*. Some say *hamantaschen* looks like Haman's hat with its three-pointed corners. (Later, families will have the opportunity to make a three-pointed Haman hat.)

Materials

hamantaschen
juice
napkins
cups
tray for serving

Procedure

- The Facilitator serves *hamantaschen* and juice.

- Remind people that the *hamantaschen* represent Haman's three-cornered hat.

- Together recite a blessing before noshing (see Blessing #8, page 488).

00:55 – 01:15
Activity: The Many Hats of Purim

Families make costumes for Purim. They will make a Purim hat for one of the main Purim figures. (Some families will want to make more than one hat. Set limits as to how many hats each family can make in accordance with time and materials available.)

Materials

2-3 sheets of tagboard 10½" x 10½"

2-3 sheets of tagboard or poster board 13" x 13"

2-3 sheets of tagboard or poster board at least 20" x 20"

18" x 24" sheets of construction paper (or a sheet of poster board)

colorful thick yarn

crepe paper streamers and ribbons in assorted colors

"jewels"(sequins, buttons, lace, beads, etc. (obtain at a sewing shop or art store)

red or purple tissue paper

yellow or gold or metallic bulletin board border

stickers

feathers

large pieces of scrap cloth at least 3' x 3'

black construction paper 12" x 18"

newspaper

several copies of the instructions for each of the following: A Crown for Ahasuerus, A Three-cornered Hat for Haman, A Head-covering for Mordecai, A Queen Hat for Esther, A Hat for a Resident of Shushan, (see Directions and Patterns)

yardstick

pencils

staplers

staples

single hole punches

gluesticks

black markers

Advance Preparation by the Facilitator

- For A Crown for Ahasuerus, draw a few circles 13" in diameter on tagboard or poster board. Cut out the circles.

- For A Three-cornered Hat for Haman, draw a few circles 10½" in diameter on tagboard or poster board. Inside the 10½" circles, draw 6" circles. Cut around the outside of the 10½" circle. Then cut out and throw away the 6" circle. The remainder looks like a bagel or doughnut.

- For A Queen Hat for Esther, draw a few circles 20" in diameter on tagboard or poster board. Cut out the circle. Fold the circle in half. Cut the fold so that you have two equal halves.

- Make a sample of each of the five hats.

- On the supply table, place all the materials needed to make the five hats.

To Make a Crown for King Ahasuerus or a Queen Esther Crown:

Materials

a few copies of A Crown for King Ahasuerus Directions (see Directions and Patterns)

red or purple tissue paper

metallic or yellow or gold bulletin board border

a few circles 13" in diameter on tagboard

"jewels" (sequins, buttons, feathers, etc.)

stickers

scissors

staples

gluesticks

pencils

Procedure

- Parents measure their child's head with the bulletin board border. They cut it, leaving an extra inch or two.

- They staple the crown to fit the child's head.

- They trace a 13" tagboard circle onto a sheet of tissue paper, then return the tagboard circle to the supply table for someone else to use,.

- They cut out the tissue paper circle.

- They fit the tissue paper circle into the middle of the crown and staple to hold it in place.

- They decorate the crown with "jewels," feathers, and stickers.

To Make a Three-Cornered Hat for Haman:

Materials
> a few copies of A Three-cornered Hat for Haman Directions (see Directions and Patterns)
> 2 or 3 pre-cut round patterns
> black construction paper
> pencils
> staplers
> staples
> scissors

Procedure

- Families trace the inside and outside of the bagel-like 10½" tagboard circle onto a piece of black construction paper. They return the tagboard circle to the supply table for someone else to use.

- They cut out the inside circle, then cut away the excess paper on the outside of the big circle.

- They pinch and staple the hat together in three places (equally spaced from one another) to create the corners.

To Make a Headcovering for Mordecai:

Materials
> a few copies of A Headcovering for Mordecai Directions (see Directions and Patterns)
> large pieces of scrap cloth
> thick rug yarn
> 1 yardstick
> black markers

Procedure

- Families cut the thick yarn into three 3'-4' strands.

- They bring the three strands together at one end and tie a knot.

- They braid the strands, then knot the other end of the braid.

- Using a yardstick and black marker, they trace a 3' x 3' square on a cloth remnant.

- They cut out the 3' cloth square.

- The fabric goes over the head and the yarn rope goes around the forehead and secures the fabric.

To Make Queen Esther's Cone Hat:

Materials
> copies of A Queen Hat for Esther Directions (see Directions and Patterns)
> 18" x 24" sheets of construction paper
> a few half moon-shaped patterns 20" in diameter made from tag board
> thick yarn
> crepe paper streamers and ribbons in assorted colors
> "jewels"(sequins, buttons, lace, etc.)
> staplers
> staples

scissors
gluesticks
pencils

Procedure

- Families trace one of the half moon tagboard shapes onto a piece of construction paper.

- They return the half moon pattern to the supply table for others to use.

- They cut the half moon shape from the construction paper.

- They cut a few lengths of crepe paper streamers.

- They staple the streamers to the middle of the straight side of the half moon shape.

- They fold the corners of the half moon shape toward each other and overlap to form a cone. The streamers should be on the outside.

- They staple the hat in this cone shape so that it fits the child's head.

- They punch one hole on each side of the hat to attach ribbon ties on both sides. (These will tie together to keep the hat on the head.)

- They cut two pieces of ribbon or string for ties and thread one through each hole, tying a knot at the end of each piece.

- They decorate the hat by gluing on "jewels," sticking on stickers.

To Make a Hat for a Resident of Shushan:

Materials

a few copies of A Hat for a Resident of Shushan Directions (see Directions and Patterns)

newspaper
decorations as desired

Procedure

- Families take a piece of newspaper, making certain it is folded along its regular fold.

- They turn the paper so that the fold is at the top.

- They take one of the upper corners, fold it toward the middle, and crease it. They do the same with the other upper corner.

- To make a rim for the hat which will secure the two folds in place, they fold the bottom edge of the paper up.

- They turn the whole thing over and fold up the other edge.

- They add feathers or other decorations.

01:15 – 01:30
Closure: Noisy Purim Tunes

End the program with parading, singing, sharing, and holiday greetings.

- Have the children parade around in their new hats.

- Sing and move to Purim music related to: the four major Purim figures, *graggers*, blotting out Haman's name, hats, hearing the story of Esther, *hamantaschen*, three corners.

Recommended Songs:

"*Al Hanisim*" (*Especially Wonderful Days* by Steve Reuben, A.R.E. Publishing, Inc.)

"*Purim's a Time*" (*Seasoned With Song* by Julie Auerbach, Tara Publications)

- Have participants share their reactions to the program. Ask families to complete one of these phrases:

  Purim is . . .

  Our favorite Purim character is . . .

  Our family enjoyed . . .

  Our family learned . . .

  This Purim, we . . .

- Send everyone off with a greeting for a *"Chag Sameach"* (Happy Holiday).

Megillat Esther

In the city of Shushan in Persia, lived a Jew named Mordecai. His relative was Hadassah, or Esther. When Esther's parents died, Mordecai took care of Esther as his own daughter.

In the kingdom of Shushan, the king was Ahasuerus. Queen Vashti dared to disobey the king. She was sent away from the kingdom. As every king needs a queen, King Ahasuerus took the beautiful and kind Esther to be his new queen. Esther went to live in the royal palace. But she kept secret from the king the fact that she was a Jew.

Soon after, King Ahasuerus promoted a man named Haman to a high position in the royal court. All the king's servants and all the people of Shushan bowed down to Haman because of his power, and because the king commanded it. But Mordecai would not bow down. When Haman saw that

Mordecai did not bow down, he was filled with anger. He swore to punish Mordecai and all the Jews in the kingdom of Persia.

Haman went to King Ahasuerus and said:

"There is a certain people who live in your kingdom. Their laws and ways are different from those of other people. If it pleases the king, let it be written that they be killed."

King Ahasuerus took the ring from his finger. He gave it to Haman, the enemy of the Jews. The King said: "Haman, you have my permission to deal as you see fit with these people who have their own laws, who do not obey the king's laws."

Soon this horrible news reached the ears of Mordecai. Into every area of the kingdom, the word of the king came to destroy the Jewish people. The Jews of the land were crying and wailing and fasting.

Megillat Esther

Many put on sackcloth and ashes.

Esther's servants came and told her of Mordecai's weeping and wailing before the king's gate. Esther's servant brought a message from Mordecai. It said: "My dear Esther, the king has made a new ruling to destroy the Jews. You must beg him not to do this. Please, go before the king and beg for the safety and lives of the Jewish people."

But Esther was afraid. Esther sent this message back to Mordecai: "Whoever goes before the king without first being asked by the king may be put to death. If the king holds out his golden scepter, then the person may live. I have not been called before the king for 30 days. I am afraid for my own life if I go before the king and make him angry."

Another message from Mordecai came to Queen Esther. "Esther, even though you are queen, do not think that you would escape the fate of your people. If you remain silent, you, too, will die under the king's new law."

Although she was frightened, Esther sent Mordecai this last message. "Mordecai, go and tell all the Jews of Shushan. They should fast for me for three days. My handmaidens and I will also fast. After three days, I will go before the king, although it is against the law. And if I die, I shall die. But I shall not forget my own people in their hour of need."

Mordecai was relieved and joyful to hear of Esther's decision. He did all that she requested of him.

On the third day, Esther put on her royal robes. She stood in the inner court of the king's house. When King Ahasuerus saw Queen Esther, he held out his golden scepter to her. She drew near and touched the top of the scepter. King Ahasuerus

Megillat Esther

asked: "Queen Esther, what is it that you desire? Even if you want half the kingdom, it shall be given to you."

"If it pleases the king, I have prepared a banquet for you and Haman today. Please come." Esther replied.

At the banquet, Queen Esther invited the king and Haman to another banquet the very next day.

That night the king could not sleep. He ordered the book of records, a history of all that had happened in the kingdom, to be read to him. It was found that Mordecai had once prevented two of the king's servants from killing the king.

"What honor was given to Mordecai for this brave act?" the king asked. "Why, nothing has been done to honor this man," the king's servant replied.

"Who is in the court?" demanded the king.

"Haman is in the court," the servant answered.

Haman had just arrived to tell the king of his desire to hang Mordecai, the Jew, on a high gallow.

"What shall be done to the man who the king desires to honor?" the king asked Haman.

Now Haman thought to himself: "Who could the king wish to honor more than I?" So Haman answered the king saying: "Dress the man the king wishes to honor in royal robes and a crown. Let the person ride on the king's horse through the city. Let this person be led by one of the king's most noble princes. Let this noble prince cry out: 'This is what shall be done to the person whom the king wishes to honor!'"

"Haman," the king commanded, "hurry. Take Mordecai who sits by the king's gate, and do all that you described. Do not fail me."

Later that day, King Ahasuerus and an angry and tired Haman hurried to Queen Esther's banquet.

Megillat Esther

"Tell me Queen Esther, what is it that you wish? Even if it be half the kingdom, it shall be yours."

"O king," Esther cried, "if I have pleased you, let my life and the lives of my people be saved. For we are threatened to be killed."

"Who is it that desires to destroy you?" boomed the king.

"It is the wicked Haman," she cried out, pointing a finger at him. "He set out the ruling to kill the Jews, my people."

King Ahasuerus rose in anger. He looked in the palace garden. There he saw the gallows that Haman made for Mordecai. The king commanded: "Hang Haman on his own gallows! Now!"

So they hanged Haman on the very gallows that he had prepared for Mordecai. The king's anger was satisfied.

Esther told the king of all that Mordecai had said and done. The king dressed Mordecai in royal robes. He told Mordecai to instruct the people of his kingdom how to treat the Jews.

In Shushan and all the kingdom, there was joy and gladness for the Jews, a feast and a good day.

Since that time, Jews keep the 14th day of the month of Adar as a time to remember their sorrow and their joy. And they called this day, "Purim," after the word *pur*, which means "lots." The *Megillah* (the Scroll of Esther) is read to celebrate the defeat of a wicked man and to recall our joyous victory over evil.

A Crown for Ahasuerus

(Directions)

1. With the bulletin board border, measure the head of the person who is going to wear the crown. Cut this border leaving an extra inch or two.

2. Form the crown into a circle and staple.

3. Trace the full-size tagboard version of the pattern below onto a piece of tissue paper. Put the pattern back on the supply table so someone else can use it.

4. Cut out the tissue paper circle.

5. Fit the tissue paper circle into the middle of the crown and staple to hold it in place.

6. Decorate the outside of the crown with jewels, sequins, and other fancies.

7. Wear your new crown while you help clean up the area where you were working.

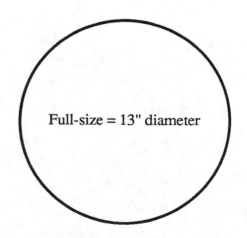

Full-size = 13" diameter

A Three-Cornered Hat for Haman

(Directions)

1. Trace the full-size tagboard version of the pattern below on a piece of 9" x 12" black construction paper. Put the pattern back near the sign so someone else can use it.

2. Cut out the inside circle, then cut away the excess paper on the outside of the big circle.

3. Fold the hat like a *hamentaschen* and put creases at the three corners.

4. Staple the corners.

5. Wear your new hat while you help clean up the area where you were working.

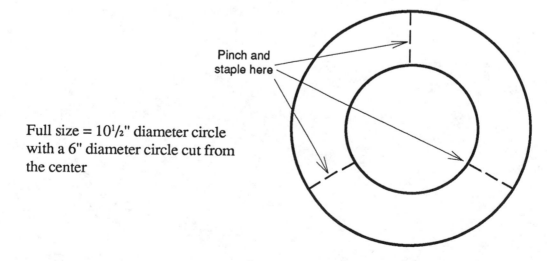

Pinch and staple here

Full size = 10½" diameter circle with a 6" diameter circle cut from the center

A Headcovering for Mordecai
(Directions)

1. Cut several strands of rug yarn into 3'-4' strands. Bring the three strands together at one end and tie a knot. Braid the strands, and then knot the other end of the braid.

2. Choose a cloth remnant. Using a yardstick and a black marker, trace a 3' x 3' square on the remnant,

3. Cut out the cloth square.

4. Put the fabric over your head and use the yarn rope to hold the fabric in place.

5. Wear your new headcovering while you help clean up the area where you were working.

A Queen Hat for Esther

(Directions)

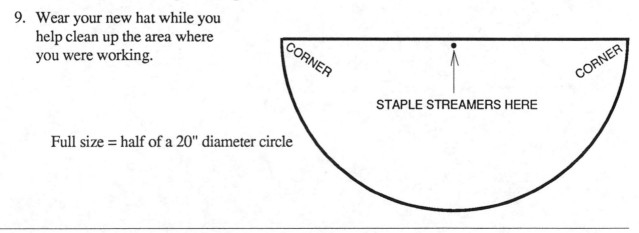

1. Trace the 20" diameter half moon shape onto an 18" x 24" piece of construction paper. Put the pattern back near the sign so someone else can use it.

2. Cut out the half moon shape from the construction paper.

3. Cut a few lengths of crepe paper streamers.

4. Staple the streamers to the middle of the straight side of the half moon shape.

5. Fold the corners of the hat toward each other and overlap to form a cone. The streamers should be on the outside.

6. Staple the hat in this cone shape so that it fits the child's head.

7. Punch holes on either side of the hat and attach ribbon ties (see sample).

8. Decorate the hat with glitter, sequins, etc.

9. Wear your new hat while you help clean up the area where you were working.

CORNER

CORNER

STAPLE STREAMERS HERE

Full size = half of a 20" diameter circle

A Hat for a Resident of Shushan

(Directions)

1. Take one whole sheet of newspaper, making certain it is folded along its regular fold.

2. Turn the paper so the fold is at the top.

3. Take one of the upper corners, fold it toward the middle, and crease it. Do the same with the upper corner.

4. To make a rim for the hat, which will secure the two folds in place, fold the bottom edge of the paper up. Turn the whole thing over and fold up the other edge.

5. Add a feather to your cap or other decorative addition.

6. Wear your new hat while you help clean up the area where you were working.

Passover: A Model Seder in 15 Easy Steps
Passover, Year 3

Postcard and/or Flier

To include:
Program Title
Sponsored by
Audience (age group, members only or
    general public, etc.)
Date
Time
Location
Cost (if applicable)
RSVP or For Further Information

Physical Set Up

tables and chairs set up for a model *Seder*
tables for supplies
table for name tags and sign-in sheet
large trash cans
trash bags
access to a sink (optional)

Holiday Symbols, Customs, Terms, and Concepts

preparations for the Passover *Seder*
Seder plate
symbols on the *Seder* plate
searching for *chametz* (leavening)
leavened versus unleavened food
setting the *Seder* table
the Four Questions
questioning
the whys behind the symbols
Elijah
15 steps for a *Seder*
Seder means "order"
the Ten Plagues

00:00 – 00:15
Mind Warmer: Seder Order Cards

Families make playing cards that introduce the
15 steps of the *Seder* and their order. Later, the
families will go through all 15 steps.

Materials

name tags
markers
sign-in sheet
2 sets per child of Seder Order Cards I and II
    on light color card stock (see Directions and
    Patterns)
1 Ziplock sandwich bag per child
crayons
scissors

Advance Preparation by the Facilitator

- On the supply table, place the following
  materials: sets of Seder Order Cards I and II
  and Ziplock sandwich bags.

- On the supply table, place the following
  materials, each in its own container:
  scissors and crayons.

Procedure

- The Facilitator greets families as they
  arrive. Have them fill out a name tag and
  sign in.

- Explain that families will be making
  playing cards for the 15 steps of the *Seder*.

- Send families to the supply table for their
  materials and directions.

- Families cut out two sheets of Seder Order Cards I and two sheets of II.

- Families play the game described on the Seder Order Cards. They shuffle the cards and race to put the *Seder* in order. Or, they turn the cards upside down and play *Memory* or *Concentration,* trying to pick two matching cards.

- Families place their Seder Order Cards in a Ziplock sandwich bag.

- The Facilitator asks families to clean up, returning materials to the supply table.

00:15 – 00:25
Introductions and Announcements

Materials

several copies of Haggadot, each different from the other

Procedure

- The Facilitator welcomes everyone on behalf of the sponsoring agency/institution.

- The Facilitator introduces himself/herself and any other official representatives of the program or the agency/institution.

- Have a member of each family introduce himself/herself and other family members. Have each family share where they are going for a *Seder* (i.e., to grandparents, to another city, having a *Seder* at home, etc.).

- Announce any upcoming events for the sponsoring agency/institution that are pertinent for this group.

- Instruct people as to how they can get on the mailing list if they are not already on it.

Setting the Stage

- The Facilitator explains that the word *Seder* means order. He or she says: There are 15 steps necessary for a *Seder*. The Haggadah, our guidebook to the *Seder,* goes through these different steps. Haggadah means "telling." The Haggadah tells the story of the Jews who go from being slaves in Egypt to being free people. (Show and pass around a few Haggadot for participants to see.)

Preparation is a major part of Passover. The six symbols for the *Seder* plate must be prepared in advance. They are: *Maror* – bitter herb, horseradish root; *Charoset* – mixture of apple, nuts, wine, and spices; *Zeroa* – shankbone, lamb bone; *Baytzah* – egg, holiday offering; *Karpas* – parsley, sprigs of parsley; *Chazeret* – leafy green, bitter lettuce.

During the next part of this program, we will go through each of the 15 steps of the *Seder*.

00:25 – 01:10
A Model Seder in 15 Easy Steps,
Including a Hunt for Leaven and a Story

This model *Seder* is instructive and experiential, containing an activity for each of the 15 steps of the *Seder*. It is intended to prepare families for their own *Seder,* not to replace the *Seder* itself.

Materials

1 copy of Seder Order Cards I and II enlarged to 8½" x 11" (see Directions and Patterns)
clotheline
15 clothespins or paperclips or masking tape
magazines with pictures of foods
4 to 5 3" x 5" blank index cards per child

1 paper plate per family, plus extras
1 paper or plastic cup per person
extra cups for holding items
towels for drying hands
salt
1 sprig of parsley per person
sliced bread for tasting
2 bowls for every 3-4 families
1 piece of *matzah* per family
$\frac{1}{3}$ of an apple per child
walnuts
1 plastic knife per child
cinnamon
2 horseradish roots or 1 horseradish root and
    1 jar of horseradish
1 or 2 macaroons per person
1 can opener
access to a sink for washing hands
1 copy of *The Magician* by Uri Shulevitz,
    adapted from the Yiddish of I.L. Peretz
    (New York: Macmillan Publishing Co.,
    Inc., 1973)
1 or 2 pitchers for water
masking tape
yeast
honey
1 6" x 9" manila envelope without clasps
    per child
1 Afikomen Bag Label per child on any
    colored paper (see Directions and Patterns)
crayons
1 set of self-adhesive velcro dots or squares
    per child
gluesticks
scissors

Advance Preparation by the Facilitator

- Enlarge each of the 15 Seder Order Cards
  on sheets I and II onto $8\frac{1}{2}$" x 11" paper.
  Color in the pictures on the enlarged copy.

- Using clothespins or paperclips, hang the
  15 Seder Order Cards on a clothesline. Or,

tape them to a wall or blackboard with
masking tape.

- Cut out pictures of foods with *chametz*
  (leavening) and foods without *chametz*
  from magazines. (There can be more than
  one food in a picture.) Have approximately
  equal numbers of both types of food. You
  will need four to five pictures per child.

- Glue the pictures onto blank 3" x 5" index
  cards.

- Hide the food pictures around the room in
  easy to find places.

- Do the following just before the program
  begins:

  - Wash the parsley.

  - Cut the apples into thirds. Cut around the
    stems and cores. Sprinkle with lemon
    juice.

  - Cut up sliced bread into bite size pieces.

  - Cut up *maror* into small pieces.

- On a supply table, place the following items
  "buffet style." (In front of each item, place
  an index card or name tag telling how much
  or how many of each item each family
  should take.)

ITEM	QUANTITY
paper plate	1 per family
paper cup	1 per person
parsley	1 sprig per person
bread	1 piece for tasting per person
matzah	1 piece per family
apples	1 segment per child
plastic knife	1 per family
walnuts	a few

maror	1 piece per person or 1 spoonful of processed horseradish per family
macaroons	1 or 2 per person
napkins	1 per person
6" x 9" manila envelope without clasps	1 per child
velcro dots or squares	1 set per child
Afikomen Bag Label	1 per child

- While families are getting their *Seder* supplies, prepare the following items to put out in each table center:

  salt in a cup
  yeast in a cup
  2 bowls per 3-4 families
  2 spoons per 3-4 families
  cinnamon in a cup
  bottle of grape juice
  crayons
  gluesticks
  scissors

Procedure

- The Facilitator explains to families that they will be participating in a 15 Step model *Seder*. The *Seder* is meant to be a real learning experience. Families should feel comfortable asking questions at any point in the *Seder*.

- The Facilitator explains the tradition of searching one's house for *chametz* (crumbs of leavening) the night before the Passover *Seder*.

  Say: I have scattered pictures of leavened and unleavened foods around the room. You will each need to find four to five food pictures. When you have found these, return to your seat. Be prepared to tell the rest of us which of your pictured foods contain *chametz*.

  Ask who in the group found food with *chametz* in it and what food it is. Then ask who in the group found food without *chametz* and what food that is.

- The Facilitator points to the enlarged Seder Order Cards. Each time a new section of the *Seder* begins, he/she points out the appropriate card. The Facilitator asks families to repeat after him/her the names of each step of *Seder* as you begin that step.

- Instruct families to go to the buffet line to pick up their materials for the model *Seder*.

Step 1: Kadesh

- Say: *Kadesh* is the first step. We recite blessing over candles, the special day, and the wine.

- Have participants pour grape juice into their cups.

- Together recite the blessing over the wine (see Blessings #1 and #2, page 487 and Blessing #5, page 488).

- Drink the grape juice.

Step 2: Urchatz

- Everyone washes their hands, or pretends to wash them. They dry them, too.

Step 3: Karpas

- Mix the salt into the water.

- Dip the parsley twice.

- Together recite the appropriate blessings (see Blessing #6, page 488).

- Eat the dipped greens.

Step 4: Yachatz

- Put the velcro "coins" where a clasp should go on your envelope. This will enable each family to use the *afikomen* bag for many years to come.

- Families color and cut out the label on the Afikomen Bag Label. They put their family name on the back. They glue the label onto a manila envelope.

- Each family breaks a *matzah* in two, taking the larger piece for the *afikomen*. Have each family put the half in their *afikomen* bag.

Step 5: Maggid

- This section of the *Haggadah* begins with the Four Questions. Have each family spend a minute coming up with a question about Passover or about the *Seder*. Those families who wish to do so may share their question.

- The *Maggid* is the section which recounts the Exodus from Egypt. The Facilitator briefly recounts the story here.

The Hebrews complained to God about being slaves in Egypt.

God heard their cries. God sent Moses to talk to Pharaoh. "Let my people go!"

Pharaoh said, "No way!"

Then there were ten plagues. (Participants drip grape juice for the ten plagues): *Dam* – blood, *Tzfarde' ah* – Frogs, *Kinim* – Lice, *Arov* – Wild Beasts, *Dever* – Blight, *Sh' chin* – Boils, *Barad* – Hail, *Arbeh* – Locusts, *Choshech* – Darkness, *Makat B' chorot* – Slaying of the firstborn.

Finally, Pharaoh said, "Leave Egypt, Hebrews!"

The people left in a hurry. They didn't even have time to wait for their bread to rise.

They crossed the Sea of Reeds on dry ground.

Then the Israelites wandered in the desert for 40 years.

- The group practices the response "*Dayenu*" (it would have been enough).

- The Facilitator reads the following lines from *Dayenu,* with families responding "*Dayenu*" They get louder with each "*Dayenu.*"

Had God brought us out of Egypt and not divided the sea for us, *Dayenu*!

Had God fed us for forty years in the desert and not given us, the Sabbath, *Dayenu!*

Had God brought us to Mount Sinai and not given us the Torah, *Dayenu*!

Had God led us into the land of Israel, and not built for us the Temple in Jerusalem, *Dayenu*!

Together sing the chorus of "*Dayenu.*"

Step 6: Rachtzah

- Participants wash their hands, or pretend to wash their hands. They dry them off.

- Together recite the blessing over washing hands (see Blessing #14, page 490).

Steps 7 and 8: Motzi and Matzah

- Families add the yeast to warm water. (If this program takes place during Passover, then ask families to imagine the yeast growing while you describe it.)

- Families stir the yeast. The Facilitator adds a little bit of honey. The honey makes the yeast grow. Stirring often, families look for bubbles over the next several minutes. The bubbles are a sign of the yeast's rising and expanding, which makes bread leaven.

- Say or sing *HaMotzi* (see Blessing #3, page 487).

- Everyone tastes the bread.

- Together recite the blessing over *matzah* (see Blessing #13, page 489).

- Everyone eats the *matzah*.

- The Facilitator asks families to identify the differences in texture, taste, and in the width or size of the bread and *matzah*.

- Identify the differences between leavened and unleavened foods.

Step 9: Maror

- The Facilitator holds up the horseradish root for everyone to see. Then hold up a jar of horseradish. Ask how the root gets into the jar.

- The Facilitator asks: Why do we eat bitter herbs on Passover? (Share the responses.)

- Together recite the blessing over *maror* (see Blessing #13, page 489).

Step 10: Korech

- The Facilitator holds up an apple, grape juice, cinnamon, and nuts. Ask families if this looks like clay or mortar for bricks. Remind the group that the Hebrews built Egyptian storehouses, not pyramids.

- The Facilitator instructs families to make their own *charoset*. Have them use the plastic knife to cut the apple segment into

small pieces. (This will act as a reminder of what it is like to be a slave and not have all the proper tools!) They mix in the grape juice and cinnamon.

- Everyone eats a Hillel sandwich made of *maror* and *charoset* between two pieces of *matzah*. This sandwich is named in honor of Rabbi Hillel, a famous Talmudic Rabbi.

Step 11: Shulchan Aruch

- It is meal time. Finish eating the symbolic foods. Eat sweet macaroons.

Step 12: Tzafon

- Somewhere in a wide open area, each parent hides their family's *afikomen* bag.

- Each parent can steer his/her child in the general direction of their bag and give them clues.

- Now each child hides their family's *afikomen* bag. The parents search for the bag, with the children offering clues.

Step 13: Barech

- Together sing "*Oseh Shalom*." Since *Birkat HaMazon* is recited during *Barech*, use that melody for the song. Here are the words:

Oseh Shalom Bimromav Hu ya' aseh Shalom Aleynu V' al Kol Yisrael, V' imru Amen.

May God, Who has created harmony in the universe, grant peace to us and to all Israel, and let us say, Amen.

- Open the door for Elijah.

- Tell the story of *The Magician*, a Passover story about Elijah.

- Sing *"Eliyahu HaNavi."*

Eliyahu HaNavi.
Eliyahu HaTishbi.
Eliyahu, Eliyahu, Eliyahu HaGiladee.
Bimheyrah Be'yameynu.
Yavo Aleynu.
Im Mashiach Ben David,
Im Mashiach Ben David.

01:10 – 01:30
Closure: Music and the Conclusion of the 15 Step Seder

End the program with singing, sharing, and holiday greetings.

Step 14: Hallel

- Sing and move to Pesach songs related to: the parts of the *Seder*, Passover blessings, the *Seder* plate, symbolic foods, *Dayenu*, slavery, freedom, order, Elijah, the ten plagues.

Recommended Songs:

"Soon It's Going to be Pesach"

(*Seasoned With Song* by Julie Auerbach, Tara Publications)

"*Al Shalosh Regalim*" (*Seasoned With Song* by Julie Auerbach, Tara Publications)

Step 15: Nirtzah

- End the music session with *"Ba'shanah Haba'ah B'yerushalayim,"* (next year in Jerusalem).

- Have participants share their reactions to the program. Ask families to complete one of these phrases:

Our favorite part of the *Seder* is . . .

Our family enjoyed . . .

Our family learned . . .

For our Passover *Seder*, we . . .

- Send everyone off with a Passover greeting, *"Chag Sameach!"* (Happy Holiday!)

Seder Order Cards I

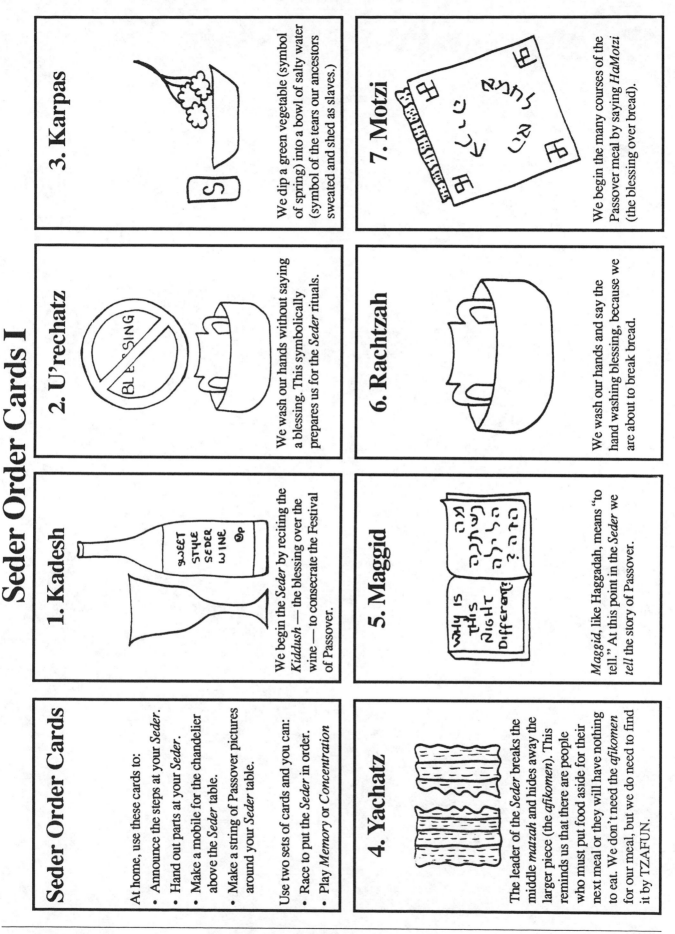

3. Karpas

We dip a green vegetable (symbol of spring) into a bowl of salty water (symbol of the tears our ancestors sweated and shed as slaves.)

7. Motzi

We begin the many courses of the Passover meal by saying *HaMotzi* (the blessing over bread).

2. U'rechatz

We wash our hands without saying a blessing. This symbolically prepares us for the *Seder* rituals.

6. Rachtzah

We wash our hands and say the hand washing blessing, because we are about to break bread.

1. Kadesh

SWEET STYLE SEDER WINE 9p

We begin the *Seder* by reciting the *Kiddush* — the blessing over the wine — to consecrate the Festival of Passover.

5. Maggid

WHY IS THIS NIGHT Different?

Maggid, like Haggadah, means "to tell." At this point in the *Seder* we *tell* the story of Passover.

Seder Order Cards

At home, use these cards to:
- Announce the steps at your *Seder*.
- Hand out parts at your *Seder*.
- Make a mobile for the chandelier above the *Seder* table.
- Make a string of Passover pictures around your *Seder* table.

Use two sets of cards and you can:
- Race to put the *Seder* in order.
- Play *Memory* or *Concentration*

4. Yachatz

The leader of the *Seder* breaks the middle *matzah* and hides away the larger piece (the *afikomen*). This reminds us that there are people who must put food aside for their next meal or they will have nothing to eat. We don't need the *afikomen* for our meal, but we do need to find it by TZAFUN.

Seder Order Cards II

11. Shulchan Orech

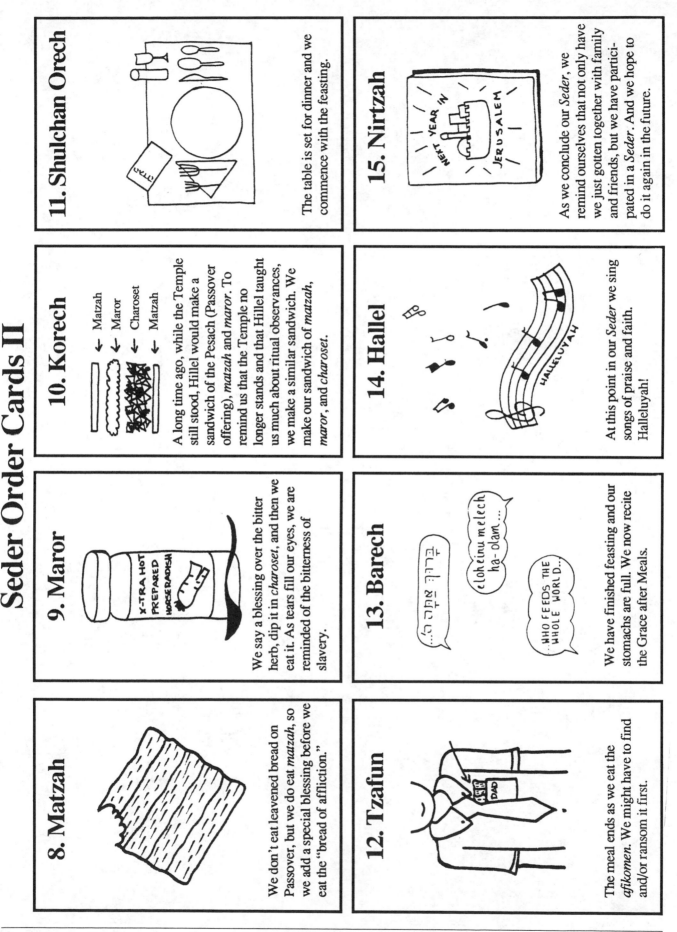

The table is set for dinner and we commence with the feasting.

10. Korech

→ Matzah
→ Maror
→ Charoset
→ Matzah

A long time ago, while the Temple still stood, Hillel would make a sandwich of the Pesach (Passover offering), *matzah* and *maror*. To remind us that the Temple no longer stands and that Hillel taught us much about ritual observances, we make a similar sandwich. We make our sandwich of *matzah*, *maror*, and *charoset*.

9. Maror

X-TRA HOT PREPARED HORSE RADISH

We say a blessing over the bitter herb, dip it in *charoset*, and then we eat it. As tears fill our eyes, we are reminded of the bitterness of slavery.

8. Matzah

We don't eat leavened bread on Passover, but we do eat *matzah*, so we add a special blessing before we eat the "bread of affliction."

15. Nirtzah

NEXT YEAR IN JERUSALEM

As we conclude our *Seder*, we remind ourselves that not only have we just gotten together with family and friends, but we have participated in a *Seder*. And we hope to do it again in the future.

14. Hallel

HALLELUYAH

At this point in our *Seder* we sing songs of praise and faith. Halleluyah!

13. Barech

בָּרוּךְ אַתָּה יְיָ

elohéinu melech ha-olam...

...WHO FEEDS THE WHOLE WORLD...

We have finished feasting and our stomachs are full. We now recite the Grace after Meals.

12. Tzafun

DAD

The meal ends as we eat the *afikomen*. We might have to find and/or ransom it first.

Afikomen Bag Label

Collect the following materials:
1 6" x 9" manila envelop without a clasp
1 set of self-adhesive velcro dots for " coins"
this label

To assemble your *afikomen* bag

1. Put the velcro "coins" where a clasp should go on your envelope.
   This will enable you to use your *afikomen* bag for many years to come.

2. Color and cut out the label below.

3. Mount the label on the front of the *afikomen* bag.

4. Use this *afikomen* bag at your *Seder* this year and in the future.

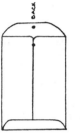

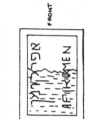

Celebrating Israel's Independence
Yom HaAatzma' ut, Year 3

Postcard and/or Flier

To include:
Program Title
Sponsored by
Audience (age group, members only, or
    general public, etc.)
Date
Time
Location
Cost (if applicable)
RSVP or For Further Information

Physical Set Up

work area: tables and chairs
tables for supplies
table for name tags and sign-in sheet
large trash cans
trash bags
1 screen or wall for projecting slides
a clear space for making the map of Israel

Holiday Symbols, Customs, Terms, and Concepts

chalutzim (pioneers of Israel)
building up the land of Israel
the land of Israel
Hebrew as the language of Israel
Israel as a place to visit
Israel as a cultural entity: food, music, dance,
    clothes, etc.
recognizable symbols of Israel such as: map,
    Western Wall, flag, seal, *felafel*, Jaffa
    oranges, Jerusalem, Masada, Dead Sea
Zionism
Israel as a State
"*Hatikvah*" (Israel's national anthem)

celebrating Israel's Independence, its date
of birth

00:00 – 00:10
Mind Warmer: If I had a Hammer

All the participants "become" *chalutzim*
(pioneers), equipped and dressed for the task
of building up the Land of Israel. Each family
makes a hammer and work apron, then comments on what they would need to build a
Jewish State.

Materials

name tags
markers
sign-in sheet
2 hammer heads per child pre-traced on grey
    or light blue construction paper (see Ham-
    mer Pattern in Directions and Patterns)
1 hammer handle per child pre-traced on
    brown construction paper (see Ham-
    mer Pattern in Directions and Patterns)
1 piece of construction paper 12" x 18" per
    child
ribbon (half inch dull gold or yellow),
    approximately two yards per child
scissors
gluesticks
single hole punches
copies of Make a Work Apron (see Directions
    and Patterns)

Advance Preparation by the Facilitator

• Outline two hammer heads per child on
  gray or light blue construction paper. Make

certain that the outline is visible for someone else to cut.

- Outline one hammer handle per child on brown construction paper. Make certain that the outline is visible for someone else to cut.

- Make a sample hammer for the families to see. Glue the hammer handle between the two halves of the hammer head.

- Make a sample of the work apron that the families will assemble. See Procedure below for detailed instructions for making the work apron.

- On the supply table, place these materials: outlines of the hammer heads, outlines of the hammer handles, the 12" x 18" construction paper, the ribbon, and copies of Make a Work Apron.

- On the supply table, place these items, each in a separate container: single hole punches, gluesticks, and scissors.

Procedure

- The Facilitator greets families as they arrive. Have them fill out a name tag for each family member and sign in.

- Let the families know that they will be getting ready to be *chalutzim* (pioneers), builders of the State of Israel. They will be equipped and dressed for this task. They will be making a hammer and a work apron.

- Show the families the sample hammer and work apron.

- Send each family to the supply tables to pick up materials. Then send them to work tables to assemble a hammer and work apron for their child.

To make the hammer:

- Each family cuts out the outline of the hammer head and handle.

- Each family "sandwiches" the handle between the two hammer heads, then glues the heads to the handles.

To make the work apron:

- Families collect the following materials: 1 piece of 12" x 18" construction paper; 2 yards of dull yellow or gold half inch wide ribbon

- They assemble the apron following these steps:

  - Make a 3" flap by folding down the short (12") edge of the construction paper. This edge is the top back of the work apron.

  - Turn the work apron over. This is the front of the apron. Make a 6$\frac{1}{2}$" flap by folding up the bottom edge. The work apron now has a pocket (see diagram on Make a Work Apron Directions).

  - Punch holes in the work apron. It is important that the second hole from the top on both sides of the work apron goes through all three layers of construction paper — the front pocket, the apron itself, and the top back flap.

  - "Sew" the work apron. Starting from the back of the top right left corner, thread the ribbon in and out of the holes. Leave an 18" tail at the beginning, and at least 18" left after the last stitch.

  - Anchor the work apron with ties by bringing each 18" tail around the side of the work apron and back through the top corner hole from the top.

- Write the child's name on the apron pocket, put in a hammer, and you're ready to help build Israel!

- With three minutes left to go, the Facilitator asks families to decide what they would need to build in a new land — a land that is a desert, a wasteland — to start a Jewish state. Request that the *chalutzim* come to the Introductions and Announcements area wearing their work aprons with the hammer in their pocket or hand.

00:10 – 00:20
Introductions and Announcements

- The Facilitator welcomes everyone on behalf of the sponsoring agency/institution.

- The Facilitator introduces himself/herself and any other official representatives of the program or the agency/institution.

- Have a member of each family introduce himself/herself and other family members. (Have families share their building projects.)

- Announce any upcoming events for the sponsoring agency/institution that are pertinent for this group.

- Instruct people as to how they can get on the mailing list if they are not already on it.

Setting the Stage

- The Facilitator says: The aprons you wear and the hammers you carry make you look like the early *chalutzim*. The *chalutzim* plowed the soil and planted trees and crops. They formed communities and built villages and cities. They wanted to create a homeland where Jews could live safely and happily. Because of these *chalutzim*, there is a country called Israel. Because of

their dreams and their hard work, we can celebrate Yom HaAtzma'ut, Israel Independence Day, the birthday of the modern State of Israel.

Yom HaAtzma'ut is a relatively new holiday as Jewish holidays go. There are even some people still alive who were there on the very first Yom HaAtzma'ut. How do Jews celebrate this new holiday? Do we eat *latkes* and *hamantaschen?* Do we light nine candles and say the four questions? What do we do? Listen to a story about how we celebrate Yom HaAtzma'ut.

00:20 – 00:35
Story: A New Holiday is Declared

Our story is based on "A New Holiday Is Declared" by Levin Kipnis. It is a modern *midrash* about the customs related to celebrating Yom HaAtzma'ut. Through it we learn how the different customs and symbols came to be associated with Yom HaAtzma'ut. The *midrash* says that each of the Jewish holidays gave something to the celebration of Israel's Independence Day.

The story appears in *Let's Celebrate Independence Day: Teacher's Guide*, and is reprinted with the permission of the Department of Education and Culture, World Zionist Organization.

Materials

shofar
yahrzeit candle
Simchat Torah flag
Israeli flag
chanukiah or Chanukah candles
picture of a white dove (optional)

Procedure

- The props needed for the telling of the story are listed in Materials above. Each prop will be referred to twice. The Facilitator holds up the prop each time it is mentioned.

A New Holiday Is Declared

A voice in the heavens calls together all of the Jewish holidays. "Gather Jewish holidays. Come, Rosh Hashanah, Yom Kippur, Sukkot, Simchat Torah, Chanukah, Passover, Shavuot, and Shabbat. For today is a special day. A new holiday is born, Yom HaAtzma'ut, Israel Independence Day."

The Holidays Show their Joy

When the holidays heard this wonderful news, they came running dressed in all their symbols to meet the new holiday.

Rosh Hashanah said: "How wonderful it is to have a new addition to our family. The Jewish holidays have a long and proud tradition."

"Let us introduce ourselves to you. As you are a new holiday, you will need symbols so that Jews can celebrate your birth around the world. Each of the holidays has a gift to present to you."

The Holidays Present their Gifts

"I am Rosh Hashanah. On Rosh Hashanah, the shofar is blown to welcome the new year. I present you this first gift, a shofar."

"I am Yom Kippur. I come ten days after Rosh Hashanah. On Yom Kippur, people light candles in memory of their loved ones. I present you a *yahrzeit* candle to light on this day."

"We are Sukkot and Simchat Torah. We are the fall holidays. Sukkot is a harvest festival. For eight days, Jews celebrate by eating in a beautiful *sukkah*. They decorate the *sukkah* with tree branches, fruits, and vegetables. When Sukkot is over, Simchat Torah is here. On Simchat Torah, people dance with the Torah and wave flags. Our gift to you is a flag."

"I am Chanukah. I celebrate a miracle of the rededication of the Temple in Jerusalem. Against all odds, the brave Maccabees made it possible for Jews to worship God freely. On Chanukah, we light flames in celebration. I give you a torch for your celebration."

"I am Passover. I celebrate the freeing of the Jewish slaves in Egypt. For 40 years, the Jews wandered in the wilderness. Finally, they arrived in the Promised Land. I offer you freedom and the Land of Israel, a land flowing with milk and honey."

"I am Shavuot. I am the spring harvest festival of the first and best fruits. On Shavuot, God gave the Ten Commandments to the Jewish People, and the Jewish People accepted them all. I offer you a gift of a white dove. This dove flies heavenward for joy and peace in the land of Israel."

"I am Shabbat. I come once a week to bring rest and prayer to all the Jewish People. Families come together to celebrate Shabbat every week. I give to you joy and rest as my gift."

Yom HaAtzma'ut Accepts the Gifts

Yom HaAtzma'ut thanked all the holidays for their gifts. "Thank you, my family, for giving me such wonderful gifts. You are so kind and so loving. I, too, want to be a special celebration for Jewish people around the world and to last for a long, long time."

"I will use your gifts as I become a very special holiday. Rosh Hashanah, I will use the shofar to announce the arrival of Israel's Independence Day."

"Yom Kippur, every household will light a *yahrzeit* candle for the soldiers and people who gave their lives in the War of Independence."

"Sukkot and Simchat Torah, flags of the State of Israel, with the blue Jewish Star and two blue stripes, will be flown from rooftops. Children will proudly march carrying you."

"Chanukah, because of your gift of light, torches will be lit as people celebrate in the streets at nights. You will light up the streets as our dancing lights our hearts."

"Passover, we Jewish people will celebrate our freedom in the Land of Israel."

"Shavuot, your dove — a sign of peace, of *shalom* — will be a special symbol of this day."

"Shabbat, you have set a tone for this special day. For I, Yom HaAtzma'ut, shall be a day of rest and joy, a day of singing and feasting."

The Celebration of Yom HaAtzma'ut

And so it happens that every year on the 5th of Iyar, Yom HaAtzma'ut decorates itself with all these symbols, gifts from the other holidays. With these gifts, Yom HaAtzma'ut joins with the other Jewish holidays as a very special day in the lives of Jews in Israel and throughout the world.

00:35 – 00:45 Snack: Yom Huledet Sameach, Israel

Yom Huledet Sameach is Hebrew for "Happy Birthday." The snack is a birthday cake or cupcakes in celebration of Yom HaAtzma'ut, the birthday of a nation. Use the appropriate number of candles to reinforce the number of years since Israel's birth. (Or, use candles in the shape of numbers.)

Materials

cake or cupcakes
regular birthday candles or candles that are
    numbers
punch
matches
plates
napkins
cups
knife (to cut the cake)

Procedure

- The Facilitator reminds participants of how old the State of Israel is, then lights the candles on the cake or cupcakes.

- Together with the group, sing "*Yom Huledet Sameach.*" Repeat these three words four times to the tune of "Happy Birthday to You."

- Together sing "Happy Birthday to You, Israel" in English (and in any other language you choose).

- All together, recite a blessing (see Blessing #8, page 488).

- Families blow out the candles. Cut and eat the cake.

00:45 – 01:10

Activity: A Walking Tour of Israel

Families go on a walking tour of Israel. Around a map of Israel laid out on the floor, they stop at different cities and sites and celebrate Yom HaAtzma'ut.

Making the Map of Israel:

Materials

Map Option #1:
map of Israel (purchase at a bookstore)
masking tape
OR

Map Option #2:
two large pieces of butcher paper 5' long
marker
masking tape
OR

Map Option # 3:
chalk to draw the map directly on the floor
OR

Map Option #4:
thick yarn
masking tape

For All Map Options:
room or area large enough for the map to be on the floor with families seated around it.
6 strips of light colored construction paper Israeli items, such as: Jaffa orange (any orange is fine — write Jaffa on it), sandals, Israeli or Hebrew T-shirt, Coca Cola bottle with Hebrew lettering, broken pieces of pottery, salt in a container representing the Dead Sea, Carmel wine bottle, a gardening tool (symbolic of a *kibbutz*), bar of Elite chocolate, box or can of food made in Israel. Use your imagination!

Advance Preparation by the Facilitator

- Make the map of Israel. Draw the map on butcher paper or on the floor with chalk. Make the map large enough for families to sit around it. The only important thing is that the outline of Israel be recognizable.

- Secure the map of Israel on the ground.

- On the six strips of construction paper, write the names of the following cities/ locations along with the activity designated for that locale:
  Jaffa: Dancing "*Mayyim*"
  Tel Aviv: A Slide Show of Israel
  Haifa: Going to the Kiosk
  The Galilee: Hebrew Ulpan
  Beersheva: Digging at a Tel
  Jerusalem: Raising the Flag at the Knesset

- Distribute the Israeli items (Jaffa oranges, sandals, etc.) around the map of Israel. This gives the map an Israeli flavor.

The Walking Tour of Israel

- Inform families that you are going on a walking tour of Israel in celebration of Yom HaAtzma'ut. Let them know that you will be their tour guide.

- Ask families to meet you at the port of Jaffa (Yaffo).

Stop #1 Israeli Dancing in Jaffa/Yaffo
In Jaffa, participants will do an Israeli dance.

Materials

cassette player or record player
cassette of Israeli dance music or Israeli music

Procedure

- Point out Jaffa on the map.

- Ask everyone to walk to Jaffa where they will do an Israeli dance.

- Ask families to join hands in a circle.

- Teach the families the dance. Keep it simple. Rather than teach an "authentic" Israeli dance, walk around in a circle, do a grapevine step, and clap a few times to an Israeli tune.

Stop #2 A Slide Show of Israel in Tel Aviv

In Tel Aviv, families watch slides of Israel (or, if desired, a short videotape).

Materials

slide projector and screen (or VCR and TV)
extension cord
slides of Israel (or videotape)
cassette player (optional)
cassette tape of Israeli music (optional)

Advance Preparation by the Facilitator

- Use slides or a professional videotape. Or, use slides or a video taken by a tourist from your community.

- Choose slides or a video that contain a number of different sites in Israel. This part should last 2-3 minutes.

- Preview whichever audiovisual materials you are using.

Procedure

- Point out Tel Aviv on the map.

- Ask participants to walk to the Hilton Hotel in Tel Aviv where they will see a slide show (or a video) of Israel.

- Present the slide show. The Facilitator narrates and points out the sites. (Or, play some Israeli music as background.)

Stop #3 A Kiosk in Haifa

In Haifa, participants enjoy a snack at a kiosk.

Materials

pita bread
chumus and/or *techina*
orange juice
bowls
plates
napkins
cups
pitchers

Advance Preparation by the Facilitator

- Cut the pita bread into small bit size pieces.

- Put the *chumus* and/or *techina* in bowls.

- Prepare and pour the orange juice into the pitchers.

Procedure

- Point out Haifa on the map. Walk to Haifa.

- Tell families that after their long walk around Israel, it is time to visit a kiosk (a stand that serves snack food).

- Point out the foods by name: pita bread, *chumus* and/or *techina*, and *mitz tapuzim* (orange juice).

- Pass around the pita and bowls of *chumus* and/or *techina* for taste testing.

- Serve small portions of *mitz tapuzim*.

Stop #4 An Ulpan in the Galilee

In the Galilee, families will learn a few words of Hebrew at an *ulpan*. The *ulpan* is housed at a *kibbutz*.

Procedure

- The Facilitator points out the Galilee on the map.

- Families walk over to the Galilee where they will spend time at an *ulpan*. The Facilitator explains that an *ulpan* is an intensive Hebrew learning experience. The *ulpan* they will visit is located on a *kibbutz*.

- Here are two lists of Hebrew words for the Facilitator to teach, one easy, and the other a little more advanced.

  Easy Hebrew:

אִמָּא	*ima*	(mother)
אַבָּא	*abba*	(father)
כֵּן	*keyn*	(yes)
לֹא	*lo*	(no)
שָׁלוֹם	*shalom*	(hello, goodbye, peace)
טֶלֶבִיזְיָה	*televizia*	(television)

  More Advanced Hebrew:

סוּס	*soos*	(horse)
כֶּלֶב	*kelev*	(dog)
תַּרְנְגוֹל	*tarnegol*	(rooster)
עַכָּבִישׁ	*akaveesh*	(spider)

- Use a combination of charades and real objects to teach the Hebrew words. First, say the word. Have everyone repeat it back. Act out or show the model of the Hebrew word. Have the participants guess what the words mean. Let them know the meaning. Have them repeat the word.

Stop #5 A Tel Near Beersheva

Participants will dig at a tel near Beersheva.

Materials

1 or 2 pails or wash basins
corn meal or sand
chocolate *gelt* or Israeli coins
shovels or spoons

Advance Preparation by the Facilitator

- Fill the pails or wash basins with corn meal or sand.

- Hide Israeli coins and/or chocolate *gelt* in the sand.

Procedure

- The Facilitator points out Beersheva on the map and walk there with the group.

- Explain that archeologists look for old things that belonged to people long ago. This helps us to learn how people lived long ago. A tel is a mound made from many villages or cities each built on the same spot over many, many years. Outside of Beersheva, there are some very important tels.

- Let several children at a time dig for objects in the tel. Explain that every child will have the opportunity to dig.

- Each child shows off what he/she finds. Pass around the coins.

Stop #6 A Pilgrimage to Jerusalem

The last stop on the Walking Tour is Jerusalem, the capital and heart of the Jewish State. Here participants will raise the Israeli flag outside of the Knesset and sing "*Hatikvah*," the Israeli national anthem.

Materials

1 copy of a telegram from the Prime Minister (see Procedure)
1 Israeli flag
1 copy of "*Hatikvah*" for each family
1 picture of the Knesset (optional)

Advance Preparation by the Facilitator

- Type out and photocopy the words to "*Hatikvah*," one for each family. (The title means "The Hope.") Here are the words and translation:

Kol Od Balayvav Penimah
Nefesh Yehudi Homiyah
U' l'fahahtay Mizrach Kadimah
Ayin L'tzion Tzofiah.
Od Lo Avdah Tikvateynu
Hatikvah Sh' not Al-payim
Lichiyot Am Chofshi B' artzeynu
B' eretz Tzion Ve' rushalayim.

So long as still within the inmost heart a Jewish soul yearns; so long as the eye looks eastward, gazing toward Zion, our hope is not lost — that hope of two millenia, to be a free people in the land, the land of Zion and Jerusalem.

- Type out a copy of the letter from the Prime Minister (see Procedure).

- Put the letter in an envelope addressed to the Facilitator/tour guide and place it next to the sign for Jerusalem.

Procedure

- The Facilitator points out Jerusalem on the map and walks there with the group.

- The group assembles at the Knesset, the Israeli Parliament building.

- The Facilitator opens the envelope and reads the following letter of greeting from the Prime Minister:

Dear Families:

On behalf of the People of Israel, I would like to express a very warm welcome to you as you join your Jewish family here in Israel. Please do not think of yourselves as visitors. This is your land, your homeland. You are family here.

This is the land that was given by God to our ancestors, Abraham and Sarah, to their children, and to all their descendents. This is the land where King David once ruled and where King Solomon built God's Holy Temple. It is a place that many Jews have loved and defended.

It is a pleasure to celebrate Yom HaAtzma'ut with you here in Jerusalem. We hope that you enjoy your stay here. You are always welcome.

B'Shalom,

_____ Prime Minister
(fill in the name of the present one)

- The Facilitator holds up the Israeli flag and raises it at the Knesset.

- Together sing "*Hatikvah*."

- The Facilitator tells the families that he/she hopes they enjoyed their Walking Tour of Israel in honor of Yom HaAtzma'ut.

- If there is extra time, allow families to roam around Israel looking at all the objects.

01:10 01:30
Closure: The Land of Milk and Honey

End the program with songs, sharing, and greetings.

- Sing and move to Yom HaAtzma'ut music related to: Israel, going on a trip, Jerusalem, building, birthdays, Hebrew, working together, *chalutzim*, oranges.

  Recommended Songs:

  "*Shalom Chaverim*." The words are: *Shalom Chaverim* (2), *Shalom* (2), *L'hitraot* (2), *Shalom* (2).

  "*Kachol-Lavan*" (Blue and White) (*Apples on Holidays and Other Days* by Leah Abrams, Tara Publications)

  "Let's Take a Trip" (*Seasoned With Song* by Julie Auerbach, Tara Publications)

- Have people share their reactions to the program. Ask each family to complete one of these phrases:

  Yom HaAtzma'ut is . . .

  Our family enjoyed . . .

  Our family learned . . .

  We hope that Israel . . .

- Send everyone off with a "*L'hitraot*" (See you again).

Hammer Pattern

For each hammer your will need:
- 2 Hammer Heads
- 1 Hammer Handle

To assemble:

1. Cut out two Hammer Head shapes and the Hammer Handle.
2. "Sandwich" the handle between the two Hammer Heads.
3. Use glue to attach the heads to the handle.
4. Place the hammer in your work apron.

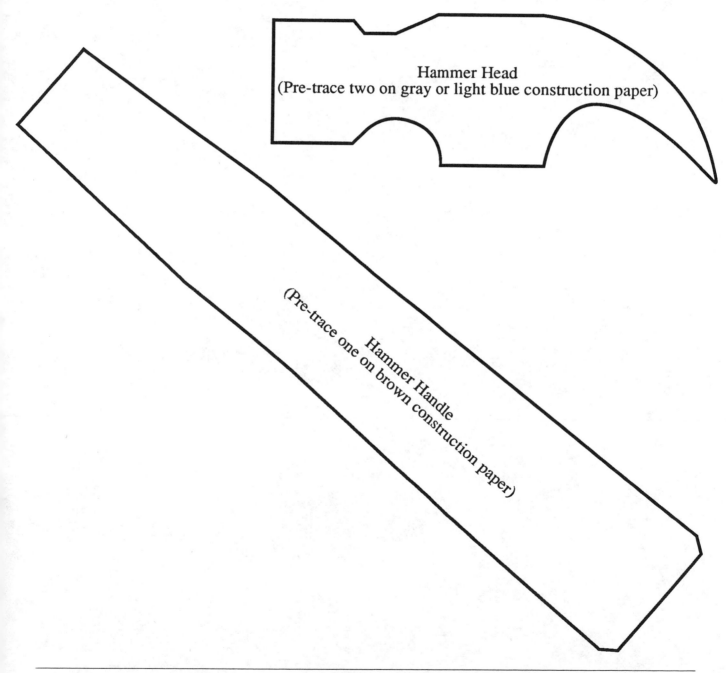

Hammer Head
(Pre-trace two on gray or light blue construction paper)

Hammer Handle
(Pre-trace one on brown construction paper)

Make A Work Apron

(Directions)

Collect the following materials:
  1 piece of 12" x 18" blue construction paper
  2 yards of dull yellow or gold half-inch braid

To assemble the apron:

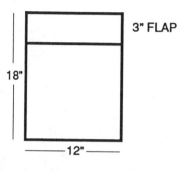

1. Make a 3" flap by folding down one short (12") edge.
   This is the top, the back of the work apron.

2. Turn the work apron over. This is the front of the apron.
   Make a 6½" flap by folding up the bottom edge. The work
   apron now has a pocket.

3. Punch holes in the work apron (see example). It is important
   that the second hole from the top on both sides of the work apron
   goes through all three layers of construction paper — the front
   pocket, the apron itself, and the top-back flap.

4. "Sew" the work apron. Starting from the back
   of the top right or left corner, thread the ribbon in
   and out of the holes. Leave an 18" tail at the beginning,
   and there should be at least 18" left after the last stitch.

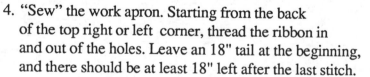

5. Anchor the work apron ties by bringing each 18" tail
   around the side of the work apron and back through
   the top corner hole from the top.

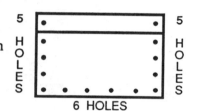

6. Write a name on the apron pocket, put in a hammer,
   and you're ready to help build Israel!

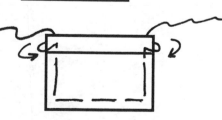

Blessings

Blessings

#1: Blessing the Shabbat (and Festival) Candles

The candles are lit Friday night (and on a festival). Light the candles first, and then cover the flames with your hands or cover your eyes and recite this blessing:

בָּרוּךְ אַתָּה, יְיָ אֱלֹהֵינוּ, מֶלֶךְ הָעוֹלָם, אֲשֶׁר קִדְּשָׁנוּ בְּמִצְוֹתָיו וְצִוָּנוּ לְהַדְלִיק נֵר שֶׁל שַׁבָּת (וְשֶׁל יוֹם טוֹב).

Baruch Atah Adonai Eloheynu Melech Ha-olam Asher Kidshanu B' mitzvotav V' tzivanu L' hadlik Ner Shel Shabbat (V' shel Yom Tov).

Blessed are You, Eternal our God, Ruler of the universe, Who sanctified us by Your commandments, and commanded us to light the Shabbat (and Festival) candles.

Now, open your fingers and look at the candles.

#2: Blessing the Wine (Kiddush)

Recite the blessing first and then drink the wine. The entire *Kiddush* can be found in a *Siddur*.

בָּרוּךְ אַתָּה, יְיָ אֱלֹהֵינוּ, מֶלֶךְ הָעוֹלָם, בּוֹרֵא פְּרִי הַגָּפֶן.

Baruch Atah Adonai Eloheynu Melech Ha-olam Boray P' ri Hagafen.

Blessed are You, Eternal our God, Ruler of the universe, Creator of the fruit of the vine.

#3: Blessing the Bread (HaMotzi)

Recite the blessing first, then eat the *challah*. Many people use two *challot* (plural of *challah*) to symbolize the double portion of manna given on Shabbat to the Jews wandering in the wilderness. *HaMotzi* is the blessing used whenever bread is served for a meal. It is not exclusively a Shabbat or holiday blessing.

בָּרוּךְ אַתָּה, יְיָ אֱלֹהֵינוּ, מֶלֶךְ הָעוֹלָם, הַמּוֹצִיא לֶחֶם מִן הָאָרֶץ.

Baruch Atah Adonai Eloheynu Melech Ha-olam Hamotzi Lechem Min Ha' aretz.

Blessed are You, Eternal our God, Ruler of the universe, Who brings forth bread from the earth.

#4: Blessing the Children

The following is recited at the Shabbat table by the parents. It is customary for the parents to place hands upon the head of the child while reciting the blessing.

For male children:

יְשִׂמְךָ אֱלֹהִים כְּאֶפְרַיִם וְכִמְנַשֶּׁה.

Y' simcha Elohim K' Efrayim V' chee' Menasheh.

May God make you as Ephraim and Menasseh.

For female children:

יְשִׂמֵךְ אֱלֹהִים כְּשָׂרָה, רִבְקָה, רָחֵל, וְלֵאָה.

Y' simech Elohim K' Sarah, Rivkah, Rachel V' Layah.

May God make you as Sarah, Rebecca, Rachel, and Leah.

End the children's blessing with the *Birkat Kochanim* as follows:

יְבָרֶכְךָ יְיָ, וְיִשְׁמְרֶךָ,

Y' varechecha Adonai v' yishmerecha.

May God bless you and keep you.

יָאֵר יְיָ פָּנָיו אֵלֶיךָ וִיחֻנֶּךָּ,

Ya' er Adonai Panav Elecha Vichuneka.

May God cause the light of God's countenance to shine upon you and be gracious unto you.

יִשָּׂא יְיָ פָּנָיו אֵלֶיךָ וְיָשֵׂם לְךָ שָׁלוֹם.

Yisa Adonai Panav Aylecha Ve'yasem Lecha Shalom.

May God set the divine countenance upon you and give you peace.

#5: Blessing Over New Things and New Seasons

בָּרוּךְ אַתָּה, יְיָ אֱלֹהֵינוּ, מֶלֶךְ הָעוֹלָם,
שֶׁהֶחֱיָנוּ וְקִיְּמָנוּ וְהִגִּיעָנוּ לַזְּמַן הַזֶּה.

Baruch Atah Adonai Eloheynu Melech Ha-olam Shehecheyanu Vekiyemanu Vehigiyanu Lazman Hazeh.

Blessed are You, Eternal our God, Ruler of the universe, Who has kept us alive, sustained us, and brought us to this season.

#6: Blessing Over That Which Grows in the Ground

בָּרוּךְ אַתָּה, יְיָ אֱלֹהֵינוּ, מֶלֶךְ הָעוֹלָם,
בּוֹרֵא פְּרִי הָאֲדָמָה.

Baruch Atah Adonai Eloheynu Melech Ha-olam Boray P'ri Ha'adamah.

Blessed are You, Eternal our God, Ruler of the universe, Who creates the fruit of the earth.

#7: Blessing Over That Which Grows on Trees

בָּרוּךְ אַתָּה, יְיָ אֱלֹהֵינוּ, מֶלֶךְ הָעוֹלָם,
בּוֹרֵא פְּרִי הָעֵץ.

Baruch Atah Adonai Eloheynu Melech Ha-olam Boray P'ri Ha'eytz.

Blessed are You, Eternal our God, Ruler of the universe, Who creates the fruit of the tree.

#8: Blessing for Pastries and Crackers

בָּרוּךְ אַתָּה, יְיָ אֱלֹהֵינוּ, מֶלֶךְ הָעוֹלָם,
בּוֹרֵא מִינֵי מְזוֹנוֹת.

Baruch Atah Adonai Eloheynu Melech Ha-olam Boray Minay M'zonot.

Blessed are You, Eternal our God, Ruler of the universe, Who creates various kinds of food.

#9: Blessing Over Other Foods

בָּרוּךְ אַתָּה, יְיָ אֱלֹהֵינוּ, מֶלֶךְ הָעוֹלָם,
שֶׁהַכֹּל נִהְיֶה בִּדְבָרוֹ.

Baruch Atah Adonai Eloheynu Melech Ha-olam Shehakol Neh'yeh Bidvaro.

Blessed are You, Eternal our God, Ruler of the universe, by Whose word all things come into being.

#10: Blessings of Sukkot

Upon Entering the Sukkah

בָּרוּךְ אַתָּה, יְיָ אֱלֹהֵינוּ, מֶלֶךְ הָעוֹלָם, אֲשֶׁר
קִדְּשָׁנוּ בְּמִצְוֹתָיו וְצִוָּנוּ לֵישֵׁב בַּסֻּכָּה.

Baruch Atah Adonai Eloheynu Melech Ha-olam Asher Kidshanu B'mitzvotav V'tzivanu Layshev Basukkah.

Blessed are You, Eternal our God, Ruler of the universe, who has made us holy through Your commandments and commanded us to dwell in the *sukkah*.

בָּרוּךְ אַתָּה, יְיָ אֱלֹהֵינוּ, מֶלֶךְ הָעוֹלָם, אֲשֶׁר
קִדְּשָׁנוּ בְּמִצְוֹתָיו וְצִוָּנוּ עַל־נְטִילַת לוּלָב.

Baruch Atah Adonai Eloheynu Melech Ha-olam Asher Kidshanu B'mitzvotav

V'tzivanu Al Netilat Lulav.

Blessed are You, Eternal our God, Ruler of the universe, who has made us holy through Your commandments and commanded us concerning the waving of the *lulav.*

#11: Chanukah Blessings

The candles are placed in the *chanukiah* from right to left. The candles are lit from left to right, beginning with the newest candle. On Shabbat, first bless then light the Chanukah candles, and then light and bless the Shabbat candles. On Saturday evening, Havdalah is recited before lighting the Chanukah candles.

Blessings for All Eight Nights:

בָּרוּךְ אַתָּה, יְיָ אֱלֹהֵינוּ, מֶלֶךְ הָעוֹלָם, אֲשֶׁר קִדְּשָׁנוּ בְּמִצְוֹתָיו וְצִוָּנוּ לְהַדְלִיק נֵר שֶׁל חֲנֻכָּה.

Baruch Atah Adonai Eloyheynu Melech Ha-olam Asher Kidshanu B' mitzvotav V' tzeevanu L' hadlik Ner Shel Chanukah.

Blessed are You, Eternal our God, Ruler of the universe, Who sanctifies us by Your commandments and commands us to kindle the Chanukah lights.

בָּרוּךְ אַתָּה, יְיָ אֱלֹהֵינוּ, מֶלֶךְ הָעוֹלָם, שֶׁעָשָׂה נִסִּים לַאֲבוֹתֵינוּ בַּיָּמִים הַהֵם בַּזְּמַן הַזֶּה.

Baruch Atah Adonai Eloheynu Melech Ha-olam Sheh' asah Nissim La' avoteynu Bayamim Hahem Bazman Hazeh.

Blessed are You, Eternal our God, Ruler of the universe, Who performed wondrous deeds for our ancestors in days of old at this season.

On the First Night of Chanukah, recite also the *Shehecheyanu* (see Blessing #5 above).

#12: Purim Blessings

Blessing Upon Reading the Megillah:

בָּרוּךְ אַתָּה, יְיָ אֱלֹהֵינוּ, מֶלֶךְ הָעוֹלָם, אֲשֶׁר קִדְּשָׁנוּ בְּמִצְוֹתָיו וְצִוָּנוּ עַל־מִקְרָא מְגִלָּה.

Baruch Atah Adonai Eloheynu Melech Ha-olam Asher Kidshanu B' mitzvotav V' tsivanu Al Mikra Megillah.

Blessed are You, Eternal our God, Ruler of the universe, Who sanctified us by Your commandments, and commands us to read the *Megillah.*

בָּרוּךְ אַתָּה, יְיָ אֱלֹהֵינוּ, מֶלֶךְ הָעוֹלָם, שֶׁעָשָׂה נִסִּים לַאֲבוֹתֵינוּ בַּיָּמִים הַהֵם בַּזְּמַן הַזֶּה.

Baruch Atah Adonai Eloheynu Melech Ha-olam Sheh' asah Nissim La' avoteynu Bayamim Hahem Bazman Hazeh.

Blessed are You, Eternal our God, Ruler of the universe, Who performed wondrous deeds for our ancestors in days of old at this season.

The *Shehecheyanu* is then recited (see #5 above).

13: Passover Blessings

Blessing Over Matzah:

בָּרוּךְ אַתָּה, יְיָ אֱלֹהֵינוּ, מֶלֶךְ הָעוֹלָם, אֲשֶׁר קִדְּשָׁנוּ בְּמִצְוֹתָיו וְצִוָּנוּ עַל אֲכִילַת מָרוֹר.

Baruch Atah Adonai Eloheynu Melech Ha-olam Asher Kidshanu B' mitzvotav V' tsivanu Al Achilat Matzah.

Blessed are You, Eternal our God, Ruler of the universe, Who sanctified us by Your commandments, and commanded us concerning the eating of *matzah.*

Blessing Over Maror:

בָּרוּךְ אַתָּה, יְיָ אֱלֹהֵינוּ, מֶלֶךְ הָעוֹלָם, אֲשֶׁר קִדְּשָׁנוּ בְּמִצְוֹתָיו וְצִוָּנוּ עַל אֲכִילַת מָרוֹר.

Baruch Atah Adonai Eloheynu Melech Ha-olam Asher Kidshanu B' mitzvotav V' tsivanu Al Achilat Maror.

Blessed are You, Eternal our God, Ruler of the universe, Who sanctified us by Your commandments, and commanded us concerning the eating of *bitter herbs*.

14: Blessing for Washing Hands

בָּרוּךְ אַתָּה, יְיָ אֱלֹהֵינוּ, מֶלֶךְ הָעוֹלָם, אֲשֶׁר קִדְּשָׁנוּ בְּמִצְוֹתָיו וְצִוָּנוּ עַל־נְטִילַת יָדַיִם.

Baruch Atah Adonai Eloheynu Melech Ha-olam Asher Kidshanu B' mitzvotav V' tsivanu Al Netilat Yadayim.

Blessed are You, Eternal our God, Ruler of the universe, Who sanctified us by Your commandments, and commanded us concerning the washing of hands.